THE ECOLOGY OF WELFARE

URBAN STUDIES SERIES

General Editor: George S. Sternlieb

The Affluent Suburb: Princeton by George S. Sternlieb, Robert William Burchell and Lynne Beyer Sagalyn

The Zone of Emergence: A Case Study of Plainfield, New Jersey by George S. Sternlieb and W. Patrick Beaton

The Ecology of Welfare: Housing and the Welfare Crisis in New York City by George S. Sternlieb and Bernard P. Indik.

Landlords and Tenants: A Complete Guide to the Residential Rental Relationship by Jerome G. Rose.

555 Families. A Social Psychological Study of Young Families in Transition by Ludwig L. Geismar.

THE ECOLOGY OF WELFARE
Housing and the Welfare Crisis in New York City

GEORGE S. STERNLIEB
Professor of Urban Planning
and Director of the Center for Urban Policy Research
Livingston College, Rutgers University

BERNARD P. INDIK
Professor of Social Work
Graduate School of Social Work
Rutgers University

with Mildred Barry
and staff

Transaction Books
New Brunswick, New Jersey
Distributed by E. P. Dutton & Co.

Printed in the United States of America
Library of Congress Catalog Number: LC-72-82193
ISBN 0-87855-041-0

This volume was prepared for the Center for Urban Policy Research
Rutgers — the State University, New Brunswick, New Jersey

CONTENTS

ACKNOWLEDGEMENTS

This study was made possible only by the aid of the over 400 welfare recipients and their families who gave us their cooperation. Though we could give them no hope of future reward, with very few exceptions, they were greatly receptive to interviewers and tried to be helpful in what at best was a complex and lengthy procedure.

One of the strongest feelings that we take with us from the study is the variation between the myth of the professional welfare recipient and the reality of so many people blunted by the vagaries of life and ill-fortune but still trying to make a reasonable life within a society with all too many barriers. Our gratitude for the positive partnership that was established between our staff and the respondents is substantial.

More than 40 people from the staff of the Center for Urban Policy Research worked on this project with great cheerfulness and enterprise. This study would have been impossible without their efforts. Mildred Barry did yeoman work in creatively administering the field interviewing staff. Audrey Greene was in charge of the video-taped group interviews and provided an unobtrusive but highly imaginative and productive format for them. Dominic Salluce together with Mary Picarella kept track of what at times seemed practically an overwhelming flood of data.

Our colleagues, Professors Ludwig Geismar, Ben Ami Gelin and Audrey Faulkner, provided most useful criticisms of the original manuscript. Glen Margo, together with William Dolphin, took much responsibility for the orderly execution of the machine computation and analysis. Mary Curtis and J. Carl Cook performed nobly in editing a very unwieldy manuscript. The errors that remain are the authors' own.

The cooperation received from the Department of Social Services of the Human Resources Administration was admirable. We are most grateful for it.

Funding for this study was secured through the Ford Foundation through the aegis of Dr. Louis Winnick and William C. Pendleton. Both of them made many helpful comments in criticisms of the literary presentation.

Large-scale efforts involved large-scale obligations. It is indeed a pleasure to express our gratitude to all the participants in the study.

PREFACE

The interplay between housing and outlook, between the physical attributes of a dwelling unit and the attitudes and responses of its inhabitants, are areas that have been subject to more ritual than research. Optimizing the mix of social inputs is still a goal rather than a reality. We measure the effectiveness of our social and economic programs by what we want to see or to happen rather than by what their consequences really are for the people involved. The relationship between the distribution of human groups with reference to material resources and the consequent social and cultural patterns that evolve from this distribution, i.e., their basic ecology, is just beginning to get large-scale, orderly attention.

This book is dedicated to one such human group—the welfare recipients of New York City. Attention to these people has long been the province of professional social workers and charitable groups, with an occasional input by irate taxpayers and municipal officials. In our own time, however, the sheer growth in the number of welfare recipients has changed this. A glance at the pages of any of the major newspapers or current events magazines indicates the extent of popular concern about the distribution of welfare monies: compare the multiple pages given over to welfare in the *New York Times Index* for 1972, with the paucity of equivalent entries a brief ten years earlier. As yet, most of this attention has come in the form of a set of a priori assertions—"They're all a bunch of con artists taking advantage of the system"—or sentiments to the effect that the expansion of the welfare rolls is a symbol of injustice generated by our entire socioeconomic system. Too often lost in this barrage of assertions are the people on welfare, where they live, what they want, like and fear and perhaps as much as anything else, just who they are. Overlooked in the statistics of X proportion of ADC mothers or Y proportion of the elderly, are the people themselves. Certainly statistical anonymity is not unique to welfare recipients; it all too frequently neutralizes the life styles of other groups in our society. The sheer fragility, however, of the welfare recipients' lives, the very specific and unique response to them of other groups in society—landlords and grocers, city officials and social workers—make much more knowledge and insight an absolute necessity.

Housing may be a major area of governmental input and support of the poor, perhaps as much because money spent on housing is easily accounted for and provides tangible results as because of its real impact on the lives and life styles of its beneficiaries. Housing lends itself to statistics about the number of structures erected, the proportion of dwelling units rehabilitated and the like. It can be seen as well as counted in contrast with many alternative social inputs. How do welfare recipients view their present housing accommodations? What would they like? What are their hopes and fears for the future, and what do these mean in terms of support systems? These are essential questions—for which there are no easily ascertainable answers.

The study that follows attempts to provide some insight into these questions. It has all of the limitations of the social sciences compounded by those of the authors. We hope, however, that if nothing more, *The Ecology of Welfare* will encourage more sophisticated future research along the lines developed herein.

Chapter 1

SOME PARAMETERS OF WELFARE

Public thinking in America has historically conceived of welfare recipients as atypical—including the old, the physically disabled and perhaps a small number of temporarily unemployed. The absolute expansion of numbers on welfare that has occurred in recent years has therefore found the majority of voters as well as many of their leaders looking to solutions which have been outpaced by the scale and complexity of the welfare phenomenon.

The increase of dependency in the North was initially viewed as resulting from the sudden influx of rural poor from the South and from Puerto Rico. The problem, therefore, was held to be transitional and was to be resolved by the acculturation of rural displacees. Novels of a generation ago are replete with anecdotal material describing the problems of adjustment to urban living. A search through that literature reveals many variations on the theme. Probably the most famous was John Steinbeck's *The Grapes of Wrath,* the odyssey of agricultural displacees who, at one point for example, find themselves completely baffled by the intricacies of modern-day plumbing.

As the tidal wave of rural migration has declined, however, some of the harsh facts are becoming more apparent. First, the number of recipients is continuing to grow in absolute terms. By June 1970, 6 percent of the United States population was receiving money payments under public assistance programs.[1] Second, the expansion in welfare has taken place largely during a period of unparalleled business prosperity. Third, and perhaps most significant, is the increasing proportion of welfare payments in relation to local government expenditures.

In the past, the amount and character of welfare payments were seen nearly exclusively as the concern of institutions and government functionaries, of technocrats of various persuasions. Welfare at a time of full employment, however, becomes a substantial and meaningful focus of popular political interest: this is something relatively new.

Is welfare a right or a privilege? Both assertions have been made by responsible parties. The National Welfare Rights Organization has asserted that it is clearly a right, but Supreme Court Judge Blackmun, in the case of Wyman v. James (U.S. 27 L Ed. 2d 408) clearly had in mind the latter description. In his opinion of January 1971 he stated:

> One who dispenses purely private charity naturally has an interset in and expects to know how his charitable funds are utilized and put to work. The public, when it is the provider, rightly expects the same. It might well expect more, because of the trust aspect of public funds and the recipient, as well as the caseworker, *has* not only an interest but an obligation.

Since 1965, it has been argued successfully that public assistance recipients have full First Amendment rights to privacy, that the equal protection clause prohibits different treatment for persons receiving and not receiving welfare, and that welfare benefits are entitlements in the nature of property rights which cannot be taken away or diminished without hearings meeting due process standards; the Supreme Court also declared unconstitutional the "substitute father" rule and residency laws.[2]

Public attitudes toward welfare in the next few years may well depend on the causes and constituents of the welfare population. Certainly, in 1971 a sharply negative public reaction was apparent. Appendix 1.1 indicates the level of state action in the area of welfare, as summarized in a HEW memorandum of July 2, 1971.

What is the future of welfare? It should be noted that the memorandum cited in Appendix 1.2 only accounts for the absolute numbers of individuals on welfare to mid-1970. In the year that followed the number of welfare recipients on a national base continued to grow. By mid-1971 it was estimated that 14.4 million Americans were receiving some form of dependency allotment.[3]

Our comparisons in this study will be based on the earlier data because the welfare increase noted there occurred during times of relatively full employment. The increase in unemployment in late 1970-1971 may account for much of the recent growth. At the same time, however, in a number of cities the administration of welfare has become more rigorous, holding down the number of recipients. Unfortunately, we do not have data on these specific and very important variables.

EXHIBIT 1.1

NUMBER OF PUBLIC ASSISTANCE RECIPIENTS BY PROGRAM[a]

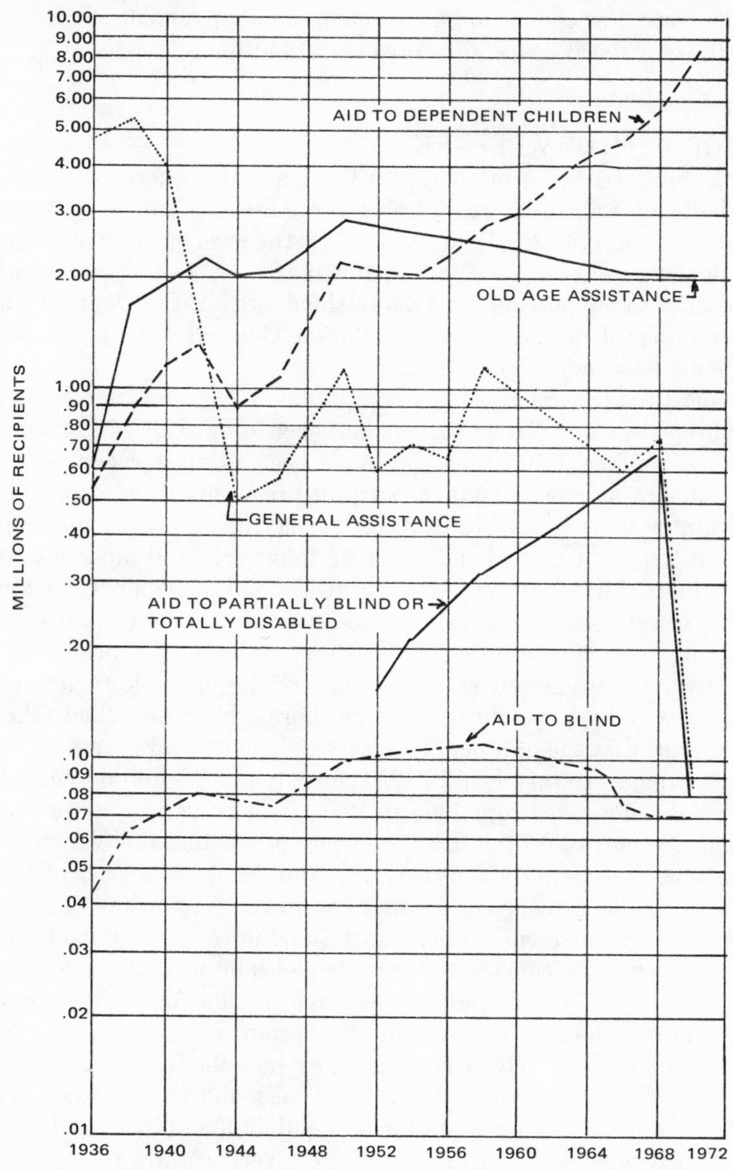

[a]Unless otherwise noted, all tables refer to New York City in 1970.

Source: Miscellaneous data from HEW.

It is difficult to foretell what events future historians may decide epitomize this era. But certainly a significant candidate for the honor must be the budgetary crossover of 1970, when for the first time New York City's expenditures on welfare exceeded the fast-growing education budget.[4] For the nation as a whole, money payments to recipients of welfare by fiscal year 1970 were over $14 billion.[5]

THE GROWTH OF WELFARE

In Exhibit 1.1 some of the gross figures on the increase in welfare recipients are indicated. From 1960 to 1970 the absolute level of population went from 179,325,671 to 203,184,772; the level of welfare recipients meanwhile rose from 7,098,000 to 10,603,100, or from 4 percent of the population to 5.2 percent. In 1936 in the depths of the Depression, the total number of categorical (i.e., excluding General Assistance) welfare recipients was under two million.

Would the proportions of our population on the welfare rolls in 1936 have been the same if the program had been administered and the categories of welfare defined as they have been in more recent years? Is there something novel about the current life styles of the population of our country or is it merely that our society has matured to the point where it will no longer abandon people to poverty and hunger as it did in the thirties? Does the striking growth in Aid to Dependent Children (ADC) reflect a basic change in familial relationships or is it that the State only now is beginning to take responsibility for problems that were always present but remained part of the invisible society of the poor? These issues remain to be more thoroughly researched. The fact is, however, that the number of welfare recipients is growing.

The national welfare load in 1960 consisted of 6.8 million people and in 1965, 8.2 million. From 1965 to 1970, it increased by more than 50 percent, in contrast to the first five years of the 1960s, in which the increase was approximately 20 percent. And the greater part of this increase is in the categorical forms of welfare.[6] There has been an increase in the inclusiveness of categories and in the proportion of people covered by these categories as contrasted with municipal assistance.*

The number of people publicly assisted in New York City has risen more sharply than in the rest of the nation. In 1948 the city had a quarter of a million welfare recipients; by 1965 the figure had risen to a half million. In 1965 one in 16 New Yorkers and one in nine children under 18 were receiving some form of public assistance. In 1960 only one in 24 residents and one in 16 children were welfare recipients. The

*See Appendix 1.2 for definition of welfare categories.

50 percent increase in New York City's welfare load in the 1960-1965 period was more than three times Chicago's increase (16 percent) and more than twice Philadelphia's increase (25 percent).

The half million New Yorkers on welfare in 1965 grew to three-quarters of a million persons by 1967. Between 1948 and 1965 the welfare rolls increased by a quarter of a million recipients. By 1968 the rolls had grown by another quarter of a million (Exhibit 1.2).[7] New York City's welfare load in early 1972 was over 1.3 million, with the net number of additional recipients running between 5,000 and 15,000 each month. Why did this growth occur?

EXHIBIT 1.2

AVERAGE ANNUAL NUMBER OF NEW YORK CITY WELFARE RECIPIENTS BY CATEGORY

YEAR	CATEGORY OF WELFARE					
	Totals	Home Relief	ADC TADC[a]	Old Age Assistance	Aid to Blind	Aid to Disabled[b]
1941	498,000[c]	389,000	43,000	55,000	2,000	9,000
1942	368,000	275,000	37,000	55,000	2,000	—
1943	124,000	39,000	28,000	56,000	2,000	—
1944	113,000	28,000	31,000	53,000	2,000	—
1945	122,000	25,000	43,000	52,000	2,000	—
1946	157,000	49,000	49,000	53,000	2,000	4,000
1947	216,000	88,000	65,000	55,000	2,000	5,000
1948	234,000	94,000	75,000	57,000	2,000	6,000
1949	264,000	110,000	86,000	60,000	3,000	7,000
1950	351,000	135,000	140,000	62,000	3,000	12,000
1951	308,000	94,000	133,000	60,000	3,000	18,000
1952	287,000	74,000	130,000	59,000	3,000	21,000
1953	256,000	55,000	120,000	56,000	3,000	23,000
1954	264,000	53,000	129,000	53,000	3,000	27,000
1955	282,000	55,000	145,000	51,000	3,000	29,000
1956	279,000	50,000	151,000	48,000	3,000	28,000
1957	295,000	52,000	166,000	47,000	3,000	27,000
1958	329,000	65,000	189,000	46,000	3,000	27,000
1959	329,000	64,000	192,000	44,000	3,000	26,000
1960	323,000	60,000	194,000	42,000	2,000	25,000
1961	346,000	53,000	230,000	36,000	2,000	24,000
1962	343,000	43,000	243,000	32,000	2,000	23,000
1963	375,000	46,000	272,000	31,000	2,000	23,000
1964	427,000	56,000	315,000	32,000	2,000	22,000
1965	484,000	67,000	361,000	33,000	2,000	22,000
1966	553,000	76,000	416,000	37,000	2,000	22,000
1967	693,000	107,000	516,000	44,000	2,000	24,000
1968	878,000	148,000	645,000	50,000	2,000	32,000
1969	1,011,000	155,000	753,000	58,000	2,000	43,000
1970	1,093,000	151,000	805,000	71,000	3,000	63,000

Source: The City of New York, Department of Social Services, Monthly Statistical Reports, Vols, 1-31, No. 12.

[a] Aid to Dependent Children of Unemployed Parents (TADC) included from 1961 to 1970 only.

[b] Aid to Disabled not included for 1942 to 1945.

[c] Figures have been rounded to the nearest thousand and therefore may not total precisely.

The question of the dynamics of welfare growth has engendered more controversy than enlightenment. The portrayal of the typical welfare recipient runs the spectrum from an able-bodied individual who has found "a good thing" to a person incapacitated (physically or otherwise) for gainful employment. Certainly a phenomenon as widespread as this one provides ample opportunity to illustrate one's own prejudice with anecdotes that fit one or the other end of the range. In the course of this study some attempt will be made to define statistically the varied characteristics of the people on present-day welfare rolls. In this section, however, only a few of the reasons that have been advanced will be explored.

EMPLOYMENT OPPORTUNITIES AND WELFARE

In the 1969 report by the New York State Joint Legislative Committee appointed to revise the State Social Services Law, an analysis was made of the linkage between employment and welfare recipiency. Data unearthed by the committee showed that until 1959 new applications for family assistance followed the level of unemployment, with roughly one year's delay. When unemployment rose the number of families needing public assistance also increased. In 1959, however, the number of cases rose on a curve independent of employment and went on rising —and continues to rise (Exhibit 1.3).

EXHIBIT 1.3

IMPORTANT SOCIAL INDICATORS

YEAR	INDICATORS					
	Gross National Product	Personal Income (Total)	Public Assistance Payments	Unemployed as Percent of Civilian Labor Force (UNADJ)	Consumer Price Index (All Items)	Consumer Price Index (Housing Only)
1960	\$503.7[a]	\$401.0	\$3.2	5.5%	103.1[b]	103.1
1961	520.1	416.8	3.4	6.7	104.2	103.9
1962	560.3	442.6	3.5	5.5	105.4	104.8
1963	590.5	465.5	3.6	5.7	106.7	106.0
1964	632.4	497.5	3.8	5.2	108.1	107.2
1965	684.9	538.9	4.0	4.5	109.9	108.5
1966	749.9	587.2	4.3	3.8	113.1	111.1
1967	793.9	629.3	4.9	3.8	116.3	114.3
1968	865.0	688.7	5.6	3.6	121.2	119.1
1969	931.4	748.9	6.6	3.5	127.7	126.7
1970 (Feb.)	—	781.5	7.6	4.7	132.5	132.2

Source: Department of Labor, Bureau of Labor Statistics, *Social Security Bulletin*, Vol. 33, No. 12, December 1970.

[a]Monetary figures are expressed in billions of dollars.

[b]Consumer price index is based on 1957 to 1959 = 100.

The committee's report points to the changing nature of job opportunities between 1960 and 1970. It cites a Department of Labor report which showed that professional and technical job opportunities for the period in question increased approximately 40 percent; jobs for skilled workers, 23 percent; and jobs for semiskilled workers only 18 percent. The Department of Labor anticipated no future increase in job opportunities for unskilled workers and a continued decrease in agricultural employment. The committee also pointed out that the proportion of adult men in the work force in surveyed slum areas of New York state dropped from 74 to 64 percent between April 1960 and November 1967. During the same period there was very little decline (77 to 75 percent) in the United States as a whole.[8]

Help-wanted advertising in New York City through 1968-1969 indicates no shortage of jobs for the able bodied. It suggests, however, that the low wage level in most of the unskilled trades has some relationship to the disinclination of the unskilled to take advantage of these "opportunities." Meanwhile New York City has ridden the crest of the national wave of increases in the cost of living. In addition, the majority of welfare growth has been accounted for, as will be discussed in detail later, by women with children and without resident husbands—the typical ADC cases. (In a small number of cases the problem may be a wifeless father with children.)

In the course of this survey, a structured probability sample of 412 welfare recipients was asked why they weren't working. In Exhibit 1.4 their reasons are given. If allowance is made for old age and for parents

EXHIBIT 1.4

REASONS FOR BEING UNEMPLOYED OR ONLY PARTIALLY EMPLOYED IN 1970 BY CATEGORY OF WELFARE

REASON NOT EMPLOYED	CATEGORY OF WELFARE									
	Home Relief		Old Age Assistance		Aid to Disabled[a]		Aid to Dependent Children		Total	
	No.	%	No.	%	No.	%	No.	%	No.	%
Laid Off	0	0.0	0	0.0	0	0.0	4	2.3	4	1.3
Acute Illness/ Accident	5	10.9	1	2.3	3	6.5	11	6.4	20	6.5
Chronic Illness	24	52.2	19	43.2	40	87.0	41	24.0	124	40.4
Needed at Home	9	19.6	1	2.3	1	2.2	110	64.3	121	39.4
Retired	7	15.2	21	47.7	1	2.2	3	1.8	32	10.4
Other	1	2.2	1	2.3	1	2.2	1	0.6	4	1.3
NA/DK	0	0.0	1	2.3	0	0.0	1	0.6	2	0.7
Total	46	100.0	44	100.0	46	100.0	171	100.0	307	100.0

Source: Housing of Welfare Recipients Survey, 1970.

[a] Aid to the Disabled includes Aid to the Blind and Veterans Assistance unless otherwise noted.

needed at home with their children, the single most frequent reason given was health problems. As the Joint Legislative Committee pointed out,

> About 60 percent of our public welfare cases involved health problems—we believe strongly that many young people get sidetracked in schools and life itself by poor teeth, poor hearing, poor sight, and undiscovered internal body deficiencies. With older persons it is more serious because of years of neglect.[9]

To the cynic the reason of poor health frequently is viewed as a socially acceptable rationalization for inactivity. There is increasing evidence, however, to indicate that it is far more than that.[10]

Certainly, however, part of the welfare increase is a result of the increasing publicity given the availability of welfare as well as the decline of the historic stigma of being on the welfare rolls. In the past there have always been poor people who did not apply for welfare assistance even though they qualified. Today a higher proportion of those who qualify are aware of the programs and are receptive to them. The welfare rights organizations and the poverty program, among others, have stimulated this awareness. In later chapters welfare recipients' membership in and/or awareness of such groups will be discussed.

Until 1971 the Department of Social Services administered welfare in New York City relatively liberally. While this may have led to some growth, it is questionable whether a major amount of it can be blamed on administrative laxity. Certainly the formal and informal communication systems within a large city such as New York will make more people more aware of the benefits that they can secure than they would be aware of in less densely habitated regions. For example, in a recent survey of poverty pockets in northwest New Jersey,[11] only one-third of the people who qualified for welfare were securing benefits in the relatively small cities and towns typical of the area. It is difficult to believe that the same ratio applies in New York City.

In any case, able-bodied males certainly do not dominate the welfare rolls. Increasingly, welfare expenditures are divided between the elderly (predominantly white) and primarily fatherless families on the Aid to Families with Dependent Children (ADC) program (typically minority group members).

In the nation as a whole, recipients of assistance under the ADC program increased from 3,080,000 in 1960 to 4,457,000 in 1965. This increase in ADC recipients exceeded the total decrease in the national welfare load by 7,000; that is, ADC more than made up for the decline in recipients in other categories. By August of 1970 there were 8,659,000 ADC recipients, three-quarters of them children. This one program includes nearly 70 percent of the total number of welfare recipients.

The growth of ADC has not occurred without interpretations. These range from causes related to slavery and the matrifocal family, to the lack of jobs for males, to the statement that welfare benefits are so generous that they outprice potential male heads of household. Determining which, if any, of these are important factors is beyond the scope of this study. It should be noted, however, that in New York City the proportion of the total Puerto Rican population receiving ADC is substantially higher than the equivalent proportion of blacks. Given the cultural patterns of strong masculine dominance among the former, it is difficult to label them subject to a matrifocal family.

The poor are not a novelty in our major cities. The older core areas' declining capacity to deal with them, however, may be relatively new. The American city is no longer a major locus of relatively unskilled factory work. Some industries which are labor intensive and demand low skills have simply been replaced by industries producing goods that respond better to capital intensification. In addition, the merchandise produced by the former type of activity is now frequently imported. In essence the United States has exported the jobs once required for its low-cost, labor-intensive merchandise. The tenement-house industries of New York, which were once basic centers of employment for agrarian newcomers from across the ocean, have substantially disappeared. There are still some remnants scattered through the Bowery and in Chinatown, but they are relatively few.[12] Again, while some of this manufacturing has moved to relatively densely populated areas in smaller communities, such as the housedress industries in the Carolinas, much of it has moved abroad. Even Puerto Rico, long the recipient of this shift, particularly in the needle trades, now faces heavy competition from such areas as Formosa, Hong Kong, Korea and other countries with relatively cheap labor.

The newcomer to the city was driven from farming by mechanization, which in cotton, for example, cut down the amount of manpower by 95 percent in one generation. Labor need diminished in equivalent proportions in many of the other areas of farm production in the United States.

But the emigrant finds little demand for his labor in the city. The limited growth in the service trades has not had much impact on his employability, since these jobs are low paid and simply not plentiful enough. As a result, the city, rather than serving as a staging ground for upward mobility, instead has become a terminus for many. In this respect, as in so many others, New York City is the classic example of the urban dilemma. While office employment has increased, blue-collar jobs are fast disappearing. Efforts to bring the poor into clerical occupations are just beginning. An estimated 40,000 jobs in the city vanished with the automation of elevators alone.

The decline of the urban job market no doubt bears some relationship to the fact that three-fourth of all welfare recipients in New York state are on the New York City welfare rolls, but it does not explain why one out of every ten recipients in the United States lives in New York City.

BACKGROUND OF THE STUDY

The purposes of this study are several. Initially it was designed as an extension of a research effort on the economics of New York City's housing stock.[13] In the course of that study, which involved substantial interviews with landlords, and the development of data on operating costs and a number of other variables, it became evident that the larger the proportion of welfare tenants in a particular building, the poorer the quality of the structure. This held even when variables such as race of tenants, age and experience of landlord, scale of landlord holdings, rent levels, rent increases over time, profitability, and repairs and maintenance costs were controlled.

The proportion of welfare tenancy, in terms of statistical analysis, is obviously tied to the maintenance variable. The primary objective, we felt, was to get a stronger feeling for the housing market from the viewpoint of the welfare tenant. How does he find housing? What does he (or society) get for his/their dollars? How and how well does the market work? And are there some obvious areas of reshaping that should be undertaken?

The proportion of welfare money that goes toward rent payments is enormous. In 1968, according to a study by the Department of Housing and Urban Development (HUD), welfare clients spent $1.1 billion for housing. This figure is identical with the total amount budgeted in 1969 for all kinds of social and rehabilitation services. It was also about one-third of the amount budgeted for cash assistance in all public assistance categories.[14] In 1969 the New York State Board of Social Welfare estimated that welfare rents in New York state alone amounted to substantially over $400 million. While the quality of environment enjoyed by welfare recipients will be discussed in detail later, it is undoubtedly true that these dollars frequently do not buy adequate housing. Is this simply a matter of economics? Of prejudice? What variables enter into the poor quality of welfare housing?

The statistical relationship between poor maintenance and welfare tenancy is subject to a host of interpretations. It may be that welfare recipients are accepted as tenants only when a building is on its last legs; or that, in the very act of letting in welfare recipients, owners feel this is the end of the structure and therefore reduce maintenance (the self-fulfilling prophecy); or that welfare recipients are destructive to the buildings they live in. And this is by no means an exhaustive list.

But housing and attitudes toward housing cannot be viewed in isolation. It is essential that they be placed within the context of the interests, worries and aspirations of welfare recipients. A number of psychological measures, therefore, are applied to provide the rough outlines of this broader framework. Much of the material which follows explores these relationships.

HOUSING'S LINKAGE TO SOCIAL TRAUMA

A generation ago a heading like the preceding would have been redundant. The social thinkers of the 1930s, reared on Jacob Riis' vision of the slum as the generator of all social ills,[15] completely accepted this relationship. Doing away with the slums was equated with victory over vice, crime, ill health, educational underachievement and most of the other social problems of the day.

The battle today, at least in some places, has shifted from improving the absolute quality of housing—the reduction of very severe overcrowding, providing more adequate toilet facilities and the like—to one of comparative quality of housing. Does the discontinuity between the housing available to the poor and the welfare recipient, and the much promulgated middle-class ideal—at least that vision of it presented in television and the popular media—generate social problems?

Resolving the older problem is simply a matter of maintenance and economics. Resolving the second is much more difficult. In any case the literature is far from adequate. Alvin Schorr puts it very bluntly:

> ...it is said that poor housing causes poverty. Research has been largely confined to the statistical correlations which fail to demonstrate a causal relationship. When poor people moved into decent housing, property deteriorated, the public concluded that poverty caused poor housing rather than the other way around. On the whole, research has abandoned the question of this unsatisfactory point.[16]

In any case, much public discussion suffers from the kind of thinking exemplified as "I'm not a horse, but if I were a horse how would I feel living in that stable?" We have attempted to avoid this pitfall here. While certain measurements of housing quality are determined from objective observation, it is our belief that not only the actual state of housing but the vision of that reality determines consumer satisfaction and response.

Certainly, the absolute quality of housing occupied by welfare recipients, as will be detailed later, still leaves much to be desired. When a male head of household who is presently on Home Relief was asked what he wanted most in a place to live, his answer was very modest: "A decent gas stove, running hot water, a clean place, more room, and no roaches and mice." When asked about his present apartment, he answered: "The place isn't fit for cattle to live in. People set fires right outside of your door and the place isn't fit to live in."

Would they still set fires if the apartments were better? That is a very important question. One of the difficulties in answering it, however, is the combination of indignation about a particular apartment and the lack of safety and overall deterioration in the area. It is very difficult to distinguish between the impact of people's problems, maintenance problems and societal problems. In the next chapter, we will discuss the methodology used in this study to clarify some very limited aspects of these factors.

Chapter 3 is concerned with the characteristics of welfare recipients: how long they have lived in New York, where they come from, their ages, household configuration, education and employment history.

In Chapter 4 attention is turned to the types of housing accommodations presently utilized by welfare recipients. Is there such a thing as a welfare building—a building largely or solely occupied by welfare recipients? If so, are a significant number of New York City's welfare recipients so housed and is this an increasing trend? How can the quality of accommodations best be appraised? How do welfare recipients find their apartments, and once settled how long do they stay? How does the Department of Social Services affect recipients' search for housing? Data on public housing's provision of accommodations for welfare recipients, as well as the function and significance of hotel residency, are also presented in this chapter.

Chapters 5 and 6 revolve around the welfare recipient's attitudes toward his housing and its location, his hopes, fears and general outlook toward life. What is the level of satisfaction with the housing accommodations? What kind of things are wanted that are not presently available? What determines satisfaction with housing—area, garbage collection, apartment maintenance, building maintenance, safety, actual apartment configuration?

Chapter 6 focuses on the personal hopes and fears of welfare recipients, using the Cantril Self-Anchoring Striving Scale technique. We have compared responses secured in the course of this study of welfare recipients with equivalent measures taken from a variety of groups.

Chapters 7 and 8 take up the costs of welfare housing; rents, operating expenses and profitability. Do welfare rents vary significantly as a function of ethnicity or category of welfare? If any alternate means of housing welfare recipients are used, much more intensive analyses of the present economics of welfare housing will be required. A step in this direction is taken in Chapter 8 which contains analyses of expenses, repairs and maintenance, and the relationship of profitability to welfare housing. Projections of alternate uses for the presently expended in welfare rents are discussed as well as alternative approaches to future funding. Particular emphasis is placed on the problems of potential alternative financing.

The final chapter of the study is devoted to a summary of the findings and their policy implications.

NOTES

1. United State Department of Health, Education and Welfare, *Public Assistance Statistics* (Washington, D.C., August 1970).

2. Beatrice Ida Vulcan, *Fair Hearings in the Public Assistance Programs of the New York City Department of Welfare*, unpublished doctoral dissertation (New York: School of Social Work, Columbia University, 1972) p. 316.

3. *Bureau of Labor Statistics Report 375*, C.P.S. Series P-23, No. 29.

4. Is the New York experience unique or a forecast of things to come? Certainly a similar situation cannot be far off in Boston where one out of every five residents is on welfare. Even some of the older suburbs are fast approaching the New York level of expenditures, though the pattern is obscured by variations in funding procedures. See George Sternlieb et al., *The Zone of Emergence* (New Brunswick, New Jersey: Transaction Books, 1972).

5. National Center for Social Statistics, *Expenditures for Public Assistance Payments 1936-1970* (Health, Education and Welfare, July 6, 1971).

6. See Appendix 1.2 for more on growth rates.

7. *Public Welfare in Transition: The Challenge/Change in Communities, Concepts, Cost.* Report of the Joint Legislative Committee to Revise the Social Services Law of New York State, 1969.

8. Joint Legislative Committee, p. 19.

9. Ibid., p. 47.

10. On the incidence, for example, of serious anemia, see George Sternlieb and Mildred Barry, *Newark: Social Needs and Social Resources* (Rutgers, 1967), p. 99. For comparable data see Jack Chernick, Bernard P. Indik and George Sternlieb, *Newark—Population and Labor Force* (Rutgers, 1968), p. 16.

11. The unpublished study was conducted by the Rutgers Center for Urban Policy Research in conjunction with the Northwest New Jersey Community Action Program, Inc., in 1971.

12. For a good description of the tenement-house industries in New York City at an earlier date, see Abraham Cahan, *The Rise of Jacob Levinsky: a Novel* (New York: Harper, 1917) and Moses Rischlin, *The Promised City* (New York: Corinth Books, 1964). For an analysis of the shift of employment opportunities in New York City, see Max Hall, ed. *Made in New York* (Cambridge, Mass.: Harvard University Press, 1959).

13. George Sternlieb, *The Urban Housing Dilemma* (New York: Housing Development Administration, 1970).

14. U.S. Department of Health, Education and Welfare, *The Role of Public Welfare in Housing:* A Report to the House Committee on Ways and Means (Washington, D.C., 1969), p. 8. It should be noted that a later estimate by HEW which included rents paid by Social Security recipients amounted to $9 billion. See *HEW and Housing* (unpublished memorandum, September 13, 1970).

15. Jacob Riis, *How the Other Half Lives: Studies Among The Tenements of New York* (New York: Charles Scribner's Sons, 1890).

16. Alvin Schorr, *Explorations and Social Policy* (New York: Basic Books, 1968), pp. 272-286. For a review of the literature, see Nathan Glazer, "Housing Problems and Housing Policies" in *The Public Interest* (Spring 1967).

Chapter 2

METHODOLOGY

This study has a number of targets. The first is to describe the character and quality of the housing available to welfare recipients. The second is to describe the welfare recipient's view of his housing and its setting, as well as his own self-image, hopes and fears. A third goal is to analyze in depth the present economics of the market in regard to the housing of welfare recipients and the possibility that reshaping the operation of the market might provide a better physical environment. This in turn involves questions such as financing, landlord attitude and the like.

There are three basic research approaches that we have used to achieve the objectives. As indicated in Chapter 1, we have relied heavily on data secured in research for *The Urban Housing Dilemma* to define the nature of welfare recipients' housing.[1] In the course of that study, which was conducted for the New York City Rent and Rehabilitation Administration, intensive analysis was undertaken of a structured probability sample of 963 buildings. This involved an interior and exterior check of maintenance, analysis of the title to the building, determination of maximum rents under the rent-control laws, and analysis of the variety of landlord and tenant inputs that may have altered those rents for a 12-year period from 1955 to 1967 for the 30,000 apartments within the structure groups. Municipal records of tax assessments and tax delinquencies were checked for each of the structures in the sample and interviews were held with the landlords of 710 of the

963 structures in the study. In addition, from one to seven years of data on operating costs were secured for 664 of these structures.[2] After a variety of checking and auditing procedures, interviews were conducted with representatives of the majority of the institutions which held mortgages on the sampled properties. What were their attitudes toward these parcels? Would they extend additional financing? Why? What was the role of the welfare variable?

This part of the study was based upon all of New York City's multiple-family rental structures that derived the bulk of their incomes from residential use and had more than 80 percent of their units rent controlled. This involves approximately one million housing units in New York City in approximately 53,000 structures. In the body of this work, the data are along those lines. New York City has a total of two million rented housing units; about 200,000 of those units are rent controlled and are excluded from this analysis. These involve units which are conversions of small structures as well as single-room occupancies. Those units which are not rent controlled under the 1943 Temporary Rent Control Law are typically structures built after 1947 which have higher rents. The proportion of welfare tenants in such units is relatively small. There are, in addition, around 100,000 decontrolled units. These typically have been decontrolled either because of their luxury status (apartments under certain strictures renting for more than $250 a month), because they have been essentially rebuilt under certain rehabilitation programs, or because they have been divided into smaller units. The welfare occupancy in these units is not known, but it certainly is smaller in both proportion and absolute number than it is in the areas of the housing market sampled here.

The level of welfare tenancy was so striking a factor affecting the decisions of the landlords and the attitudes of the institutional mortgage grantors toward the parcel's desirability as collateral, as to call for much more analysis than was possible within the limitations of *The Urban Housing Dilemma.* Through the cooperation of the Human Resources Administration and the Housing Development Administration, the master check tape (from which almost all New York City welfare payments are made) was secured for March 1968, approximately the same time as the rent-control data had been developed. This enabled us to cross-tabulate the results secured in the rent-control study with the definitive level of welfare recipients recorded in the tape. (In the earlier study some cross-tabulations had been attempted based upon the landlord's judgement of the degree of welfare tenantry. For comparison of the landlords' statements and the data obtained from the actual welfare tape, see Chapter 5.)

ANHATTAN BY CATEGORY OF WELFARE

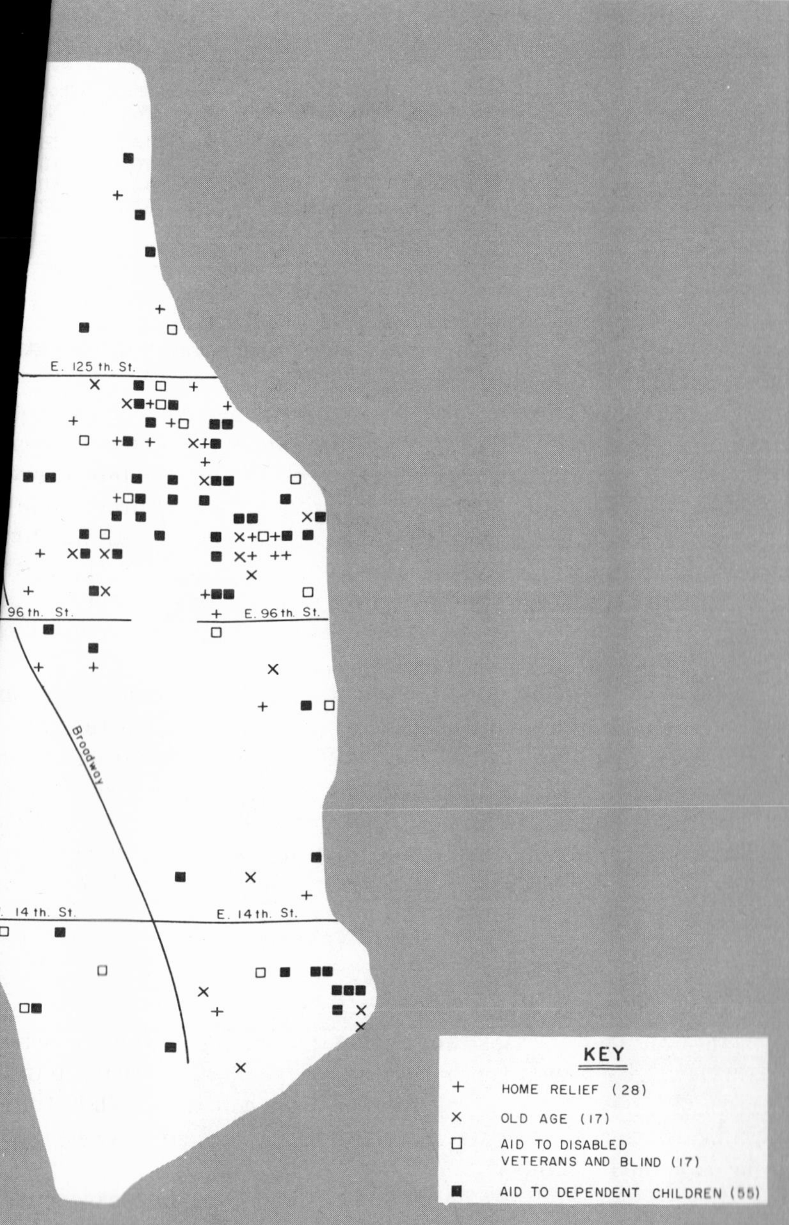

A similar tape of welfare recipients was secured in February 1970. This, in turn, permitted analysis of the changes in the level of welfare tenancy densities in specific buildings over time and provided insight into the question of whether the general expansion of the welfare rolls has increased the number of "welfare" buildings, enlarged the proportion of welfare recipients within buildings that had already housed welfare recipients, or led to the dispersion of welfare recipients throughout the city. In addition it served as a base for the development of other samples. This analysis provided a basic view of the owners and infrastructure of the city's private residential buildings by their degree of welfare tenancy.

THE ATTITUDES OF WELFARE RECIPIENTS

In order to secure insight into the attitudes of welfare recipients, a series of semi-structured group interviews were held with welfare recipients, in which their own views of housing and the costs and benefits attendent to it were discussed.[3] There was a single discussion leader matched, as best we could, to the ethnicity of the majority of the participants.

To minimize the potential interference of the primary researchers in the interviews, the interviews were video taped. The video-tape camera requires neither extraordinary lighting nor studio conditions of any kind. While the intrusiveness of the camera and its operator may have some effect on the interviews, in general, after five or ten minutes it does not seem to be a deterrent to open discussion.

Whatever the constraints imposed by this approach, the virtues of preserving the interviews for detailed review and study are considerable. Verbal interaction requires much more than an ear—the facial expressions, the intensities and all the elements that are recorded visibly are, in the authors' opinions, extremely important. These tapes, each of which lasted from one and a half to two and a half hours, were reviewed individually, with colleagues and with students, to provide a systematic and thorough analysis of the welfare recipient's view of his housing and environment.

The interviews were, by design, relatively unstructured. Prior to the interviews the discussion leader had memorized a list of ten topics which were to be introduced if the conversation lagged. They included: my apartment, my rent, the landlord, the janitor, the neighborhood, transportation, maintenance of the apartment and building, the Welfare Department, safety and the like. Other than these the interviewer's remarks were limited to "How did you find your present apartment?" In general, little intervention was required.

The group interviews were collected from February to April 1970 as follows:

1. February 21, 1970: Members of the Welfare Rights Organization, New Brunswick, New Jersey.
2. February 24, 1970: Younger welfare recipients in New York City.
3. March 6, 1970: Welfare Rights Group, typically ADC mothers, in Newark, New Jersey.
4. March 10, 1970: Welfare Rights Group in New York City.
5. April 10, 1970: Spanish-speaking welfare recipients in New York City.
6. April 23, 1970: Old Age Recipients in New York City.

Participants were each paid a $5 fee for their services.

These interviews enabled us to identify major areas of concern. These were followed up in detail in the structured interviews.

THE PROBABILITY SAMPLE

A random sample of welfare cases was drawn from the February 1970 check tape mentioned earlier which listed almost all welfare cases receiving aid during that month.[4] From this sample, as the accompanying exhibit shows, 412 interviews were completed out of the total sample of 500.

EXHIBIT 2.1

RESPONDENTS VERSUS NON-RESPONDENTS BY BOROUGH

BOROUGH	STATUS OF INTERVIEW					
	Respondents		Non-respondents		Total Sample	
	No.	%	No.	%	No.	%
Manhattan	117	75.5	38	24.5	155	100.0
Brooklyn	158	89.3	19	10.7	177	100.0
Bronx	108	82.4	23	17.6	131	100.0
Queens	24	77.4	7	22.6	31	100.0
Richmond	5	83.3	1	16.7	6	100.0
Total	412	82.4	88	17.6	500	100.0

Source: Housing of Welfare Recipients Survey, 1970.

Exhibit 2.1 analyzes the sample ratios by borough versus the completions by borough. There is no considerable skew in the geographic distribution of successfully completed interviews. Similarly, Exhibit 2.2 indicates respondents versus non-respondents by category of welfare. For definitions of the welfare categories see Appendix 1.2. Exhibits 2.3, 2.4, 2.5 and 2.6 give the locations of the respondents.

The reasons for failing to secure interviews with the 88 non-respondents vary, and are summarized in Exhibit 2.7. Only 28 cases refused to

EXHIBIT 2.2

RESPONDENTS VERSUS NON-RES
BY CATEGORY OF WELFARE

CATEGORY OF WELFARE	Tot No.
Home Relief	92
Old Age Assistance	71
Aid to Disabled	74
Aid to Dependent Children	263
Total	500

Source: Housing of Welfare Recipients Survey,

participate. In 33 additional cases, no
peated call-backs.

The 20 cases which are listed as "mo
ber of individuals who were found to re
listed on the check tape. In a substantia
able to find adequate forwarding addres
ment of Social Services or through con
friends. Those who were not found typic
listed premises a considerable length of t
amounted to a year or more, as nearly
neighbors.

Wherever possible the interviewer and t
for ethnicity and language. In a number o
the aged, there were considerable difficult
views. Such problems were epitomized by
deaf mute in a home for the aged in the B
Brooklyn. In this particular case the intervie
attendant. Even with help, however, the inte
a no response (Case No. 2-337-3).

VARIATIONS IN WELFARE CATEGORY

In a number of cases the information secure
terviews about what type of welfare respondent
jibe with data secured from the basic payroll t
indicates the respondents' lack of knowledge, in
be explained so simply.

In 28.2 percent of the entire sample of 412, var
tween the welfare category derived from the che
gory described by the recipient household membe

EXHIBIT 2.4
BOROUGH OF BROOKLYN BY CATEGORY OF WELFARE

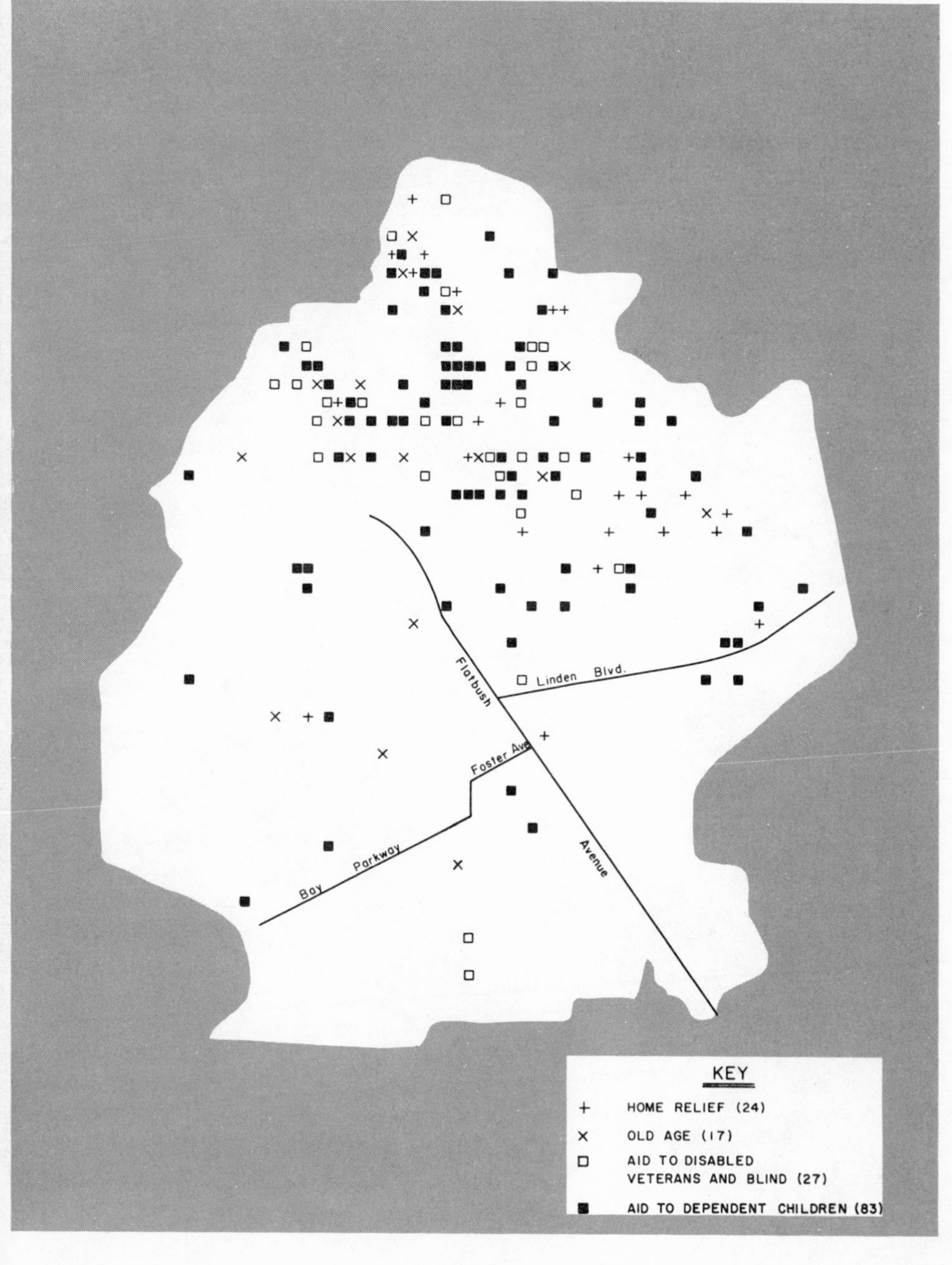

EXHIBIT 2.5
BOROUGH OF THE BRONX BY CATEGORY OF WELFARE

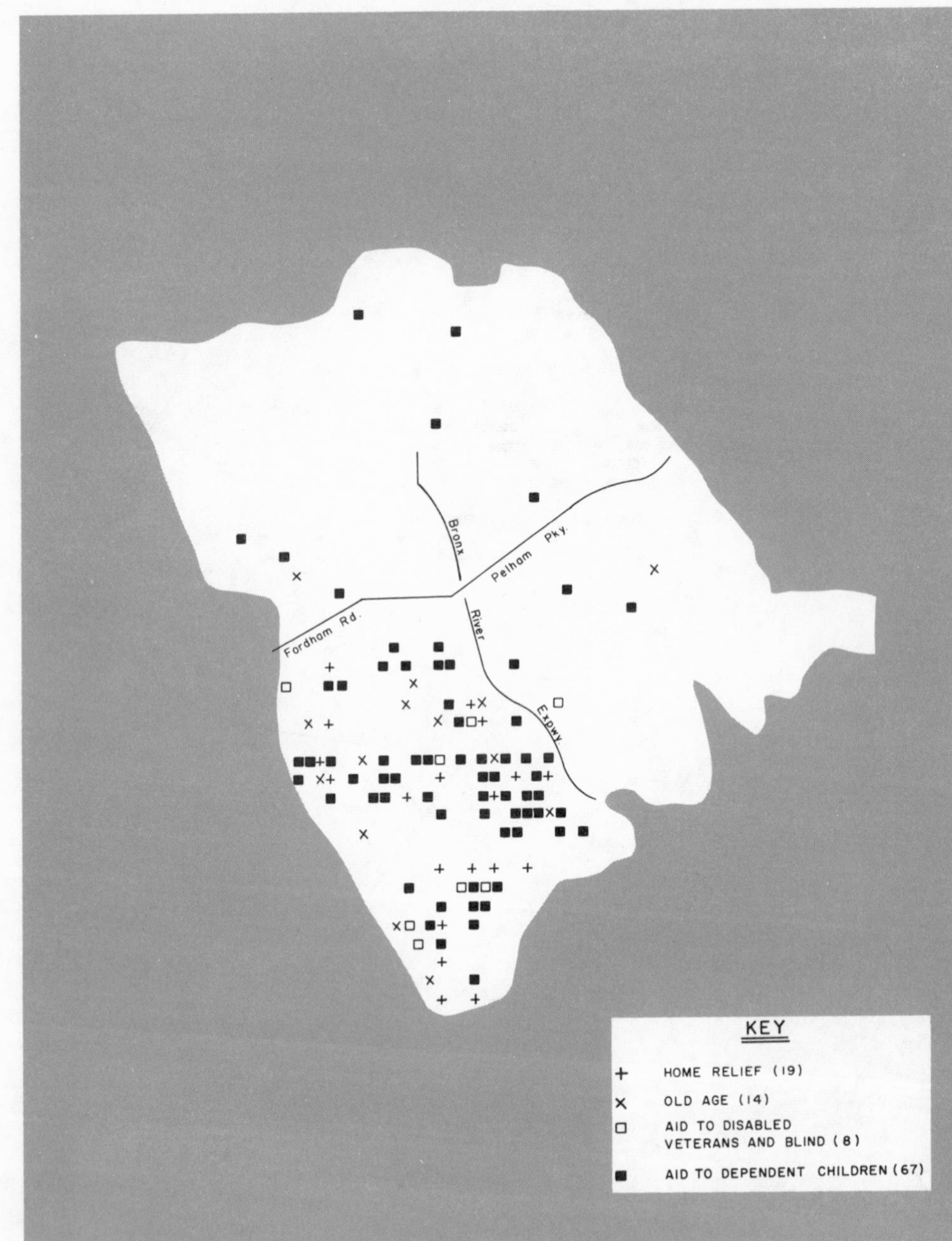

EXHIBIT 2.6

BOROUGHS OF QUEENS AND RICHMOND BY CATEGORY OF WELFARE

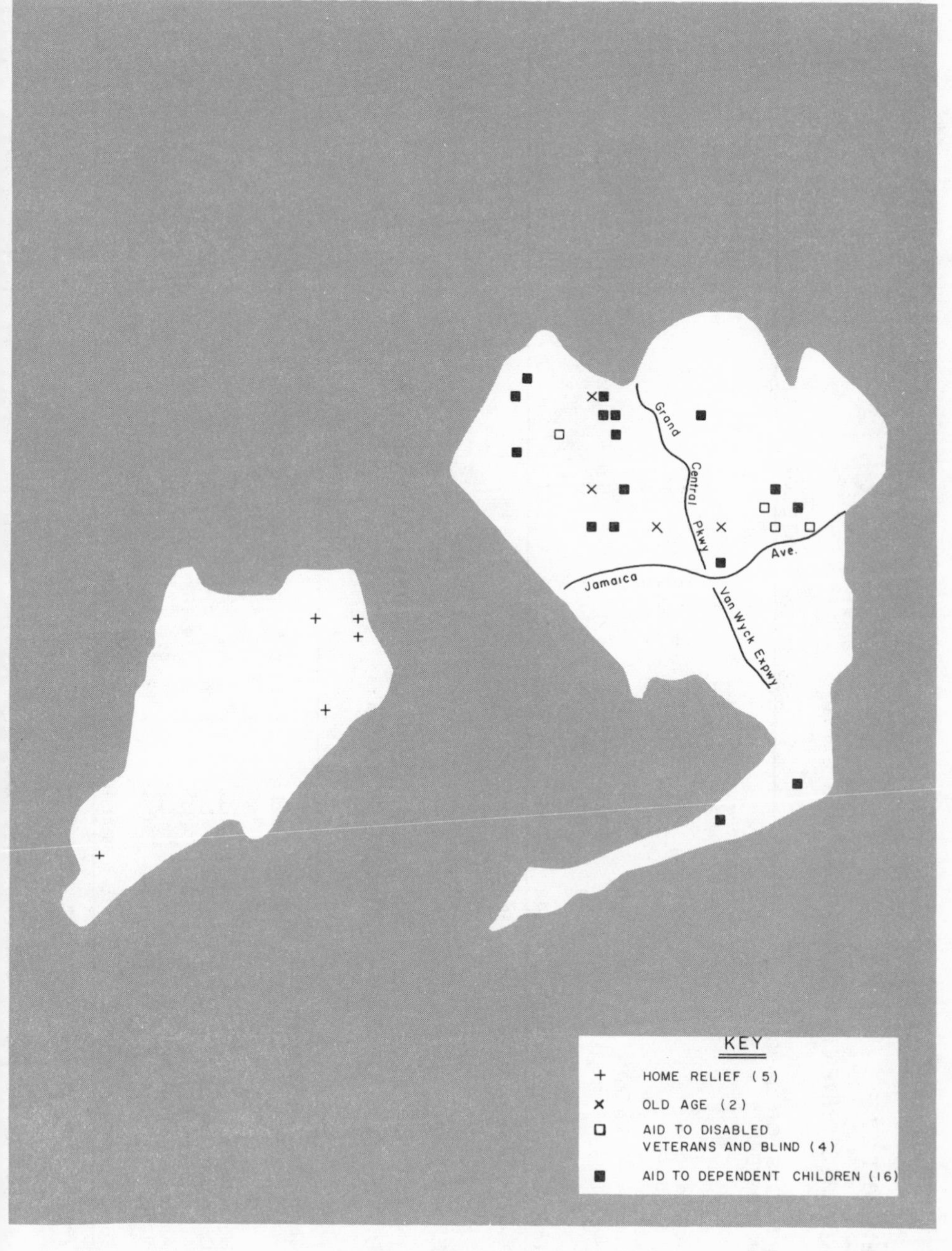

EXHIBIT 2.7

NON-RESPONDENTS BY CATEGORY OF WELFARE

REASONS FOR LACK OF INTERVIEW	CATEGORY OF WELFARE									
	Home Relief		Old Age Assistance		Aid to Disabled		Aid to Dependent Children		Total	
	No.	%	No.	%	No.	%	No.	%	No.	%
No One Home	0	0.0	1	6.7	1	5.9	3	7.9	5	5.7
Refused	5	27.8	3	20.0	7	41.2	13	34.2	28	31.8
Moved	4	22.2	2	13.3	4	23.5	10	26.3	20	22.7
Condemned, Vacant	0	0.0	0	0.0	0	0.0	1	2.6	1	1.1
No Contact	9	50.0	8	53.3	5	29.4	11	28.9	33	37.5
Other	0	0.0	1	6.7	0	0.0	0	0.0	1	1.1
Total	18	100.0	15	100.0	17	100.0	38	100.0	88	100.0

Source: Housing of Welfare Recipients Survey, 1970.

EXHIBIT 2.8

TYPE OF WELFARE ASSISTANCE CLAIMED BY RESPONDENT COMPARED TO DEPARTMENT OF SOCIAL SERVICES CATEGORY

TYPE OF ASSISTANCE CLAIMED BY RESPONDENTS	CATEGORY OF WELFARE									
	Home Relief		Old Age Assistance		Aid to Disabled		Aid to Dependent Children		Total	
	No.	%	No.	%	No.	%	No.	%	No.	%
Home Relief	10	13.3	2	3.6	5	8.8	26	11.6	43	10.4
Old Age Assistance	7	9.3	26	47.3	2	3.5	1	0.4	36	8.7
Aid to Disabled	36	48.0	9	16.4	39	68.4	25	11.1	109	26.5
Aid to Dependent Children	7	9.3	1	1.8	0	0.0	140	62.2	148	35.9
NA/DK	15	20.0	17	30.9	11	19.3	33	14.7	76	18.4
Total	75	100.0	55	100.0	57	100.0	225	100.0	412	100.0

Source: Housing of Welfare Recipients Survey, 1970.

proportionately according to ethnicity; discrepancies were noted with 15.6 percent of the whites, 20.6 percent of the blacks and fully 40.9 percent of the Spanish-speaking respondents. This may indicate a language problem. In part, recipients' errors regarding their welfare category may also have been a function of relative differences in their length of tenure on welfare. When the groups were analyzed by age, however, it was clear that errors affected the center much more than the wings of the sample, with approximately one-fourth of the 26 to 57 age category making such mistakes as compared to less than 10 percent of the younger and older groups.

Exhibit 2.8 outlines the variations between the respondent's description of the type of welfare received and the check tape data. Note particularly the variation in definition of Home Relief. There is some evidence, based on information secured by the interviewers, that people disabled by drug addiction increasingly have been included within this grouping. The data are summarized in Exhibit 2.9.

EXHIBIT 2.9

CLASSIFICATION CHANGE BY CATEGORY OF WELFARE

	CATEGORY OF WELFARE									
CLASSIFICATION CHANGE	Home Relief		Old Age Assistance		Aid to Disabled		Aid to Dependent Children		Total	
	No.	%	No.	%	No.	%	No.	%	No.	%
Yes	50	66.7	12	21.8	10	17.5	44	19.6	116	28.2
No	9	12.0	26	47.3	36	63.2	142	63.1	213	51.7
Unable To Determine	16	21.3	17	30.9	11	19.3	39	17.3	83	20.1
Total	75	100.0	55	100.0	57	100.0	225	100.0	412	100.0

Source: Housing of Welfare Recipients Survey, 1970.

Fully 18.4 percent of the respondents did not even volunteer a guess as to what category of welfare they were in. In part their reluctance may reflect a distaste for verbalizing their situation. Fully 30.9 percent of the 55 Old Age Assistance recipients, 20 percent of Home Relief cases, and nearly that same proportion of the other disabled categories would not discuss their welfare category. Only 14.7 percent of the ADC category declined, however. This may indicate either a variation in the level of information or a disinclination to acknowledge the realities of welfare aid, particularly among the Old Age Assistance recipients.

WHO WAS INTERVIEWED

In over three-fourth of the cases (76.2 percent), the interviews were conducted with the actual heads of household. In 8.3 percent of the cases they were with the wives of the heads of household. In an additional 5.1 percent of the cases they were with the sons or daughters of the heads of household. The remainder were with other people, typically members of the family. In only one case was an interview conducted with someone outside of the household group.

There is some variation between the several categories of welfare recipients interviewed; ADC recipients made up the largest proportion of interviews held with either the head of household or wife. These total over 90 percent of the cases. The low figure is the 73 percent achieved among the Home Relief recipients. It should be noted in this context that 4 percent of the households indicated that they typically had someone outside of the immediate family living with them.

Overall, 22.3 percent of the interviews were with males, 77.7 percent with females. The low figure for males, as would be guessed, is in the ADC category, with only 7.6 percent; the high is in the Aid to Disabled category, at 47.4 percent.

Appendix 2.1 contains the structured interview which was used in this study. Field testing of the instrument was undertaken with welfare recipients outside New York in order to secure a mutual understanding between interviewers and the interviewed on the meaning of the several questions. The instrument was further translated into Spanish as well as Italian and Yiddish when needed. The introductory elements of the interview need little elaboration. The specialized application and principal findings of the Semantic Differential are described in Appendix 5.1; the Cantril Self Anchoring Striving Scale is detailed in Appendix 6.1.

NOTES

1. George Sternlieb, *The Urban Housing Dilemma* (New York: Housing Development, Administration, 1970).

2. A full description of the methodologies employed can be found in *The Urban Housing Dilemma.*

3. For the use of focused interviewing in terms of its heuristic function prior to the setting up of quantitative procedures, see Robert K. Merton *et al. The Focused Interview* 2nd ed. (New York: Columbia University, Bureau of Applied Research, September 1952).

4. A small proportion of cases were not posted to the tape because of processing lags. Similarly a few closed cases are still on the tape pending notification by the local Department of Social Services centers.

Chapter 3

WHO ARE THE WELFARE RECIPIENTS?

For many years urbanists, liberal as well as conservative, viewed the growth of welfare as essentially related to the migration of the poor from obscure hidden pockets of poverty in the agrarian South to the urban North—as a Southern problem transported to Northern cities. How realistic is this model? The discussion which follows touches first on the geographic origins of welfare recipients. How long have they lived in New York? Where did they come from? What kind of place did they live in before they came to the city? And why did they come to New York?

After a brief glance at racial backgrounds and other characteristics of our sample of *individual* recipients, such as marital status, age, education and the like, we will focus on some of the attributes of salient *groups* in the welfare sample: first, age groups, second, households with small children, and finally, their employment and employability.

LENGTH OF RESIDENCE

Exhibit 3.1 presents the answers to the question "How long have you lived in New York City" by category of welfare recipient. Of the total sample, 22.8 percent responded that they have always lived in New York. An additional 42.5 percent have been residents of the city for 15 or more years. Overall, more than 75 percent of the welfare population have lived in New York ten years or more or have "always lived here."

EXHIBIT 3.1

LENGTH OF RESIDENCE IN NEW YORK CITY BY CATEGORY OF WELFARE

LENGTH OF RESIDENCE	CATEGORY OF WELFARE									
	Home Relief		Old Age Assistance		Aid to Disabled		Aid to Dependent Children		Total	
	No.	%	No.	%	No.	%	No.	%	No.	%
Less than One Year	0	0.0	0	0.0	1	1.8	2	0.9	3	0.7
One to Two Years	6	8.0	1	1.8	2	3.5	13	5.8	22	5.3
Three to Four Years	3	4.0	1	1.8	2	3.5	15	6.7	21	5.1
Five to Nine Years	3	4.0	6	10.9	4	7.0	32	14.2	45	10.9
Ten to 14 Years	7	9.3	1	1.8	7	12.3	37	16.4	52	12.6
15 or Over	42	56.0	36	65.5	26	45.6	71	31.6	175	42.5
Always Lived Here	14	18.7	10	18.2	15	26.3	55	24.4	94	22.8
Total	75	100.0	55	100.0	57	100.0	225	100.0	412	100.0

Source: Housing of Welfare Recipients Survey, 1970.

EXHIBIT 3.2

LENGTH OF RESIDENCE IN NEW YORK CITY BY ETHNICITY

LENGTH OF RESIDENCE	ETHNICITY									
	White		Negro		Spanish Speaking		Other[a]		Total	
	No.	%	No.	%	No.	%	No.	%	No.	%
Less than One Year	0	0.0	0	0.0	3	1.8	0	0.0	3	0.7
One to Two Years	0	0.0	3	1.7	19	11.6	0	0.0	22	5.3
Three to Four Years	0	0.0	4	2.2	17	10.4	0	0.0	21	5.1
Five to Nine Years	1	1.6	19	10.6	25	15.2	0	0.0	45	10.9
Ten to 14 Years	1	1.6	20	11.1	31	18.9	0	0.0	52	12.6
15 or Over	26	40.6	84	46.7	61	37.2	4	100.0	175	42.5
Always Lived Here	36	56.3	50	27.8	8	4.9	0	0.0	94	22.8
Total	64	100.0	180	100.0	164	100.0	4	100.0	412	100.0

Source: Housing of Welfare Recipients Survey, 1970.

[a]Respondents from oriental background.

Only 11.1 percent indicate a residency under five years. Even if it is assumed that some respondents exaggerated their length of stay in New York City because they are afraid of residency requirements or think they have been especially selected for investigation, there is no question that most are actually long-time residents of the city.

As would be anticipated, the preceding generalization is especially true of people receiving Old Age Assistance. In this category more than four out of five (83.7 percent) were either born in or have lived in New York for 15 or more years. In the case of ADC the situation is more mixed. Nearly one-fourth (24.4 percent) have "always lived in New York," with 31.6 percent more having lived in the city for 15 years or longer. While there are obviously more recent immigrants among the ADC recipients, only slightly over one-fourth of them (26.7 percent) have been in the city less than ten years. Thus, earlier assumptions that Northern welfare recipients are primarily recent immigrants from the South are substantially called into question by the data. Recent attempts to revitalize minimum residence requirements are misplaced: less than 1 percent of the sample have lived in New York City under one year.

Exhibit 3.2 analyzes the data on length of residence by ethnicity of respondent. Only 3.2 percent of the whites have been in New York under 15 years. This percentage contrasts very sharply with the data for the Spanish-speaking group, which has the highest degree of recent immigration. Here 13.4 percent have been in the city for less than three years, with an additional 10.4 percent in New York for three to four years. This data provides an interesting contrast with that for black respondents. Fewer than 2 percent of black welfare recipients have been in the city for less than two years, with only an additional 2.2 percent at the three-to-four-year mark. Indeed, nearly three-quarters (74.5 percent) have always lived in the city or have lived there for 15 years or more.

Certainly, in terms of length of residence in New York, black welfare recipients are quite different from Puerto Rican recipients. Black recipients' knowledge of the housing market, at least as gauged by the longevity of their experience in New York, is probably more extensive.

PLACE OF ORIGIN

Exhibit 3.3 shows the previous state of residence by category of welfare recipient. Again, the variations in origin are quite clear. The data are detailed for the 317 respondents who were not born in New York. The previous place of residence for more than half of the 317 respon-

EXHIBIT 3.3

PREVIOUS STATE OF RESIDENCE BY CATEGORY OF WELFARE

PREVIOUS RESIDENCE	CATEGORY OF WELFARE									
	Home Relief		Old Age Assistance		Aid to Disabled		Aid to Dependent Children		Total	
	No.	%	No.	%	No.	%	No.	%	No.	%
New Jersey	4	6.6	2	4.4	0	0.0	2	1.2	8	2.5
Pennsylvania	2	3.3	2	4.4	3	7.1	5	3.0	12	3.8
Other Northern or Western State	4	6.6	3	6.7	6	14.3	7	4.1	20	6.3
Southern State	18	29.5	10	22.2	16	38.1	58	34.3	102	32.2
Out of Country	33	54.1	28	62.2	17	40.5	96	56.8	174	54.9
New York State	0	0.0	0	0.0	0	0.0	1	0.6	1	0.3
Total	61	100.0	45	100.0	42	100.0	169	100.0	317	100.0

Source: Housing of Welfare Recipients Survey, 1970.

EXHIBIT 3.4

TYPE OF LOCALE BEFORE MOVING TO NEW YORK CITY BY CATEGORY OF WELFARE

PREVIOUS LOCALE	CATEGORY OF WELFARE									
	Home Relief		Old Age Assistance		Aid to Disabled		Aid to Dependent Children		Total	
	No.	%	No.	%	No.	%	No.	%	No.	%
Large City	27	44.3	15	33.3	17	40.5	47	27.8	106	33.4
Small City	13	21.3	11	24.4	9	21.4	37	21.9	70	22.1
Small Town	11	18.0	13	28.9	8	19.0	60	35.5	92	29.0
Rural	10	16.4	6	13.3	8	19.0	25	14.8	49	15.5
Total	61	100.0	45	100.0	42	100.0	169	100.0	317	100.0

Source: Housing of Welfare Recipients Survey, 1970.

dents not born in New York is "out of the country" (including Puerto Rico). An additional one-third (32.2 percent) come from the southern states. Migration from the North, including other parts of New York state, has been relatively slight. Not presented here are similar data on place of birth within the United States.[1]

When asked how many places within the United States they have lived in before coming to the city, most (95.5 percent) of the Spanish-speaking respondents indicate a direct move to New York. A similar answer is given by 60.7 percent of the white non-Spanish-speaking respondents[2] (the remnants of older immigrant groups) but by only 3.9 percent of the blacks. Three-quarters of those blacks who did not move directly to New York indicate an interim shift (usually within a southern state) in contrast to barely 10.7 percent of whites and only 1.3 percent of the Spanish-speaking group. Indeed for the entire group of 317, three-quarters (74.8 percent) have moved only once. An additional 13.6 percent have two moves in addition to the move to New York, while the balance had more than two. Welfare recipients may be mobile but the mobility is essentially within the city rather than outside it.

One-third of the respondents who were not born in New York come from large cities (over 300,000 population). An additional 22.1 percent come from small cities, and only 29 percent and 15.5 percent from small town and rural backgrounds, respectively. In general, as presented in Exhibit 3.4, the ADC cases tend to come from small town or rural backgrounds with 35.5 percent and 14.8 percent, respectively, originating there. Home Relief cases, on the other hand, number only 34.4 percent in these two categories combined. Small town or rural origins are indicated by 39.3 percent of the whites, 41.9 percent of the blacks and 47.4 percent of the Spanish-speaking individuals who were not born in New York.

When these data are analyzed by borough, however, there is an interesting skew. Brooklyn has most of the small town and rural émigrés, with 58.9 percent of the 118 respondents in that category; Manhattan has only 35.8 percent, and the Bronx is in the middle at 40 percent. Again, the thesis of rural unpreparedness, given the relative length of residence in New York City, is somewhat diminished in persuasiveness.

REASONS FOR MOVING

Some 317 respondents have moved to New York; approximately one-third of them indicate they did so "for a better job." An additional 17 percent point to the fact that they already had families in New York.

EXHIBIT 3.5

CATEGORY OF WELFARE BY ETHNICITY

ETHNICITY	CATEGORY OF WELFARE									
	Home Relief		Old Age Assistance		Aid to Disabled		Aid to Dependent Children		Total	
	No.	%	No.	%	No.	%	No.	%	No.	%
White	8	10.7	23	41.8	15	26.3	18	8.0	64	15.5
Negro	32	42.7	16	29.1	24	42.1	108	48.0	180	43.7
Spanish Speaking	35	46.7	14	25.5	17	29.8	98	43.6	164	39.8
Other	0	0.0	2	3.6	1	1.8	1	0.4	4	1.0
Total	75	100.0	55	100.0	57	100.0	225	100.0	412	100.0

Source: Housing of Welfare Recipients Survey, 1970.

EXHIBIT 3.7

AGE OF RESPONDENT BY BOROUGH

AGE	BOROUGH											
	Manhattan		Brooklyn		Bronx		Queens		Richmond		Total	
	No.	%	No.	%	No.	%	No.	%	No.	%	No.	%
15 to 18	1	0.9	3	1.9	0	0.0	0	0.0	0	0.0	4	1.0
19 to 25	10	8.5	16	10.1	21	19.4	4	16.7	1	20.0	52	12.6
26 to 36	30	25.6	50	31.6	28	25.9	5	20.8	2	40.0	115	27.9
37 to 47	25	21.4	27	17.1	22	20.4	3	12.5	1	20.0	78	18.9
48 to 57	17	14.5	30	19.0	10	9.3	1	4.2	1	20.0	59	14.3
58 to 67	18	15.4	15	9.5	9	8.3	7	29.2	0	0.0	49	11.9
68 and Over	16	13.7	17	10.8	17	15.7	4	16.7	0	0.0	54	13.1
NA/DK	0	0.0	0	0.0	1	0.9	0	0.0	0	0.0	1	0.2
Total	117	100.0	158	100.0	108	100.0	24	100.0	5	100.0	412	100.0

Source: Housing of Welfare Recipients Survey, 1970.

EXHIBIT 3.6

PERCENTAGE OF WELFARE TENANTS BY ETHNICITY (1968)

ETHNICITY OF TENANTS	NUMBER AND PERCENTAGE OF WELFARE TENANTS														Total Structures	
	None		1% to 10%		11% to 20%		21% to 30%		31% to 40%		41% to 60%		61% to 100%			
	No.	%	No.	%	No.	%	No.	%	No.	%	No.	%	No.	%	No.	%
All White	15,491	75.7	2,921	14.3	779	3.8	330	1.6	486	2.4	453	2.2	0	0.0	20,460	100.0
All Negro	2,812	36.4	666	8.6	1,081	14.0	938	12.2	820	10.6	666	8.6	733	9.5	7,716	100.0
All Spanish	842	22.5	287	7.7	314	8.4	380	10.2	668	17.8	930	24.8	322	8.6	3,743	100.0
Subst. Negro	823	49.5	230	13.8	41	2.5	156	9.4	296	17.8	118	7.1	0	0.0	1,664	100.0
Subst. White	1,713	50.1	1,025	30.0	365	10.7	151	4.4	165	4.8	0	0.0	0	0.0	3,419	100.0
Subst. Spanish	688	23.2	143	4.8	1,009	34.0	470	15.8	476	16.0	185	6.2	0	0.0	2,971	100.0
Mixed Spanish	255	12.0	20	0.9	420	19.8	378	17.8	398	18.7	327	15.4	327	15.4	2.125	100.0
All Three Mixed	3,822	41.8	2,448	26.8	838	9.2	985	10.8	229	2.5	660	7.2	157	1.7	9,139	100.0
NA/DK	552	46.7	172	14.5	177	15.0	131	11.1	131	11.1	20	1.7	0	0.0	1,183	100.0
Total	26,998	51.5	7,912	15.1	5,024	9.6	3,919	7.5	3,669	7.0	3,359	6.4	1,539	2.9	52,420	100.0

Sources: George Sternlieb, *The Urban Housing Dilemma* (New Brunswick, New Jersey, Rutgers University Press, 1970).
New York City Department of Social Service Data Processing Administration, March 1968.

The majority of the other responses typically have to do with economic improvement. Fully one out of six come with a specific job which has been secured prior to coming to the city. There are nine responses from Cubans who refer to political problems. None of the other subcategories is clear-cut enough to warrant quantification here; the emphasis throughout is on economic betterment.

In no case, however, is there a clear-cut response indicating that the generosity of New York City's welfare laws is an inducement to move. A number of Puerto Ricans indicate, however, that the superior health facilities available in New York influenced their decision to emigrate. Also mentioned in several instances is the hope of securing better housing.

CHARACTERISTICS OF WELFARE RECIPIENTS

RACE

Of the total number of respondents, 15.5 percent are white, 43.7 percent black and 39.8 percent Spanish-speaking. Exhibit 3.5 lists the type of welfare received by ethnic group. The black and Spanish-speaking respondents are comparable in category, with the exception of recipients of Aid to the Disabled. Non-Spanish-speaking whites are heavily represented in the Old Age Assistance category, making up 41.8 percent of that group though only 15.5 percent of the total recipients in all categories. The majority of white respondents in New York are not, however, Old Age Assistance recipients.

The shift in the racial composition of major American cities needs no elaboration. The linkage of race/ethnicity to limitations on economic advancement and concomitantly with welfare is all too clear-cut. Thus, most welfare recipients suffer from dual discrimination—first as a function of their race/ethnicity and second as a function of their welfare status. Exhibit 3.6 shows the racial/ethnic concentrations of welfare recipients by degree of welfare tenancy in the building they reside in, pyramided for the entire rent-controlled sample universe of 52,000 buildings. Fully three-fourths of the buildings inhabited solely by whites have no welfare tenants. Less than half of the all-black buildings and less than a quarter of the all-Spanish buildings have no welfare tenants. In the reverse situation, that is, in buildings heavily tenanted by welfare recipients, minority groups predominate. Thus, there is a dual form of segregation, both in terms of welfare recipiency and ethnic discrimination.

AGE

As would be expected, there is considerable variation by age in type of welfare. Fully 42.2 percent of the ADC group are between 26 and 36,

EXHIBIT 3.8

AGE AND ETHNICITY OF WELFARE RESPONDENTS

AGE	White		Negro		Spanish Speaking		Other[a]		Total	
	No.	%	No.	%	No.	%	No.	%	No.	%
ETHNICITY BY AGE										
15 to 18	0	0.0	3	1.7	1	0.6	0	0.0	4	1.0
19 to 25	5	7.8	24	13.3	23	14.0	0	0.0	52	12.6
26 to 36	11	17.2	48	26.7	55	33.5	1	25.0	115	27.9
37 to 47	7	10.9	35	19.4	36	22.0	0	0.0	78	18.9
48 to 57	8	12.5	32	17.8	19	11.6	0	0.0	59	14.3
58 to 67	9	14.1	21	11.7	17	10.4	2	50.0	49	11.9
68 and Over	24	37.5	17	9.4	12	7.3	1	25.0	54	13.1
NA/DK	0	0.0	0	0.0	1	0.6	0	0.0	1	0.2
Total	64	100.0	180	100.0	164	100.0	4	100.0	412	100.0
AGE BY ETHNICITY										
15 to 18	0	0.0	3	75.0	1	25.0	0	0.0	4	100.0
19 to 25	5	9.6	24	46.2	23	44.2	0	0.0	52	100.0
26 to 36	11	9.6	48	41.7	55	47.8	1	0.9	115	100.0
37 to 47	7	9.0	35	44.9	36	46.2	0	0.0	78	100.0
48 to 57	8	13.6	32	54.2	19	32.2	0	0.0	59	100.0
58 to 67	9	18.4	21	42.9	17	34.7	2	4.1	49	100.0
68 and Over	24	44.4	17	31.5	12	22.2	1	1.9	54	100.0
NA/DK	0	0.0	0	0.0	1	100.0	0	0.0	1	100.0
Total	64	15.5	180	43.7	164	39.8	4	1.0	412	100.0

Source: Housing of Welfare Recipients Survey, 1970.

[a] Unless otherwise noted, the "other" category refers to respondents from oriental background.

EXHIBIT 3.9

AGE AND WELFARE CATEGORY OF RESPONDENTS

AGE OF RESPONDENT	CATEGORY OF WELFARE BY AGE									
	Home Relief		Old Age Assistance		Aid to Disabled		Aid to Dependent Children		Total	
	No.	%	No.	%	No.	%	No.	%	No.	%
15 to 18	0	0.0	0	0.0	0	0.0	4	1.8	4	1.0
19 to 25	6	8.0	0	0.0	6	10.5	40	17.8	52	12.6
26 to 36	12	16.0	0	0.0	8	14.0	95	42.2	115	27.9
37 to 47	17	22.7	0	0.0	9	15.8	52	23.1	78	18.9
48 to 57	19	25.3	0	0.0	15	26.3	25	11.1	59	14.3
58 to 67	17	22.7	6	10.9	19	33.3	7	3.1	49	11.9
68 and Over	4	5.3	49	89.1	0	0.0	1	0.4	54	13.1
NA/DK	0	0.0	0	0.0	0	0.0	1	0.4	1	0.2
Total	75	100.0	55	100.0	57	100.0	225	100.0	412	100.0
	AGE BY WELFARE CATEGORY									
15 to 18	0	0.0	0	0.0	0	0.0	4	100.0	4	100.0
19 to 25	6	11.5	0	0.0	6	11.5	40	76.9	52	100.0
26 to 36	12	10.4	0	0.0	8	7.0	95	82.6	115	100.0
37 to 47	17	21.8	0	0.0	9	11.5	52	66.7	78	100.0
48 to 57	19	32.2	0	0.0	15	25.4	25	42.4	59	100.0
58 to 67	17	34.7	6	12.2	19	38.8	7	14.3	49	100.0
68 and Over	4	7.4	49	90.7	0	0.0	1	1.9	54	100.0
NA/DK	0	0.0	0	0.0	0	0.0	1	100.0	1	100.0
Total	75	18.2	55	13.3	57	13.8	225	54.6	412	100.0

Source: Housing of Welfare Recipients Survey, 1970.

with an additional 19.6 percent under 26, while 23.1 percent are between 37 and 47 years old. Only 3.5 percent of heads of ADC households are 58 and over. In the Home Relief category, on the other hand, 28 percent are 58 and over, with only 24 percent under 36, 22.7 percent at the 37 to 47 level, and 25.3 percent from 48 to 57.

In the Old Age Assistance group, only 10.9 percent of the respondents are under 67 with 89 percent 68 and over. Note the substantial variation in age of welfare recipients by borough as shown in Exhibit 3.7. The proportion under age 26 in the Bronx is nearly twice that of the other major boroughs. The impact on housing and landlord choice of tenant merely as a function of the youth of the household has considerable import.

Exhibit 3.8 shows the age of welfare respondents by ethnicity. As mentioned earlier, and as might have been guessed from the categories of welfare by ethnic group, whites tend to be relatively elderly, with more than 50 percent over 58 years old compared to barely 20 percent of the black respondents and even less than that for the Spanish-speaking group.

The era of mass welfare recipiency in this country is too new for definitive studies of intergenerational welfare dependency. The limited evidence to date does not show an extensive amount of this phenomenon.[3] The potential of such growth is evident, however, particularly in the skews in age. Notice that the black respondents are intermediate between the whites and Spanish-speaking in age distribution, perhaps because of the lack of recent emigration by blacks. The higher age of black respondents may also indicate that fears of intergenerational dependency have been somewhat exaggerated. Obviously, this problem should be investigated by concerned agencies. If the child-bearing groups are defined quite arbitrarily as those with heads of households under the age of 37, it is clear that this population has vast potential for internal expansion—assuming that the children continue their parents' pattern of dependency. Fully three out of five welfare recipients are under the age of 37. The age distribution very closely follows variations in the type of welfare. Less than 15 percent of the ADC cases are outside our child-bearing category (Exhibit 3.9).

HOUSEHOLD SIZE

Exhibit 3.10 gives data on the total number of people in the household by the ethnicity of the respondent. Five out of every eight (62.5 percent) of the white households are comprised of only one or two people. This is true for only 36.6 percent of the black households and

EXHIBIT 3.10

SIZE OF HOUSEHOLD BY ETHNICITY

NUMBER IN HOME	ETHNICITY									
	White		Negro		Spanish Speaking		Other		Total	
	No.	%	No.	%	No.	%	No.	%	No.	%
One	24	37.5	33	18.3	15	9.1	2	50.0	74	18.0
Two	16	25.0	33	18.3	23	14.0	1	25.0	73	17.7
Three	10	15.6	29	16.1	31	18.9	1	25.0	71	17.2
Four	4	6.3	25	13.9	43	26.2	0	0.0	72	17.5
Five	5	7.8	22	12.2	20	12.2	0	0.0	47	11.4
Six	1	1.6	14	7.8	15	9.1	0	0.0	30	7.3
Seven	1	1.6	11	6.1	9	5.5	0	0.0	21	5.1
Eight	2	3.1	6	3.3	3	1.8	0	0.0	11	2.7
Nine or More	1	1.6	7	3.9	5	3.0	0	0.0	13	3.2
Total	64	100.0	180	100.0	164	100.0	4	100.0	412	100.0

Source: Housing of Welfare Recipients Survey, 1970.

EXHIBIT 3.11

SIZE OF HOUSEHOLD BY BOROUGH

NUMBER IN HOME	BOROUGH											
	Manhattan		Brooklyn		Bronx		Queens		Richmond		Total	
	No.	%	No.	%	No.	%	No.	%	No.	%	No.	%
One	32	27.4	26	16.5	12	11.1	4	16.7	0	0.0	74	18.0
Two	23	19.7	28	17.7	19	17.6	3	12.5	0	0.0	73	17.7
Three	16	13.7	33	20.9	18	16.7	4	16.7	0	0.0	71	17.2
Four	17	14.5	19	12.0	30	27.8	5	20.8	1	20.0	72	17.5
Five	12	10.3	15	9.5	12	11.1	6	25.0	2	40.0	47	11.4
Six	8	6.8	14	8.9	8	7.4	0	0.0	0	0.0	30	7.3
Seven	3	2.6	11	7.0	5	4.6	2	8.3	0	0.0	21	5.1
Eight	3	2.6	3	1.9	3	2.8	0	0.0	2	40.0	11	2.7
Nine or More	3	2.6	9	5.7	1	0.9	0	0.0	0	0.0	13	3.2
Total	117	100.0	158	100.0	108	100.0	24	100.0	5	100.0	412	100.0

Source: Housing of Welfare Recipients Survey, 1970.

for less than a quarter (23.1 percent) of the Spanish-speaking households. Conversely, households with five or more people are found with only one out of six of the white respondents, but double that proportion of black and Spanish-speaking respondents.

Fully one-third of the minority-group welfare recipients, therefore, need large housing units in a city of predominantly small apartments, while most of the white welfare recipients are elderly and childless. Comparatively few elderly households are found among the Spanish-speaking respondents, with the blacks intermediate. The relative difficulty of finding housing for large households will be considered more fully in the next chapter.

The number of large families and their attendant problems varies substantially by borough. In Brooklyn, for example, nearly one-third of the welfare-receiving families are comprised of five or more individuals and 7.6 percent have eight or more. By way of contrast, in Manhattan the former pattern holds true for less than one-quarter of the respondents, and barely 5 percent have eight or more members. The Bronx pattern is similar to the Brooklyn one (Exhibit 3.11).

In Exhibit 3.12 these data are analyzed by category of welfare recipients. While nearly three out of ten of the total sample are households with five or more people, size varies substantially by category of welfare. Less than 11 percent of the Old Age Assistance recipients have five or more people in their household, while about one-third (33.4 percent) of the ADC cases do.

Indeed, nearly one out of ten of the families in the ADC category (8.9 percent) has seven or more members. In order to put this figure in perspective, an analysis of size of housing unit is shown by borough. The analysis indicates that little has been built to accommodate large families (Exhibit 3.13).

Children Under Ten

What are the ages of the children involved? The total number of persons in the household under the age of ten by category of welfare appears in Exhibit 3.14. Two hundred and sixteen or slightly more than half of the households have such children, for a grand total of 494 children under ten. One hundred and seventy-six out of the 225 ADC households have children under the age of ten (78.2 percent), and a substantial proportion (36.4 percent) have three or more children in this age group. An additional 30.1 percent have two children.

In Exhibit 3.15 these data are cross-tabulated by the ethnicity of the recipient. As would be anticipated from the age distribution, less than three out of ten of the white households have children within this age

EXHIBIT 3.12

SIZE OF HOUSEHOLD BY CATEGORY OF WELFARE

NUMBER IN HOME	CATEGORY OF WELFARE									
	Home Relief		Old Age Assistance		Aid to Disabled		Aid to Dependent Children		Total	
	No.	%	No.	%	No.	%	No.	%	No.	%
One	19	25.3	27	49.1	28	49.1	0	0.0	74	18.0
Two	14	18.7	18	32.7	14	24.6	27	12.0	73	17.7
Three	10	13.3	2	3.6	5	8.8	54	24.0	71	17.2
Four	8	10.7	2	3.6	3	5.3	59	26.2	72	17.5
Five	3	4.0	4	7.3	5	8.8	35	15.6	47	11.4
Six	9	12.0	0	0.0	1	1.8	20	8.9	30	7.3
Seven	5	6.7	1	1.8	0	0.0	15	6.7	21	5.1
Eight	5	6.7	1	1.8	0	0.0	5	2.2	11	2.7
NA/DK	2	2.7	0	0.0	1	1.8	10	4.4	13	3.2
Total	75	100.0	55	100.0	57	100.0	225	100.0	412	100.0

Source: Housing of Welfare Recipients Survey, 1970.

EXHIBIT 3.13

RENTED HOUSING
NUMBER OF ROOMS AND BOROUGH

NUMBER OF ROOMS BY BOROUGH

BOROUGH	One		Two		Three		Four		Five		Six or More		Not Reported		Total	
	No.	%	No.	%	No.	%	No.	%	No.	%	No.	%	No.	%	No.	%
Bronx	6,681	5.8	22,727	12.0	158,312	23.3	139,273	21.7	68,116	22.3	27,324	16.8	0	0.0	422,433	20.2
Brooklyn	21,799	18.8	39,814	21.0	191,052	28.1	225,062	35.0	105,891	34.7	60,857	37.5	0	0.0	644,475	30.7
Manhattan	78,405	67.6	93,437	49.3	185,546	27.3	158,177	24.6	71,324	23.4	39,224	24.2	0	0.0	626,113	29.9
Queens	8,693	7.5	32,752	17.3	140,261	20.6	111,486	17.4	53,174	17.4	30,779	19.0	0	0.0	377,145	18.0
Richmond	483	0.4	909	0.5	5,500	0.8	8,394	1.3	6,462	2.1	4,144	2.6	0	0.0	25.892	1.2
Total	116,061	100.0	189,639	100.0	680,671	100.0	642,392	100.0	304,967	100.0	162,328	100.0	0	0.0	2,096,058	100.0

BOROUGH BY NUMBER OF ROOMS

BOROUGH	No.	%	No.	%	No.	%	No.	%	No.	%	No.	%	No.	%	No.	%
Bronx	6,681	1.6	22,727	5.4	158,312	37.5	139,273	33.0	68,116	16.1	27,324	6.5	0	0.0	422,433	100.0
Brooklyn	21,799	3.4	39,814	6.2	191,052	29.6	225,062	34.9	105,891	16.4	60,857	9.4	0	0.0	644,475	100.0
Manhattan	78,405	12.5	93,437	14.9	185,546	29.6	158,177	25.3	71,324	11.4	39,224	6.3	0	0.0	626,113	100.0
Queens	8,693	2.3	32,752	8.7	140,261	37.2	111,486	29.6	53,174	14.1	30,779	6.2	0	0.0	377,145	100.0
Richmond	483	1.9	909	3.5	5,500	21.2	8,394	32.4	6,462	25.0	4,144	16.0	0	0.0	25,892	100.0
Total	116,061	5.5	189,639	9.0	680,671	32.5	642,392	30.6	304,967	14.5	162,328	7.7	0	0.0	2,096,058	100.0

Source: New York City Housing and Vacancy Survey, 1968.

EXHIBIT 3.14

NUMBER OF CHILDREN UNDER AGE TEN IN HOUSEHOLD BY CATEGORY OF WELFARE

CATEGORY OF WELFARE	NUMBER OF CHILDREN UNDER AGE TEN													
	One		Two		Three		Four		Five		Six		Total	
	No.	%	No.	%	No.	%	No.	%	No.	%	No.	%	No.	%
Home Relief	8	26.7	9	30.0	3	10.0	7	23.3	3	10.0	0	0.0	30	100.0
Old Age Assistance	1	33.3	1	33.3	1	33.3	0	0.0	0	0.0	0	0.0	3	100.0
Aid to Disabled	2	28.6	3	42.9	1	14.3	0	0.0	1	14.3	0	0.0	7	100.0
Aid to Dependent Children	59	33.5	53	30.1	39	22.2	16	9.1	6	3.4	3	1.7	176	100.0
Total	70	32.4	66	30.6	44	20.4	23	10.6	10	4.6	3	1.4	216	100.0

Source: Housing of Welfare Recipients Survey, 1970.

EXHIBIT 3.15

NUMBER OF CHILDREN UNDER AGE TEN IN HOUSEHOLD BY ETHNICITY

CHILDREN UNDER TEN	ETHNICITY									
	White		Negro		Spanish Speaking		Other		Total	
	No.	%	No.	%	No.	%	No.	%	No.	%
None	46	71.8	82	45.6	65	39.6	3	75.0	196	47.6
One	9	14.1	30	16.7	30	18.3	1	25.0	70	16.9
Two	4	6.3	32	17.8	30	18.3	0	0.0	66	16.0
Three	1	1.6	18	10.0	25	15.2	0	0.0	44	10.7
Four	3	4.7	11	6.1	9	5.5	0	0.0	23	5.6
Five	1	1.6	6	3.3	3	1.8	0	0.0	10	2.4
Six	0	0.0	1	0.5	2	1.2	0	0.0	3	0.7
Total	64	100.0	80	100.0	164	100.0	4	100.0	412	100.0

Source: Housing of Welfare Recipient Survey, 1970.

category, but slightly more than half (54.4 percent) of the black households are represented in this group. The Spanish-speaking households have a slightly higher proportion of households with three or more children under the age of ten: 23.7 percent, as compared to 19.9 percent of the black households and only 7.9 percent of the white households.

Children Ten to Eighteen

The number of children in the household between the ages ten and 18 by category of welfare received appears in Exhibit 3.16. The ADC categories have by far the great bulk here, with 136 out of their 225 households having children ten to 18. Seventy-four out of the 225 ADC cases (32.9 percent) have two or more such children. Again, when these data are cross-tabulated by ethnicity, most children of ages ten to 18 are black or Spanish-speaking; only 21.9 percent of the white households having such children are in this age group (Exhibit 3.17).

The problem of wear and tear on housing, which is popularly linked with ethnicity as well as welfare, may be more a function of the size of the household and the youth of its members than of any other single variable. Certainly, the city's problems in housing children are evident (see Appendix 3-1).

EXHIBIT 3.16

TOTAL NUMBER IN HOUSEHOLD AGES TEN TO EIGHTEEN BY CATEGORY OF WELFARE

	CATEGORY OF WELFARE									
CHILDREN IN HOUSEHOLD TEN TO EIGHTEEN	Home Relief		Old Age Assistance		Aid to Disabled		Aid to Dependent Children		Total	
	No.	%	No.	%	No.	%	No.	%	No.	%
None	53	70.7	48	87.3	50	87.7	89	39.6	240	58.3
One	10	13.3	4	7.3	4	7.0	62	27.6	80	19.4
Two	6	8.0	1	1.8	1	1.8	41	18.2	49	11.9
Three	2	2.7	1	1.8	1	1.8	21	9.3	25	6.1
Four	1	1.3	1	1.8	1	1.8	9	4.0	12	2.9
Five	3	4.0	0	0.0	0	0.0	2	0.9	5	1.2
Six	0	0.0	0	0.0	0	0.0	1	0.4	1	0.2
Total	75	100.0	55	100.0	57	100.0	225	100.0	412	100.0

Source: Housing of Welfare Recipients Survey, 1970.

The Aged

One hundred and sixty-nine of the 412 households (41 percent) that were interviewed during the study contain at least one resident over the age of 50. Approximately one-fourth of the households (26.6 percent) contain two such individuals, with an additional 4.7 percent having

EXHIBIT 3.17

TOTAL NUMBER IN HOUSEHOLD
AGES TEN TO EIGHTEEN BY ETHNICITY

CHILDREN IN HOUSEHOLD TEN TO EIGHTEEN	ETHNICITY									
	White		Negro		Spanish Speaking		Other		Total	
	No.	%	No.	%	No.	%	No.	%	No.	%
None	50	78.1	105	58.3	82	50.0	3	75.0	240	58.3
One	8	12.5	32	17.7	39	23.8	1	25.0	80	19.4
Two	2	3.1	21	11.7	26	15.9	0	0.0	49	11.9
Three	2	3.1	12	6.7	11	6.7	0	0.0	25	6.1
Four	1	1.6	6	3.3	5	3.0	0	0.0	12	2.9
Five	1	1.6	3	1.7	1	0.6	0	0.0	5	1.2
Six	0	0.0	1	0.6	0	0.0	0	0.0	1	0.2
Total	64	100.0	180	100.0	164	100.0	4	100.0	412	100.0

Source: Housing of Welfare Recipients Survey, 1970.

three or more; the mean number is 1.37. There is significant variation, however, when these data are analyzed by ethnicity. Forty-five out of 64 (70.3 percent) of the white households have people over the age of 50 as contrasted with only 72 of the 180 black households (40 percent) and 49 of the 164 Spanish-speaking households (29.9 percent). To state the converse, only an average of three out of ten of the white households has people under the age of 50, while the same holds true for six out of ten of the blacks and seven out of ten of the Spanish-speaking families.

In Exhibit 3.18 these data are analyzed by category of welfare recipient. Naturally, the aged are the single largest group receiving Old Age Assistance. Notice however, that in absolute number the other

EXHIBIT 3.18

HOUSEHOLDS WITH MEMBERS OVER AGE FIFTY
BY CATEGORY OF WELFARE

NUMBER OF HOUSEHOLD MEMBERS OVER AGE 50	CATEGORY OF WELFARE									
	Home Relief		Old Age Assistance		Aid to Disabled		Aid to Dependent Children		Total	
	No.	%	No.	%	No.	%	No.	%	No.	%
One	23	56.1	39	70.9	30	76.9	24	70.6	116	68.6
Two	15	36.6	13	23.6	8	20.5	9	26.5	45	26.6
Three	3	7.3	2	3.6	1	2.6	1	2.9	7	4.1
Four	0	0.0	1	1.8	0	0.0	0	0.0	0	0.6
Total	41	100.0	55	100.0	39	100.0	34	100.0	169	100.0

Source: Housing of Welfare Recipients Survey, 1970.

categories are quite close. Interestingly, no less than 15 of the 24 total sample welfare cases in Queens have someone in the household over the age of 50 (62.5 percent). The other boroughs are each at approximately 40 percent.

The data indicate that in the great majority of the ADC cases there is no elderly relative to "stay home with the children" and permit mother (or father) to seek employment. While other arrangements can be made, e.g., sharing child supervisory chores with a neighbor or using nursery school facilities, these typically impose some financial strain or difficulty. And even though the data indicate that approximately 15 percent of the ADC families have an elderly relative within the household, we do not know how many of them are physically able or willing to care for children.

Unfortunately we have no way of knowing how earlier ethnic groups handled this problem. Did the female Italian needleworkers of yore have the advantage of extended families within the household? Certainly, some of the popular literature[4] would imply this kind of pattern.

EDUCATION

More than two-thirds of the Spanish-speaking respondents indicate they have less than a high school education—68.3 percent. The equivalent figure for the black population is only 33.9 percent, while for the whites it is intermediate at 50.1 percent. Six of the 64 whites, one of the 180 blacks and 22 of the 164 Puerto Ricans said that they have no formal education at all.

EXHIBIT 3.19

AMOUNT OF EDUCATION
BY CATEGORY OF WELFARE

	CATEGORY OF WELFARE									
EDUCATION	Home Relief		Old Age Assistance		Aid to Disabled		Aid to Dependent Children		Total	
	No.	%	No.	%	No.	%	No.	%	No.	%
None	5	6.7	12	21.8	7	12.3	5	2.2	29	7.0
One to Two Years	4	5.3	7	12.7	3	5.3	9	4.0	23	5.6
Three to Four Years	9	12.0	10	18.2	4	7.0	17	7.6	40	9.7
Five to Six Years	5	6.7	3	5.5	8	14.0	21	9.3	37	9.0
Seven to Eight Years	21	28.0	13	23.6	8	14.0	38	16.9	80	19.4
Nine to Ten Years	12	16.0	3	5.5	13	22.8	51	22.7	79	19.2
11 to 12 Years	17	22.7	4	7.3	13	22.8	72	32.0	106	25.7
13 to 25 Years	2	2.7	2	3.6	1	1.8	12	5.3	17	4.1
NA/DK	0	0.0	1	1.8	0	0.0	0	0.0	1	0.2
Total	75	100.0	55	100.0	57	100.0	225	100.0	412	100.0

Source: Housing of Welfare Recipients Survey, 1970.

Exhibit 3.19 shows educational attainment by welfare category. Less than four out of ten of the ADC recipients have more than two years of high school; yet as a group they have more formal education than any of the other categories.[5] This low average level of education is a clear deterrent to employment over and above any of the many other inhibitors.

While the importance of education as a prerequisite for entry into the job market perhaps has been exaggerated, there is no question that a great many of the welfare recipients are inadequately prepared—in terms of formal education—for work. On the other hand, a reasonable case can be made that a substantial proportion of the blacks and Puerto Ricans may have secured at least the formal prerequisites. Nevertheless, fulfillment of the educational requirement has not kept these individuals off the welfare rolls.

MARITAL STATUS

As shown in Exhibit 3.20 only 20.6 percent of the heads of households are married. An additional 17.7 percent, substantially concentrated in

EXHIBIT 3.20

MARITAL STATUS OF WELFARE RECIPIENTS BY ETHNICITY

	ETHNICITY									
MARITAL STATUS	White		Negro		Spanish Speaking		Other		Total	
	No.	%	No.	%	No.	%	No.	%	No.	%
Married	13	20.3	35	19.4	37	22.6	0	0.0	85	20.6
Widowed	22	34.4	29	16.1	19	11.6	3	75.0	73	17.7
Divorced	11	17.2	9	5.0	16	9.8	0	0.0	36	8.7
Separated	5	7.8	69	38.3	70	42.7	0	0.0	144	35.0
Single	13	20.3	38	21.1	20	12.2	1	25.0	72	17.5
Common Law	0	0.0	0	0.0	2	1.2	0	0.0	2	0.5
Total	64	100.0	180	100.0	164	100.0	4	100.0	412	100.0

Source: Housing of Welfare Recipients Survey, 1970.

the white group, are widowed. Respondents who reply that the head of household is divorced number 8.7 percent for the entire group, while 35 percent are separated from their spouses. Again, there is an evident skew in the last category, with fully 38.3 percent of the blacks, and 42.7 percent of the Spanish-speaking versus only 7.8 percent of the whites indicating that they are separated. Single respondents number 17.5 percent. Common-law associations are referred to by only two respondents.

This distribution follows the category of welfare. Of the ADC respondents, only 18.7 percent answer that they are presently married, an additional 7.6 percent say that they are widowed, 10.7 percent are divorced and nearly half (48.4 percent) are separated. One out of seven are listed as single.

If the variation in divorce versus separation is analyzed by ethnicity, it may very well be a function of cultural folkways, unfamiliarity with legal mechanisms and financial incapacity to secure legal separation. In any case, however, to the landlord interested in securing a tenant, the configuration of the minority welfare household is frequently a handicap.

EMPLOYMENT AND EMPLOYABILITY

Exhibit 3.21 contains the response to the question "Has the head of household been employed at any time within the last year?" Barely one-fourth of the total sample (25.7 percent) answer affirmatively. While there is little variation between boroughs, there is significant variation between categories of welfare recipients. The high figure is the 38.7 percent of heads of households of Home Relief cases who have worked within the last year. The low figure is the 19.3 percent of disabled recipients. A very interesting 24.4 percent of the ADC cases show affirmative responses here, with an additional 20 percent of the Old Age Assistance recipients in the same category.

EXHIBIT 3.21

EMPLOYMENT STATUS OF HEAD OF HOUSEHOLD DURING THE PAST YEAR BY CATEGORY OF WELFARE

	CATEGORY OF WELFARE									
HEAD OF HOUSEHOLD EMPLOYED AT ANY TIME DURING YEAR?	Home Relief		Old Age Assistance		Aid to Disabled		Aid to Dependent Children		Total	
	No.	%	No.	%	No.	%	No.	%	No.	%
Yes	29	38.7	11	20.0	11	19.3	55	24.4	106	25.7
No	46	61.3	44	80.0	46	80.7	170	75.6	306	74.3
Total	75	100.0	55	100.0	57	100.0	225	100.0	412	100.0

Source: Housing of Welfare Recipients Survey, 1970.

Of the 106 welfare recipients who say that the head of household had worked sometime during the past year, nearly three-fourths (73.6 percent) say that this was full-time employment; 18.9 percent refer to part-time activity, while the balance (5.7 percent) refer to on-the-job training. The lowest level of full-time employment occurs in the ADC cases, with 67.3 percent of the 55 cases showing such involvement.

When the welfare recipients are further asked why they are not employed or only partially employed, they give a number of reasons (Exhibit 3.22). In approximately four out of ten cases the reasons involve chronic illness, with a similar proportion saying that they are needed at home. One out of ten of the cases (concentrated in the Old Age Assistance category) are retired. The only other answer of any proportional significance is the 6.5 percent who indicate that acute illness or accident necessitates unemployment.

There is substantial variation between the several categories of welfare on this answer, as shown in Exhibit 3.22. The highest frequency of acute illness or accident occurs in the Home Relief cases: 11.1 percent in contrast to 2.3 percent of the Old Age Assistance group. Chronic illness

EXHIBIT 3.22

REASONS FOR BEING UNEMPLOYED OR ONLY PARTIALLY EMPLOYED LAST YEAR BY CATEGORY OF WELFARE

	CATEGORY OF WELFARE									
REASON NOT EMPLOYED	Home Relief		Old Age Assistance		Aid to Disabled		Aid to Dependent Children		Total	
	No.	%	No.	%	No.	%	No.	%	No.	%
Laid Off	0	0.0	0	0.0	0	0.0	4	2.3	4	1.3
Acute Illness/Accident	5	10.9	1	2.3	3	6.5	11	6.4	20	6.5
Chronic Illness	24	52.2	19	43.2	40	87.0	41	24.0	124	40.4
Needed at Home	9	19.6	1	2.3	1	2.2	110	64.3	121	39.4
Retired	7	15.2	21	47.7	1	2.2	3	1.8	32	10.4
Other	1	2.2	1	2.3	1	2.2	1	0.6	4	1.3
NA/DK	0	0.0	1	2.3	0	0.0	1	0.6	2	0.7
Total	46	100.0	44	100.0	46	100.0	171	100.0	307	100.0

Source: Housing of Welfare Recipients Survey, 1970.

accounts for nearly nine out of ten of the responses in the disabled category, in contrast to 24.0 percent of ADC cases who give the same response. The other two categories (Home Relief and Old Age Assistance) are at 52.2 and 43.2 percent, respectively. The response "needed at home" accounts for nearly two-thirds of the ADC cases (64.3 percent) and 20 percent of the Home Relief group with the other two categories at a much lower level. The "retired" responses are highest among the Old Age Assistance recipients, with 47.7 percent giving this as their answer.

Chapter 4

THE WELFARE RECIPIENT'S HOUSING

In this chapter we shall examine the structures that house welfare recipients, and their quality and type as a function of welfare category and ethnicity. We shall first describe the type and quality of welfare housing, and then review the density patterns of welfare housing. Has the growth of welfare expenditures in New York City been attended by a growth in the number of buildings that house welfare recipients—that is, a geographical expansion of the locus of welfare housing? Or rather is it accompanied by greater density of welfare recipients within specific structures?

A brief discussion of the use of hotels and public housing then follows. How frequently are "emergency" measures used? What is the role of New York's public housing and how many welfare recipients does it shelter? Has this number changed over time?

A fourth concern of this chapter is the maintenance of apartments, the number of housing violations in welfare buildings and overcrowding. Then, an analysis of the turnover rates of welfare recipients is attempted—how many of them must find new housing each year. The ways that welfare recipients hunt for new housing are discussed, as well as the problems of prejudice.

Finally the welfare recipients' views and use of city services in order to find their housing are presented.

TYPE OF HOUSING

New York City has a higher proportion of apartments and rental units to total dwelling units than any other major American city. Welfare housing accommodations are obviously influenced by this fact. Fully 78.2 percent of the sample respondents live in apartments, only 11.7 percent live in public housing, and 4.1 percent live in rented or owned houses, while the balance are typically in single-room occupancy (SRO) facilities. Exhibit 4.1 lists this distribution by category of welfare recipient.

EXHIBIT 4.1

TYPE OF HOUSING ACCOMMODATIONS
BY CATEGORY OF WELFARE

	CATEGORY OF WELFARE									
TYPE OF ACCOMMODATIONS	Home Relief		Old Age Assistance		Aid to Disabled		Aid to Dependent Children		Total	
	No.	%	No.	%	No.	%	No.	%	No.	%
House	3	4.0	2	3.6	1	1.8	11	4.9	17	4.1
Apartment	62	82.7	39	70.9	41	71.9	180	80.0	322	78.2
Public Housing	6	8.0	7	12.7	5	8.8	30	13.3	48	11.7
Other[a]	4	5.3	7	12.7	10	17.5	4	1.8	25	6.1
Total	75	100.0	55	100.0	57	100.0	225	100.0	412	100.0

Source: Housing of Welfare Recipients Survey, 1970.
[a]Typically single room occupancy (SRO).

Public housing is used slightly more frequently by persons receiving Old Age Assistance and Aid to Dependent Children, with roughly 13 percent of each of these groups in public housing compared to 8 percent and 8.8 percent respectively for Home Relief and Aid to Disabled recipients. Persons in the Old Age Assistance program also typically are in SROs, and for the disabled, some kind of institutional accommodation is not uncommon. Both of these are included in the "other" category (Exhibit 4.1). In the ADC case, less than 2 percent are in "other" forms of accommodation. (Despite the publicity given to the number of welfare recipients in hotel accommodations, this, as will be discussed later, is a small factor in proportion to the total number.)

Exhibit 4.2 gives data on the type of housing accommodation by ethnicity. Our information indicates that 16.1 percent of the black sample are in public housing, as compared to half that number (7.9 percent) of Spanish-speaking respondents and an even smaller percentage (6.3 percent) of whites. The great majority of respondents, regardless of ethnicity or welfare category, are housed in apartments. SROs are more frequent among the whites, with 9.4 percent so housed as compared to 7.2 percent of blacks, and only 3 percent of Spanish-speaking individuals. SROs are typically homes for the aged, rooming houses and the like.

The type of housing accommodations for welfare recipients was also compared by borough. Slightly over 20 percent of Manhattan respondents are in public housing as opposed to only 12 percent of the Brooklyn people, and less than 3 percent of those in the Bronx. Manhattan also had the bulk of "other" accommodations, with 9.4 percent, compared to the total sample of 6.1 percent.

One-fifth of the housing units in the total sample are furnished (20.6 percent). The several categories of welfare differ significantly in their use of furnished housing. No less than 41.8 percent of Old Age Assistance respondents occupy furnished accommodations, but only 10.7 percent of the ADC cases. The other categories of welfare recipients fall somewhere between these extremes, though closer to the ADC group.[1]

EXHIBIT 4.2

TYPE OF HOUSING ACCOMMODATION BY ETHNICITY

	ETHNICITY									
TYPE OF ACCOMMODATIONS	White		Negro		Spanish Speaking		Other[a]		Total	
	No.	%	No.	%	No.	%	No.	%	No.	%
House	3	4.7	9	5.0	5	3.0	0	0.0	17	4.1
Apartment	51	79.7	129	71.7	141	86.0	1	25.0	322	78.2
Public Housing	4	6.3	29	16.1	13	7.9	2	50.0	48	11.7
Other[b]	6	9.4	13	7.2	5	3.0	1	25.0	25	6.1
Total	64	100.0	180	100.0	164	100.0	4	100.0	412	100.0

Source: Housing of Welfare Recipients Survey, 1970.

[a]These include respondents with oriental background.

[b]Typically SRO.

JURIDICAL STATUS

The question of whether a respondent has a lease or the exact legal status of his tenancy is complicated by the rent-control laws in New York City. Under the laws, the landlord's capacity to evict a tenant and to raise rents is very limited. A further complication is that many people don't know if they have a lease. (This is true of middle-class people as well as the poor.) In any case, 39 percent of the total sample say that they have leases. A higher proportion of ADC cases say that they have a lease (47.1 percent) than do any of the other recipient categories. Affirmative answers are also given by 22.8 percent of the Aid to Disabled category, 26.4 percent and 36 percent of the Old Age Assistance and Home Relief categories respectively. One hundred and forty-six of the 160 respondents gave the length of their leases. In most of the cases (72.6 percent) they are for two years; 15.1 percent indicate one-year terms, with the balance holding three-year leases.

Given the rent-control laws in New York, the statutory tenant in many ways is in a position fully comparable to that of a tenant with a formal lease. A lease, therefore, may have more psychological than legal significance. The feeling of belonging, of clear-cut rights, that may occur with the lease can be quite important. In any case, only a minority of welfare recipients believe that they hold a lease.

Forty-seven of the 412 respondents said that they share their rent in some form. In all but a few cases, rent is shared with another member of the nuclear family. Among ADC cases only 7 percent share rent payments, compared to 20 percent in each of the other categories. Most welfare households are essentially in charge of their own rent payments.

QUALITY OF HOUSING

Few topics are more controversial than the quality of the buildings occupied by welfare recipients. Close to half a billion dollars a year is spent on rent for people on welfare in New York state alone. Yet, newspapers repeatedly publish stories about the inadequacies of the housing facilities that are secured. In a HEW study in 1968, it was estimated that at least half of all assistance recipients live in housing that is deteriorated, dilapidated, unsafe, unsanitary and overcrowded. "This includes over 4,000,000 persons of which an estimated 1.1 million are receiving Old Age Assistance, ADC, or AFDC. Approximately 800,000 adults and 2.5 million children are involved." It is further noted that state and local studies consistently report higher proportions of defective housing for ADC than for the other public assistance categories. In the study, the proportion of ADC clients living in substandard housing was estimated at 60 percent.[2]

A Louis Harris study conducted in 1969 in New York City evaluated slightly more than 400 buildings using an eight-item checklist in a number of selected transitional neighborhoods. Analysis by welfare status showed that 44 percent of the people on welfare lived in the worst buildings in contrast to 9 percent the best. Altogether 33 percent of the buildings were categorized "worst" and 23 percent "best." In general, housing tended to parallel income distributions.[3]

EXHIBIT 4.3

PROPORTION OF RENT-CONTROLLED APARTMENTS OCCUPIED BY WELFARE RECIPIENTS BY BUILDING CATEGORY

	TYPE OF STRUCTURE								
	Old Law Structures		New Law Structures			Structures Built After 1929		Small Structures	
CATEGORY OF WELFARE	Five to 19 Units	20 Units or More	Five to 19 Units	20 to 49 or More	50 Units or More	Ten to 49 Units	50 Units or More	Three and Four Units	Total
Total Number of Apartments in Sample	1,080	3,120	1,032	3,636	8,640	4,200	8,640	408	30,756
Proportion Occupied by Welfare Recipients	16.1%	12.0%	4.7%	13.1%	10.7%	2.9%	2.0%	9.0%	5.9%
Home Relief	4.1	2.9	0.6	2.5	2.0	0.2	0.2	1.2	1.1
Old Age Assistance	2.2	1.8	0.6	1.7	1.9	1.1	0.9	2.9	1.0
Aid to Blind	0.1	0.1	0.1	0.1	0.1	0.0	0.1	0.0	0.1
Aid to Dependent Children	8.5	6.1	3.2	8.1	5.7	1.3	0.5	4.7	3.2
Veteran's Assistance	0.1	0.3	0.1	0.0	0.1	0.0	0.1	0.0	0.1
Aid to Disabled	1.1	0.8	0.1	0.7	0.9	0.3	0.2	0.2	0.4
	DISTRIBUTION OF WELFARE-RECIPIENT-OCCUPIED RENT-CONTROLLED APARTMENTS BY TYPE OF WELFARE AND BUILDING CATEGORY								
Home Relief	25.5%	24.2%	12.8%	19.1%	18.7%	6.9%	10.0%	13.3%	18.6%
Old Age Assistance	13.7	15.0	12.8	13.0	17.8	37.9	45.0	32.2	16.9
Aid to Blind	0.6	0.8	2.1	0.8	0.9	0.0	5.0	0.0	1.7
Aid to Dependent Children	52.8	50.8	68.1	61.8	53.3	44.8	25.0	52.2	54.2
Veteran's Assistance	0.6	2.5	2.1	0.0	0.9	0.0	5.0	0.0	1.7
Aid to Disabled	6.8	6.7	2.1	5.3	8.4	10.3	10.0	2.2	6.8
Total	100.0%	100.0%	100.0%	100.0%	100.0%	100.0%	100.0%	100.0%	100.0%

Source: George Sternlieb, *The Urban Housing Dilemma,* 1970.

EXHIBIT 4.4

TENANTS ON WELFARE AND STRUCTURE CATEGORIES

	PERCENTAGE OF TENANTS ON WELFARE BY STRUCTURE CATEGORY											
	PERCENT ON WELFARE										Total Structures	
BUILDING CATEGORY	0%		1 to 9%		10 to 19%		20 to 32%		33 to 99%			
	No.	%	No.	%	No.	%	No.	%	No.	%	No.	%
Old Law Structures												
Five-19 Units	6,500	48.3	700	5.0	1,900	14.2	1,800	13.3	2,600	19.2	13,400	100.0
20 Units or More	600	30.8	500	28.3	300	17.5	200	11.7	200	11.7	1,800	100.0
New Law Structures												
Five-19 Units	7,100	59.2	700	5.8	1,100	9.2	1,500	12.5	1,600	13.3	12,000	100.0
20-49 Units	3,000	30.3	2,400	24.6	1,900	19.7	1,200	12.3	1,300	13.1	9,900	100.0
50 Units or More	900	36.7	1,200	50.8	100	5.8	100	2.5	100	4.2	2,400	100.0
Structures Built After 1929												
Ten-49 Units	400	61.7	200	33.3	0	3.3	0	0.8	0	0.8	700	100.0
50 Units or More	700	65.8	400	34.2	0	0.0	0	0.0	0	0.0	1,100	100.0
Small Structures												
Three and Four Units	9,300	79.7	0	0.0	0	0.0	500	4.2	1,900	16.1	11,700	100.0
Total	28,500	53.7	6,100	11.6	5,400	10.2	5,300	10.0	7,700	14.5	53,000	100.0

	STRUCTURE CATEGORY BY PERCENTAGE OF TENANTS ON WELFARE											
	No.	%	No.	%	No.	%	No.	%	No.	%	No.	%
Old Law Structures												
Five to 19 Units	6,500	22.8	700	10.9	1,900	35.1	1,800	34.0	2,600	33.6	13,400	25.4
20 Units or More	600	1.9	500	8.3	300	5.8	200	4.0	200	2.7	1,800	3.4
New Law Structures												
Five to 19 Units	7,100	24.9	700	11.4	1,100	20.3	1,500	28.4	1,600	20.9	12,000	22.6
20 to 49 Units	3,000	10.5	2,400	39.6	1,900	35.8	1,200	23.0	1,300	16.9	9,900	18.6
50 Units or More	900	3.1	1,200	19.9	100	2.6	100	1.1	100	1.3	2,400	4.5
Structures Built After 1929												
Ten to 49 Units	400	1.6	200	3.9	0	0.4	0	0.1	0	0.1	700	1.4
50 Units or More	700	2.5	400	6.0	0	.0	0	.0	0	.0	1,100	2.0
Small Structures												
Three and Four Units	9,300	32.7	0	.0	0	.0	500	9.4	1,900	24.5	11,700	22.0
Total	28,500	100.0	6,100	100.0	5,400	100.0	5,300	100.0	7,700	100.0	53,000	100.0

Source: George Sternlieb, *The Urban Housing Dilemma,* 1970.
Note: Numbers may not add precisely because of rounding.

AGE AND CONFIGURATION

New York City's low-income rental housing is old. Forty percent of the inventory was built before the Crash of 1929, with nearly 200,000 units dating back to the nineteenth century. And most post-World War II private housing is, or at least has been considered to be, far too costly for welfare recipients. They therefore must depend substantially on the 1.2 million units of rent-controlled housing built before 1947.

Exhibit 4.3 shows the disposition of 1,771 welfare recipients from the master check tape of New York City's Welfare Department as of February 1970, within a structured probability sample of 963 substantially rent-controlled structures incorporating 30,756 apartments. The exhibit indicates the number of apartments within each of the eight age/size of structure groups, and the proportion occupied by welfare recipients. The balance of the data is concerned with the subcategories of welfare—16.1 percent of the 1,080 apartments in the five-to-19-unit Old Law structures are occupied by welfare recipients; Home Relief makes up 4.1 percent of the 16.1 percent; Old Age Assistance, 2.2 percent and so forth.[4]

Our information indicates that the proportion of apartments occupied by welfare recipients differs markedly according to the structure's age. The oldest units tend to have the greatest proportion of welfare recipients. The poorest quality structures sampled are usually the Old Law (five to 19 units) buildings which were built prior to 1902. Nearly one out of six of these apartments is occupied by welfare recipients. In the larger Old Law structures—those of 20 units or more—the equivalent figure is 12 percent. The New Law structures similarly have a relatively small proportion (4.7 percent) of the buildings containing five to 19 units occupied by welfare recipients, but 13.1 percent of the buildings of 20 to 49 units and 10.7 percent of the 50-unit-or-more categories are so occupied.

Contrast this with the structures built after 1929, the most modern in the city's rent-controlled stock. Less than 3 percent of the apartments in this better housing is used by welfare recipients.

Exhibits 4.4 and 4.5 contain data extrapolated by building category for the approximately 53,000 structures and 908,000 apartments represented by the rent-controlled sample. (Such extrapolations compound error and are to be viewed as indications rather than definitive measurements.) Nearly one-third of the Old Law structures (five to 19 units) have 20 percent or more of their units occupied by persons on welfare. This is also true for slightly more than one-fourth of each of the two smaller categories of New Law structures, while 23.4 percent of the Old Law structures with 20 units or more are so occupied.

Notice the great contrast with structures built after 1929. None of the

EXHIBIT 4.5

TENANTS ON WELFARE AND NUMBER OF APARTMENTS PER BUILDING CATEGORY

BUILDING CATEGORY	PERCENT ON WELFARE 0% No.	%	1 to 9% No.	%	10 to 19% No.	%	20 to 32% No.	%	33 to 99% No.	%	Total Apartments No.	%
PERCENTAGE OF TENANTS ON WELFARE BY NUMBER OF APARTMENTS PER CATEGORY												
Old Law Structures												
Five to 19 Units	59,000	48.3	6,000	5.0	17,000	14.2	16,000	13.3	23,000	19.2	121,000	100.0
20 Units or More	14,000	30.8	13,000	28.3	8,000	17.5	5,000	11.7	5,000	11.7	47,000	100.0
New Law Structures												
Five to 19 Units	61,000	59.2	6,000	5.8	9,000	9.2	13,000	12.5	14,000	13.3	103,000	100.0
20 to 49 Units	90,000	30.3	73,000	24.6	58,000	19.7	36,000	12.3	39,000	13.1	296,000	100.0
50 Units or More	62,000	36.7	87,000	50.8	10,000	5.8	4,000	2.5	7,000	4.2	170,000	100.0
Structures Built After 1929												
Ten to 49 Units	32,000	61.7	17,000	33.3	2,000	3.3	a	0.8	a	0.8	52,000	100.0
50 Units or More	51,000	65.8	27,000	34.2	0	0.0	0	0.0	0	0.0	78,000	100.0
Small Structures												
Three and Four Units	32,000	79.7	0	0.0	0	0.0	2,000	4.2	6,000	16.1	40,000	100.0
Total	402,000	44.2	229,000	25.2	105,000	11.5	77,000	8.5	95,000	10.5	908,000	100.0
NUMBER OF APARTMENTS PER CATEGORY BY PERCENTAGE OF TENANTS ON WELFARE												
	No.	%	No.	%	No.	%	No.	%	No.	%	No.	%
Old Law Structures												
Five to 19 Units	59,000	14.6	6,000	2.6	17,000	16.4	16,000	20.9	23,000	24.4	121,000	13.4
20 Units or More	14,000	3.6	13,000	5.8	8,000	7.8	5,000	7.1	5,000	5.7	47,000	5.2
New Law Structures												
Five to 19 Units	61,000	15.2	6,000	2.6	9,000	9.0	13,000	16.7	14,000	14.4	103,000	11.4
20 to 49 Units	90,000	22.4	73,000	31.9	58,000	55.6	36,000	47.1	39,000	40.8	296,000	32.7
50 Units or More	62,000	15.6	87,000	37.9	10,000	9.5	4,000	5.5	7,000	7.4	170,000	18.8
Structures Built After 1929												
Ten to 49 Units	32,000	7.9	17,000	7.5	2,000	1.6	a	0.6	a	0.5	52,000	5.7
50 Units or More	51,000	12.8	27,000	11.7	0	0.0	0	0.0	0	0.0	78,000	8.6
Small Structures												
Three and Four Units	32,000	8.0	0	0.0	0	0.0	2,000	2.2	6,000	6.8	40,000	4.4
Total	402,000	100.0	229,000	100.0	105,000	100.0	77,000	100.0	95,000	100.0	908,000	100.0

Source: George Sternlieb, *The Urban Housing Dilemma,* 1970.
Note: Numbers may not add precisely because of rounding.
[a] Less than 500

50-unit-or-more buildings in this age group have 20 percent of all their tenants on welfare. For small buildings, with ten to 49 units, the equivalent figure is 1.6 percent. In any case, the extrapolations indicate that there are 7,700 buildings with one-third or more of their tenants on welfare and an additional 5,300 units housing 20 to 32 percent welfare tenants out of the total of 53,000 structures.

Of the total number of apartments represented by the sample—approximately 908,000—about 95,000 are in structures with one-third or more welfare tenants, with an additional 77,000 at 20 percent to 32 percent[5] (Exhibit 4.5).

The top 10 percent of each of the Old Law categories and both of the smaller categories of New Law structures has 35 percent or more of their apartments occupied by welfare recipients. The equivalent figure for the largest (and generally in best condition) New Law structures is 11 percent, while for the largest (50-unit-and-over) post-1929 structures the figure is only 2 percent. The high mean for any category of structures is the 15.3 percent average for the Old Law, five-to-19-unit category of structures. Second highest is 13.2 percent for the intermediate-sized New Law buildings. The mean, by contrast for the large post-1929s, is 0.9 percent.

The data are given in more detail in Exhibit 4.6, which analyzes by percentile the proportion of welfare recipients within structures that

EXHIBIT 4.6

TOTAL NUMBER OF WELFARE RECIPIENTS
IN RENT CONTROL SAMPLE

	DISTRIBUTION OF STRUCTURES WITH WELFARE RECIPIENTS			
BUILDING CATEGORY	Total Structures	Number of Buildings With Welfare Recipients	Number of Apartments Per Building	Mean Percentage of Apartments With Welfare Recipients
Old Law Structures				
Five to 19 Units	13,400	6,900	900	29.7%
20 Units or More	1,800	1,200	2,600	17.7
New Law Structures				
Five to 19 Units	12,100	4,900	900	27.4
20 to 49 Units	9,900	6,900	3,000	19.0
50 Units or More	2,400	1,500	7,100	8.0
Structures Built After 1929				
Ten to 49 Units	700	300	3,400	5.5
50 Units or More	1,100	400	7,700	2.6
Small Structures				
Three and Four Units	11,900	2,400	400	39.1
Total	53,300	24,500	26,000	

Source: George Sternlieb, *The Urban Housing Dilemma,* 1970.

EXHIBIT 4.7

ETHNICITY OF TENANTS BY PERCENTAGE ON WELFARE

PERCENTAGE ON WELFARE	Total Structures		All White		All Negro		All Spanish		Subst. Negro (Bal. Mixed)		Subst. White (Bal. Mixed)		Subst. Spanish (Bal. Mixed)		Mixed Spanish (Other White)		All Three Mixed		NA/DK	
	ETHNICITY OF TENANTS																			
	No.	%	No.	%	No.	%	No.	%	No.	%	No.	%	No.	%	No.	%	No.	%	No.	%
0%	270	51.5	155	75.7	28	36.4	9	22.5	8	49.5	17	50.1	7	23.2	3	12.0	38	41.8	6	46.7
1% to 9%	66	12.6	25	12.4	4	4.9	2	5.0	1	6.7	9	26.4	1	4.8	0	0.9	21	23.4	2	14.5
10% to 19%	52	9.9	7	3.5	13	16.5	3	7.9	2	9.6	3	9.7	9	28.7	3	12.4	11	12.4	2	15.0
20% to 32%	53	10.0	8	3.8	10	13.4	5	13.3	2	9.4	3	9.0	7	24.4	5	25.2	11	12.1	1	11.1
33% to 100%	84	16.0	9	4.6	22	28.8	19	51.3	4	24.9	2	4.8	6	18.9	11	49.5	9	10.4	2	12.8
Total	524	100.0	205	100.0	77	100.0	37	100.0	17	100.0	34	100.0	30	100.0	21	100.0	91	100.0	12	100.0

Source: George Sternlieb, *The Urban Housing Dilemma,* 1970.
Note: Numbers may not add precisely because of rounding.

have such tenants. It is clear that while welfare tenants are found in most of the categories, their prevalence within structures varies substantially. If the small structure group is disregarded, i.e., those of three or four units which by sample design have at least one unit occupied by a welfare household, the high figure is in the Old Law category, with 29.7 percent of the small units so occupied. A close second is the equivalent sized New Law structures, with 27.4 percent of the apartments occupied by welfare tenants. This is more than five times the proportion to be found in the post-1929 structures, where buildings with 50 units or more house welfare recipients in less than 3 percent of their apartments.

ETHNIC SEGREGATION PATTERNS

Exhibit 4.7 gives the ethnicity of welfare tenants in a particular structure. Sixteen percent of the projected sample structures have one-third or more of their apartments occupied by welfare recipients. Note, however, the skew in the racial composition of the total tenants in such structures. Less than 5 percent of the all-white structures have more than one-third of the occupants on welfare. On the other hand, more than half, 51.3 percent, of the all-Spanish-speaking structures are so tenanted, and the all-black buildings are in the middle, with 28.8 percent.

Slightly over 4,000 of the projected 52,400 structures are either all black or all Spanish-speaking and have more than one-third of their recipients on welfare. The level of compaction is very clear; it involves approximately half of all such heavily welfare-tenanted structures. It is evident, therefore, that such buildings—and their inhabitants—are in a dual minority status—in terms of their welfare recipients and in terms of the tenants' ethnicity. These tenants are twice out of the mainstream. The psychological impact of this dual minority status upon them may be most severe.

HOUSING BY ETHNICITY AND BY BOROUGH

The proportion of white welfare recipients by borough is constant for Manhattan, Brooklyn and the Bronx, ranging from 13 percent to 15.2 percent respectively. Queens, however, is at 33.3 percent and Staten Island is at 40 percent. Notice, however, that only 24 cases out of the 412 total sample are housed in Queens and only five in Staten Island; so obviously, these latter figures are open to a considerable margin of error. The pattern, however, is clear. When attention is focused on black recipients, omitting Staten Island, the lower percentage is in the Bronx at 40.7 percent with the somewhat higher percentage in Queens at 45.8

percent. Among Spanish-speaking welfare recipients, however, the pattern in quite different, with a low of 20.8 percent in Queens and a high of 46.3 percent in the Bronx.

It is clear, therefore, that welfare recipients are substantially segregated, whether from choice, economic necessity, landlord-tenant selection procedures or for other reasons.

Segregation Patterns by Welfare Category

It is difficult to separate the several factors that produce variance in housing type and location among the several categories of welfare. Certainly, it is logical, if not desirable, that SROs dominate among Old Age Assistance recipients. The predominance of ADC families within certain kinds of housing may also have a logic beyond landlord discrimination. In any case, the types of structures vary, to a great degree, according to different categories of welfare.

Of all the welfare recipients within the New Law structures with five to 19 units, 60 percent are ADC. This contrasts sharply with the equivalent figure for the post-1929 structures where only 20 percent of the relatively few welfare recipients are on ADC. The pattern of Old Age Assistance is substantially the reverse of this latter relationship. Most welfare recipients who are in the best rent-controlled structure stock (post-1929) are Old Age Assistance recipients.

Again, the lack of apartments with a large number of rooms would to some degree tend to generate this skew. Generally, ADC families have more difficulty finding adequate housing since their families are larger. Certainly, the type of housing which they find leaves much to be desired.

This seems the case not only in New York but nationwide. For example, several regions consistently show a higher proportion of substandard housing for ADC families than for the total adult category of welfare recipients. A 1967 study estimated that 60 percent of ADC families were living in housing which was substandard and/or overcrowded. However, only 39 percent of Old Age Assistance households occupied rental housing in 1965, compared to 66 percent of ADC families in 1967.[6]

In a housing market with a pronounced scarcity of accommodations and a plenitude of applicants, landlords will discriminate against what they view as high wear-and-tear families, which tends to be synonymous with families having children. This discrimination occurs in middle-class accommodations as well as those for the poor. But when discrimination is further complicated by the fatherless status of many ADC cases, the size of family, the number of minors involved, as well

EXHIBIT 4.8

DEGREE OF WELFARE TENANTRY 1968 TO 1970 IN RENT CONTROL SAMPLE STRUCTURE

DEGREE OF WELFARE TENANTRY (1968)

PERCENTAGE OF WELFARE TENANTRY	None		1% to 10%		11% to 20%		21% to 30%	
	No.	%	No.	%	No.	%	No.	%
None	370,000	74.9	66,000	28.0	16,000	20.0	11,000	20.4
1% to 10%	73,000	14.8	120,000	50.8	5,000	6.3	0	0.4
11% to 20%	9,000	1.8	39,000	16.5	16,000	20.0	4,000	7.4
21% to 30%	11,000	2.2	4,000	1.7	18,000	22.5	6,000	11.1
31% to 40%	8,000	1.6	6,000	2.5	15,000	18.8	12,000	22.2
41% to 60%	11,000	2.2	1,000	0.4	9,000	11.3	17,000	31.5
61% to 99%	12,000	2.4	0	0.0	1,000	1.3	4,000	7.4
Total	494,000	100.0	236,000	100.0	80,000	100.0	54,000	100.0

PERCENTAGE OF WELFARE TENANTRY	31% to 40%		41% to 60%		61% to 99%		Total	
	No.	%	No.	%	No.	%	No.	%
None	5,000	11.4	3,000	7.7	2,000	13.3	473,000	49.2
1% to 10%	0	0.0	0	0.0	0	0.0	198,000	20.6
11% to 20%	1,000	2.3	1,000	2.6	1,000	6.7	71,000	7.4
21% to 30%	2,000	4.5	2,000	5.1	0	0.0	43,000	4.5
31% to 40%	13,000	29.5	3,000	7.7	0	0.0	57,000	5.9
41% to 60%	19,000	43.2	15,000	38.5	2,000	13.3	74,000	7.7
61% to 99%	4,000	9.1	15,000	38.5	10,000	66.7	46,000	4.8
Total	44,000	100.0	39,000	100.0	15,000	100.0	962,000	100.0

Source: New York City Department of Social Service Data Processing Administration, March 1968.

EXHIBIT 4.9

SHIFT IN WELFARE DENSITIES – APRIL 1968 TO FEBRUARY 1970 – BY CATEGORY OF STRUCTURES

PROPORTION OF APARTMENT UNITS WITH WELFARE TENANTS	CATEGORY OF STRUCTURES															
	Old Law				New Law						Post-1929					
	Five to 19 Units (n=120)		20 Units and Over (n=120)		Five to 19 Units (n=121)		20 to 49 Units (n=122)		50 Units and Over (n=120)		Ten to 49 Units (n=120)		50 Units and Over (n=120)		Small Three and Four Units (n=119)		Total Sample (n=962)	
	'70	'68	'70	'68	'70	'68	'70	'68	'70	'68	'70	'68	'70	'68	'70	'68	'70	'68
0% to 0%	62	58	36	37	73	71	32	37	30	44	72	74	77	79	91	94	473	494
1% to 10%	3	9	28	37	3	9	26	37	59	63	37	40	42	41	–	–	198	236
11% to 20%	11	20	19	20	4	12	15	19	14	5	7	4	1	0	–	–	71	80
21% to 30%	11	10	9	12	5	12	14	11	3	3	1	1	–	–	0	5	43	54
31% to 40%	8	11	13	4	10	8	14	6	7	4	2	1	–	–	3	10	57	44
41% to 60%	13	6	14	10	14	5	16	10	6	1	–	–	–	–	11	7	74	39
61% to 100%	12	6	1	0	12	4	5	2	1	0	1	0	–	–	14	3	46	15
PERCENT OF TOTAL BUILDING CATEGORY																		
0% to 0%	51.7	48.3	30.0	30.8	60.3	58.7	26.2	30.3	25.0	36.7	60.0	61.7	64.2	65.8	76.5	79.0	49.2	51.4
1% to 10%	2.5	7.5	23.3	30.8	2.5	7.4	21.3	30.3	49.2	52.5	30.8	33.3	35.0	34.2	–	–	20.6	24.5
11% to 20%	9.2	16.7	15.8	16.7	3.3	9.9	12.3	15.6	11.7	4.2	5.8	3.3	0.8	–	–	–	7.4	8.3
21% to 30%	9.2	8.3	7.5	10.0	4.1	9.9	11.5	9.0	2.5	2.5	0.8	0.8	–	–	4.2	4.2	4.5	5.6
31% to 40%	6.7	9.2	10.8	3.3	8.3	6.6	11.5	4.9	5.8	3.3	1.7	0.8	–	–	2.5	8.4	5.9	4.6
41% to 60%	10.8	5.0	11.7	8.3	11.6	4.1	13.1	8.2	5.0	0.8	–	–	–	–	9.2	5.9	7.7	4.1
60% to 99%	10.0	5.0	0.8	–	9.9	3.3	4.1	1.6	0.8	–	0.8	–	–	–	11.8	2.5	4.8	1.6
Subtotal	27.5	19.2	23.3	11.6	29.8	14.0	28.7	14.7	11.6	4.1	2.5	0.8	–	–	23.5	16.8	18.4	10.3
1970 AS A PERCENTAGE OF 1968																		
0% to 0%		107.0		97.4		102.7		86.5		68.1		97.2		97.3		96.8		95.7
1% to 10%		33.3		75.6		33.8		70.3		93.7		92.5		102.3		–		84.1
11% to 20%		55.1		94.6		33.3		78.3		278.6		175.8		–		–		89.2
21% to 30%		110.8		75.0		41.4		127.8		100.0		100.0		–		–		80.4
31% to 40%		72.8		327.3		125.8		234.7		175.8		212.5		–		29.8		128.3
41% to 60%		216.0		141.0		282.9		159.8		600.0		–		–		155.9		187.8
61% to 100%		200.0		–		300.0		256.3		–		–		–		472.0		306.1

Source: New York City Department of Social Service Data Processing Administration, March 1968.

as welfare status and ethnic group membership, their competition in the housing market is severely hampered.

SHIFTS IN WELFARE DENSITY

From April 1968 to February 1970, the number of welfare cases in New York City increased by 21.4 percent. Was this accompanied by a wider range in the housing occupied by welfare recipients or rather did the proportion of welfare tenants within welfare structures increase? In order to answer this question, comparison was made of the master check tape listings of the Welfare Department of April 1968 and February 1970.

Considerable methodological problems arise in answering this question. Because of difficulties in street coding, approximately 17 percent of the 1970 welfare cases could not be computer matched to specific addresses. This was true of roughly the same proportion in 1968. In any case, in 1970 there were 2,577 identifiable cases in the 963 structures in the rent-control sample. Within the same structures in 1968 there were 1,771 cases. Was the shift into non-welfare tenanted structures or does it rather represent an increase in the density of welfare recipients within structures?

Exhibit 4.8 presents a comparison of 962 structures within the rent-control sample in terms of the degree of welfare tenantry which they had in 1968 and 1970. It is clear that while the total number of welfare recipients housed in the sample structures rose by half during 1968-1970, this by no means indicates comparable increases in the number of structures housing welfare recipients. For example, in 1968 there were 494 structures with no welfare tenants; the equivalent for 1970 was 473. Conversely, while about one-fifth of the low-density welfare structures had no increase in welfare tenants by 1970, if the comparatively high-density welfare structures are analyzed over time the increase in their number is evident. There were 44 structures in 1968 with 31 percent to 40 percent of their tenants on welfare. By 1970 the equivalent figure was 57. Similarly the structures with 41 to 60 percent of their tenants on welfare went from 39 to 74. It is evident that welfare tenancy has become substantially intensified within structures.

Exhibit 4.9 shows the changes in degree of welfare tenantry by category of structure. The structures are divided into eight size/age categories based on the rent-control study. The incidence of welfare tenants is secured from the Welfare Department's check tapes as previously detailed. It is evident that most welfare intensification has taken place in the older structures, with relatively little impact on the post-1929 structures.

The densities by building category in 1968 and 1970 are projected for the total universe represented by the rent-controlled structures. By 1970, 4,300 of the 53,000 structures represented in this pyramiding had over 60 percent of their tenants on welfare, compared to 1,531 such tenants in 1968. The group with 41 percent to 60 percent welfare tenants had grown from 2,845 to over 5,500; the number of structures at the 21 percent to 30 percent and 31 percent to 40 percent levels remained relatively constant, as did the number of structures which have no welfare tenants whatsoever in both periods. (There are slightly over 28,000 buildings in this group). A major shift has taken place in the 1 percent to 20 percent welfare-tenanted structures, which numbered 8,400 in 1970 while in 1968 they had numbered 12,700. Despite this, it is evident that the concentration of welfare tenants has been increasing and has resulted in a considerable enlargement in the number of what for all intents and purposes can be referred to as welfare buildings. According to the projection, 18 percent of the buildings in the sample had more than 30 percent welfare tenants by 1970.

Analysis of the concentration of welfare recipients by category of welfare within structures from 1968 to 1970 confirms the overall findings. Rather than greater dispersion there is significant intensification of densities.

THE USE OF HOTELS

New York City's Welfare Department began using significant numbers of hotel facilities to house transients in the late sixties. By January 1971 some 97 hotels containing 1,100 welfare families (5,000 people in all) were being used to house welfare recipients. Six hotels had 50 or more welfare households.

The characteristics of the hotel residents have varied over time. Basically, they are divided between essentially SROs (typically men without families) and accommodations for very large families. While the average stay in hotels is 4.5 months, this period is heavily weighted by families containing six or more individuals, for whom the city is having increasing difficulty in finding housing. While, as will be discussed later, approximately 50 percent of all new admissions to public housing are on welfare, this has not adequately met the increased needs of welfare recipients.

Hotels have not generally been used to house the newcomer on welfare, but rather the person who has lost his apartment, whether through eviction (approximately 27 percent of present cases), or fire (approximately 30 percent), or any of a vast number of other causes. Not least among the latter has been the closing down of hazardous structures by the Health Department.

THE LAW OF LARGE NUMBERS

In every aspect of New York life, the law of large numbers is evident. The actual proportion of welfare recipients in hotels, for example, is less than half of 1 percent of the total, but that is 5,000 people.

Their living conditions in many cases are deplorable. The old hotels used by the Welfare Department were never designed for family life. While policing by the department has recently improved conditions, in some cases families have been distributed throughout a number of different floors. The difficulty of parental supervision under these circumstances and the accompanying increase in vandalism, public safety hazards and the like require no amplification. Another problem is providing schooling for the children. While this issue is outside the range of our discussion, there is question of whether conventional approaches can in any way cope with the education of these children.

A case study of a 37-year-old Puerto Rican woman living with one of her children, a 17-year-old boy, and two nieces in a two-room hotel accommodation gives some feeling for the situation of hotel residents. The respondent has custody of the two nieces because both parents are heroin addicts. The mother is in jail right now.

The hotel's better days are three generations past. She has been there for a year and a half "because the building where I used to live was evacuated." Her goal in life is "to get an apartment in the projects."

> I was living on the West Side of Manhattan in an apartment, then the landlord who also owns a hotel called the____and when he sold the apartment building he asked us to move to a room in that hotel at his own expenses for moving. Then he also sold that hotel and got us a room in this one...this is a very small apartment as you can see, I have only one bedroom and the bed I have in the living room. [She sleeps with her two nieces in the one room, her son uses the living room.]...the apartment maintenance is very poor because the owner wants me to move out. Anything I need to repair, he won't do it because of that. My door is broken since last New Year's Eve because he was drunk and somebody from the outside was complaining about the noise, so he was looking apartment by apartment to find out where the noise came from. So I wasn't here when he smacked my door and then he'd push it and break it—so he refused to repair it. I put a piece of wood and fix it up a little bit myself.

The problems of roaches and other vermin are also evident. She had moved to New York directly from Puerto Rico hoping for a "good job." Her major fears are of drug addiction and her major hope is "getting into the projects" (Case No. 1-1-145).

Another interview with a 40-year-old black welfare recipient living with her eight children in a two-room facility at a midtown Manhattan hotel provides further insight. She has been there for over two months. Her welfare grant is currently $1,496. The rent alone is $1,188 a month, leaving $308 for food, clothing and other necessities. She has been on welfare for 12 years. The hotel had 24 open violations at the time of the interview.

When asked how she found the apartment she said, "My house was being torn down and welfare sent us here." Asked in another context whether she found welfare assistance useful in securing housing, she said, "No, I hate it here. There's not enough room for cooking facilities or anything—I want a decent place to live, and they send me to worse slums than was torn down. There's no water in the morning, the building isn't safe. The garbage cans are piled up, and while there are no rats, the mice are a problem."

Asked what she would like to do in the future she said, "I'd like to go to school and get a better place to live. I'd like to live like a human. I don't want to see my kids go down" (Case No. 1-4-148).

Even in a time of housing shortage, hotels should be used strictly as the most temporary quarters for the family unexpectedly deprived of living facilities. Their increasing use beyond these limits reflects the inadequate supply of housing, particularly for large families with low incomes. Recent publicity on the misuse of hotels has resulted in some improvement. But unless the housing market conditions are fundamentally bettered, any improvement can only be temporary.

THE ROLE OF PUBLIC HOUSING

The role of New York City's Public Housing in relation to welfare households has frequently been misunderstood. Many people assume that the bulk of public housing apartments are occupied by welfare recipients and vice versa, that the bulk of welfare recipients are in public housing. In New York City, neither of these statements is at all true. Even on the national level, where a higher proportion of welfare recipients have been in public housing, welfare recipients are a decided minority.

Nationally in 1967, approximately 200,000 welfare households occupied rental units in public housing projects, according to a study conducted by HEW. These recipient families, in turn, occupied 31 percent of the 640,000 public housing units under HUD management. Fully 36 percent—or 72,000—were headed by aged or disabled persons. The remaining 128,000, or 64 percent, of the recipients' households received

AFDC. Welfare recipients occupied 31 percent of public housing units, but as a group public housing residents comprised only 3 percent of the recipients in the adult categories and 11 percent of the AFDC families.[7]

This relationship has evolved through a number of circumstances. First is the fact that, particularly in New York, public housing has been the sanctuary for the working-class poor. Even when the federal government has assumed the capital costs of construction, the rents have frequently excluded welfare recipients.[8] The gross income for all of New York City's publicly housed families averaged $5,664 in January 1970.[9]

In addition, the standards set for acceptance of tenants into public housing tend to exclude welfare recipients. These standards assume that certain characteristics such as a history of crime or broken families will produce housing problems for other tenants as well as for the housing administrators.

In 1968 the requirements for admission to public housing in New York City were substantially reduced. However, there had already been some increase in the percentage of welfare tenants in public housing. The data for 1960 to 1969 are as follows:

1960	12.1%	1965	12.5%
1961	11.8	1966	13.0
1962	11.7	1967	14.6
1963	12.0	1968	16.8
1964	12.2	1969	20.4

The increases in the past decade are further highlighted by the fact that from December 1969 to September 1970, the figures went from 20.4 percent to 23.2 percent. The absolute number of units in New York City's public housing occupied by welfare recipients moved from 30,300 to 34,700 in this period. Currently about 50 percent of all persons admitted are on welfare.

ETHNICITY IN PUBLIC HOUSING

New York City had, in January 1970, approximately 150,000 public housing units. Slightly under one-third of the *housing units* (32.6 percent) house whites; 35.1 percent are occupied by blacks; with Puerto Rican and others of Spanish-speaking origins making up the balance of 22.3 percent. If the data are analyzed in terms of total *population* the result is somewhat different. Only 26.4 percent of the total population is white, while 47.4 percent is black and 26.2 percent is Puerto Rican and others.

A disproportionate number of the white public housing occupants are elderly: nearly 23,000 of 48,700 white families (46.7 percent) were headed by individuals 60 years and over in January 1970. This can be said of only 19.1 percent of the blacks and a bare 11.9 percent of the Puerto Ricans. Overall, 26.5 percent of the heads of household in New York City's public housing are over 60 years of age.

Of the white families in public housing 9.6 percent are on welfare (56 percent are 60 years and over, typically Old Age Assistance recipients). Of the 67,500 black families, 24.2 percent are on welfare, and 22 percent of these heads of household are 60 years old or over. Among Puerto Ricans, 29.2 percent of all the families in public housing are on welfare, with 1,730 out of the 9,725 (18 percent) of the heads of household 60 years old and over.

These percentages reflect the number of minors in public housing. There are over 100,000 school children in the 150,000 units of public housing in New York in kindergarten through junior high. The total number of minors for the projects as a whole was 1.7 per dwelling unit. Again, there is substantial variation among the several ethnic groups. For white families the mean number of minors per household is 1.0; for blacks it is 2.0; while for Puerto Ricans it is 2.3.

FUTURE USE OF PUBLIC HOUSING

The total turnover in New York City's public housing is only 5 percent to 6 percent a year. The likelihood that significant amounts of public housing will be open to welfare recipients in any one year is obviously limited. The growth in the proportion of welfare recipients being housed in public housing units does, however, represent a change in the kind of applicant accepted, as well as the growth of welfare among people who are already public housing residents.

While determining the concentration of welfare families within specific projects is beyond the scope of this work, some housing developments are more dependent upon welfare tenants than others. Is there some maximum percentage of welfare families in the massive projects which dominate New York City's public housing beyond which negative social effects will be felt? Unfortunately, social science research in this area is permeated with folklore rather than clear findings.

In the group interviews conducted among welfare recipients in public housing, however, some feeling was expressed (by ADC mothers particularly) that the lack of adult supervision, characteristic of units occupied by fatherless families with minors, presents very severe problems.

Social scientists have been vigorous in their criticism of negative attitudes toward welfare families. But senseless and unthinking prejudices against the fatherless family have been reversed without proper attention to the realistic problems of child supervision.

Reporting of actual vandalism and tenant problems is far from precise. "Problem" families, which are responsible for serious deterioration of their housing and/or the subjects of complaints by their neighbors, are identified in the procedural forms used by the management of New York's public housing units. Complaints involve households on welfare more than twice the proportion of their total incidence in public housing. Again, there are serious difficulties in determining the meaning of this finding. The potential for future problems, however, should not be underestimated.

The problems of tenants not paying rents are not exclusively the prerogative of the private sector but have also occurred among welfare recipients in public housing. A number of public housing authorities point to a serious lack of communication with welfare workers about tenant problems in this area.

Social Services

If nothing more, the concentration of welfare recipients within a particular structure makes possible a reasonably efficient application of ameliorative measures. Child care centers, public health facilities and training programs are obviously more feasible. Whether these have been realized in fact is another question. Their potential must be measured against the problem potential of dual segregation by race and welfare status.

Attitudes Toward Public Housing

Later in this study the attitudes of welfare recipients toward public housing will be examined in greater detail.[11] For the moment, however, despite the shortcomings characteristic of the massive structures that most residents live in, we must note that public housing in New York City is regarded quite positively.

One elderly Negro couple and their grandson exemplified this attitude as they pointed out that the move into public housing had satisfied all of their needs. When asked where they stood on a ladder of personal position running from zero to ten, the latter being the very top of the scale, they stated that their present position was at ten, while five years before, prior to residence in public housing, it was zero.

INTERIOR MAINTENANCE OF HOUSING

In the rent control study, 953 of the buildings sampled had an interior maintenance check conducted by field examiners.[12] The basic goal of the examiners was not to appraise the absolute quality of the structure but to rank it within one of the eight age/size categories of structures.

EXHIBIT 4.10

INTERIOR MAINTENANCE RATING AND PERCENTAGE OF WELFARE TENANTS

INTERIOR MAINTENANCE RATING	PERCENTAGE OF WELFARE TENANTS BY INTERIOR MAINTENANCE RATING											
	PERCENT ON WELFARE											
	0%		1 to 9%		10 to 19%		20 to 32%		33 to 100%		Total Structures	
	No.	%	No.	%	No.	%	No.	%	No.	%	No.	%
1 to 59	3,000	32.8	600	6.5	1,200	13.4	1,400	15.6	2,900	31.7	9,100	100.0
60 to 75	8,400	42.9	2,500	12.6	2,700	13.9	2,500	12.5	3,600	18.1	19,700	100.0
76 to 89	11,500	67.0	2,000	11.8	1,400	7.9	1,300	7.5	1,000	5.9	17,200	100.0
90 to 100	4,800	77.1	1,000	16.5	100	1.8	100	1.5	200	3.1	6,300	100.0
Total	27,800	53.1	6,100	11.7	5,400	10.4	5,300	10.1	7,700	14.7	52,300	100.0
	INTERIOR MAINTENANCE RATING BY PERCENTAGE OF WELFARE TENANTS											
	No.	%	No.	%	No.	%	No.	%	No.	%	No.	%
1 to 59	3,000	10.8	600	9.6	1,200	22.5	1,400	27.0	2,900	37.8	9,100	17.5
60 to 75	8,400	30.4	2,500	40.6	2,700	50.4	2,500	46.9	3,600	46.5	19,700	37.7
76 to 89	11,500	41.4	2,000	33.0	1,400	25.0	1,300	24.3	1,000	13.2	17,200	32.9
90 to 100	4,800	17.4	1,000	16.8	100	2.1	100	1.8	200	2.5	6,300	12.0
Total	27,800	100.0	6,100	100.0	5,400	100.0	5,300	100.0	7,700	100.0	52,300	100.0

Source: G. Sternlieb, *The Urban Housing Dilemma,* 1970.

Note: Numbers may not add precisely because of rounding.

How did the maintenance quality of the structure compare with others within its subcategory? For the purposes of this study we also analyzed the interior maintenance rating as a function of the proportion of welfare recipients tenanted in the building.

Barely 25 percent of the buildings with 20 percent to 32 percent of tenants on welfare and less than 16 percent of buildings with an even larger proportion of welfare tenants were rated at 76 and over on a scale on which the highest positive score was 100. In contrast, nearly 70 percent of the other structures so rated had no welfare tenants.

It is very clear that the rating of the internal maintenance of the buildings is directly related to the proportion of welfare recipients in the building. Less than 11 percent of the structures with no welfare tenants are included in the poorest category of structures (those rated under the 60 level). Nearly four out of ten of the buildings with one-third or more of their units occupied by welfare tenants are, however, in this lowest category. In absolute numbers, based on extrapolations, this proportion involves close to 3,000 buildings. Similarly, approximately 42,000 apartments are in buildings with one-third or more of their tenants on welfare which are rated under the 60 level, and a nearly equivalent number have the same low rating and have 10 percent to 32 percent welfare tenants (Exhibits 4.10 and 4.11).[13]

While three-fourths of the structures rated in the good to very good category (76 to 100) had no welfare tenants, less than one-third of the structures graded 1 to 59 are without welfare tenants; over 30 percent have one-third or more of their units so occupied. Only 3 percent of the 90 to 100 rated structures have any welfare tenants.

The instructions to field supervisors and interior maintenance checkers were set up to equalize the ratings within each building category; some level of skew may have entered into the overall evaluations. These data were, therefore, rerun with ratings for *each* of the eight structure categories divided into three segments in terms of quality. Again, however, the close relationship of low maintenance rating and high levels of welfare is very apparent.

The quality of interior maintenance is highly dependent on the level of welfare tenancy; even rent levels are a less significant variable. The sum of the measured effects on maintenance for the ten most significant variables is R^2=.3874. Welfare tenancy accounts for more than one-third of this variation. The variables included age and size of structure, Planning Area, rent level, repair and maintenance expenditures, mortgage data and a variety of landlord characteristics as well as tenant ethnicity. Clearly there are elements at work other than those measured, and future efforts should be directed toward uncovering them.

EXHIBIT 4.11

INTERIOR MAINTENANCE RATING AND PERCENTAGE OF WELFARE TENANTS

INTERIOR MAINTENANCE RATING	PERCENTAGE OF WELFARE TENANTS BY INTERIOR MAINTENANCE RATING											
	PERCENT ON WELFARE											
	0%		1 to 9%		10 to 19%		20 to 32%		33 to 100%		Total Apartments	
	No.	%	No.	%	No.	%	No.	%	No.	%	No.	%
1 to 59	30,000	22.8	18,000	13.9	25,000	18.8	17,000	13.0	42,000	31.5	132,000	100.0
60 to 75	100,000	31.1	85,000	26.4	54,000	16.9	41,000	12.8	41,000	12.8	322,000	100.0
76 to 89	165,000	55.2	84,000	28.3	25,000	8.2	16,000	5.4	9,000	3.0	299,000	100.0
90 to 100	100,000	67.5	41,000	27.6	1,000	0.7	3,000	1.9	3,000	2.3	148,000	100.0
Total	395,000	43.8	229,000	25.4	105,000	11.6	77,000	8.6	95,000	10.6	901,000	100.0
	INTERIOR MAINTENANCE RATING BY PERCENTAGE OF WELFARE TENANTS											
	No.	%	No.	%	No.	%	No.	%	No.	%	No.	%
1 to 59	30,000	17.7	18,000	8.0	25,000	23.7	17,000	22.3	42,000	43.8	132,000	14.7
60 to 75	100,000	25.3	85,000	37.2	54,000	51.9	41,000	53.3	41,000	43.3	322,000	35.7
76 to 89	165,000	41.7	84,000	36.9	25,000	23.4	16,000	20.7	9,000	9.3	299,000	33.2
90 to 100	100,000	25.3	41,000	17.9	1,000	1.0	3,000	3.6	3,000	3.6	148,000	16.4
Total	395,000	100.0	229,000	100.0	105,000	100.0	77,000	100.0	95,000	100.0	901,000	100.0

Source: G. Sternlieb, *The Urban Housing Dilemma,* 1970.

Note: The percentages presented here vary from Exhibit 4.10 as a result of the variation in the size of buildings concerned.

Ethnicity

The poorest rated structures contained nearly one-fourth of the residences of Spanish-speaking welfare recipients—23.8 percent—and 13.9 percent of the blacks', while only 4.7 percent of the whites'.

Conversely, when top rated structures are analyzed by the ethnicity of their welfare inhabitants, 39.1 percent of the whites live in such structures as compared to 15.9 percent of the Spanish-speaking respondents and only 5.6 percent of the blacks.

Welfare Category

There is surprisingly little variation among the several categories of welfare recipients in terms of their evaluation of maintenance. In a later section of this study the welfare recipients' attitudes and expressions of satisfaction or dissatisfaction with their housing will be discussed in detail. However, 43 percent of the total sample said that their building maintenance was either very good or good. An additional 27.4 percent answered that it was fair. The balance, 29.6 percent, gave negative or very negative responses. The degrees of variation among the several welfare categories in this variable are relatively small. A more positive response was secured from Old Age Assistance recipients, who tend to live in slightly better rated structures than did the other welfare recipients. A shade less than one-third of the three other categories of welfare recipients indicated significant dissatisfaction with the level of their building maintenance.

Borough Variation

The sample distribution among the several boroughs unfortunately does not permit an adequate analysis in depth of variation on the part of Queens residents. However, only five of the 24 respondents were negative about their building's maintenance while for the more significant group in the Bronx the equivalent figure was no less than 37 percent. In Manhattan 23.9 percent of the welfare tenants gave a negative rating to their building maintenance; Brooklyn was intermediate at 28.5 percent. Due to the size of the sample in the three latter boroughs, each of which is over 100, it seems reasonable to conclude that the level of consumer satisfaction with building maintenance among welfare respondents in the Bronx is significantly lower than in the other boroughs.

VIOLATIONS

The number of violations of the New York City Building Code on individual structures is subject to the frequency of inspection, the size of the structure and the vagaries of procedures involved. Even allowing for this, however, there is a clear-cut association between structures

EXHIBIT 4.12

OPEN VIOLATIONS BY PERCENTAGE OF WELFARE TENANTS

PERCENT ON WELFARE	Total Structures	OPEN VIOLATIONS: PERCENTILES 10	20	30	40	50	60	70	80	90	Interquartile Range (25% to 75%)	Mean
None	28,500	0	0	0	100	100	100	300	500	900	0 to 400	3.9
1% to 9%	6,100	0	0	100	200	400	500	700	900	1,600	0 to 800	6.2
10% to 19%	5,400	0	0	100	300	500	600	1,000	1,400	2,000	0 to 1,300	8.1
20% to 32%	5,300	0	0	100	300	400	500	900	1,200	2,500	700 to 1,000	7.9
33% to 100%	7,700	0	0	0	100	200	600	1,100	1,500	3,500	0 to 1,200	10.6
Total	53,000											

Sources: George Sternlieb, *The Urban Housing Dilemma,* 1970.
New York City Department of Social Service Data Processing Administration, March 1968.

EXHIBIT 4.13

NUMBER OF ROOMS PER APARTMENT BY TOTAL NUMBER OF PERSONS IN HOUSEHOLD

NUMBER OF ROOMS PER APARTMENT	TOTAL NUMBER OF PEOPLE IN HOUSEHOLD: 1 No.	1 %	2 No.	2 %	3 No.	3 %	4 No.	4 %	5 No.	5 %	6 No.	6 %	7 No.	7 %	8 No.	8 %	9 No.	9 %	Total No.	Total %	Overcrowded Units No.	Overcrowded Units %
One	30	81.1	5	13.5	0	0.0	0	0.0	1	2.7	1	2.7	0	0.0	0	0.0	0	0.0	37	100.0	7	18.9
Two	8	40.0	7	35.0	2	10.0	1	5.0	0	0.0	0	0.0	1	5.0	0	0.0	1	5.0	20	100.0	3	15.0
Three	19	21.1	30	33.3	24	26.7	15	16.7	1	1.1	0	0.0	1	1.1	0	0.0	0	0.0	90	100.0	2	2.2
Four	11	8.1	21	15.6	33	24.4	32	23.7	21	15.6	8	5.9	5	3.7	1	0.7	3	2.2	135	100.0	17	12.6
Five	4	4.7	8	9.3	7	8.1	18	20.9	14	16.3	17	19.8	7	8.1	7	8.1	4	4.7	86	100.0	18	20.9
Six	1	3.3	1	3,3	4	13.3	4	13.3	6	20.0	2	6.7	6	20.1	2	6.7	4	13.3	30	100.0	6	20.0
Seven to Eight	0	0.0	1	9.1	1	9.1	2	18.2	3	27.3	2	18.2	1	9.1	1	9.1	0	0.0	11	100.0	0	0.0
Nine and Over	1	33.3	0	0.0	0	0.0	0	0.0	1	33.3	0	0.0	0	0.0	0	0.0	1	33.3	3	100.0	–	–
Total	74	18.0	73	17.7	71	17.2	72	17.5	47	11.4	30	7.3	21	5.1	11	2.7	13	3.2	412	100.0	53	
Overcrowded	–	–	5	6.8	0	0.0	1	1.4	2	4.3	9	30.0	14	66.7	10	90.9	12	92.3		12.9		

Source: Housing of Welfare Recipients Survey, 1970.

with a considerable number of violations and the proportion of welfare tenants (Exhibit 4.12). The extrapolation presented in the exhibit is of the 963 structures in the rent control sample projected for the total universe of 53,000 buildings which they represent.

Buildings with one-third or more of their tenants on welfare have a mean of 10.6 open violations. The mean number for the projected 28,500 structures with no welfare tenants is only 3.9. The violations in other categories support the thesis that the proportion of welfare tenants is substantially associated with the number of violations.

When data on ethnic patterns and violations are analyzed, there is little variation. Buildings that house Spanish-speaking welfare recipients have more violations, with 36.4 percent of the Spanish-speaking respondents in buildings with seven or more violations, compared with 27.4 percent for blacks. The equivalent for whites is 23.5 percent.

CROWDING

One of the prime targets of proponents of governmental intervention in housing markets has been to reduce the level of crowding which has historically typified the slums. The image, all too frequently corroborated by fact, is that of a one-room apartment inhabited by entire families. The negative social effects of crowding have been well documented by social scientists. How substantial is crowding among welfare recipients?

Exhibit 4.13 compares the number of rooms per apartment by the total number of people per household based on the sample survey. The mean number of persons per household is 3.61. (This calculation takes the nine-or-more-person households, which number 3.2 percent of the total sample, as having only nine persons, which, of course, underestimates the problem somewhat.) The evidence shows that 18 percent of the welfare recipients are one-person households, with a similar proportion in the two-person category. Three- or four-person households are at the 17 percent and over level, with 11.4 percent at the five-person level, 7.3 percent at the six-person level, 5.1 percent at the seven-person level and 5.9 percent over that. In sum, nearly one in five (18 percent) of the welfare households in the sample require accommodations for six or more persons. Considering the relative lack of housing accommodations for families of this scale in New York, pressures are obvious.

How well is New York City meeting the housing challenge? There is no universally accepted measuring stick of an appropriate relationship between number of rooms and size of household. In Exhibit 4.13 we have drawn a stepped diagonal line to indicate what is considered a level of overcrowding by frequently used standards.[14]

The reader should be warned that the standards imposed here are quite arbitrary. For example, there are 15 four-person households occupying three-room apartments. To observers unfamiliar with middle-class housing standards in New York, this may seem an intolerable level of density. It is not at all uncommon, however, even among the more affluent, for the city is characterized by relatively small units.

On the other hand, a seven-person household in a five-room apartment would be categorized as overcrowded. Some persons may question this evaluation, which certainly depends on the character and caliber of the apartment in question, the size of the rooms and so forth.

In any case, accepting the levels specified in the exhibit, 12.9 percent of the welfare families are "overcrowded." But this condition is far from universal. It holds true, for example, for 12 out of 13 of the largest categories of households, those with nine or more people in them, and similarly for ten out of the 11 eight-person households. Two-thirds of the 21 households with seven persons are overcrowded by the standards of this presentation. This drops to less than one-third of the 30 households with six persons in them, and only two out of the 47 with five persons. The only other category with any significant crowding incidence is in the five out of 73 two-person households who occupy one room which, by the standards used here, are overcrowded.[15]

Overcrowding by Ethnicity

An earlier part of this work analyzed the size of households by ethnicity. It is worthwhile restating these data in the context of overcrowding. Nearly two-thirds of the white welfare households consist of only one or two persons. Among blacks slightly over one out of three households this size is found and among Spanish-speaking households it is less than one out of four. The opposite is evident in households with five or more members. Among whites, such households number less than one out of six, but among blacks and Spanish-speaking households they are approximately two out of six.

The relatively large size of minority group households is corroborated by the number of rooms used. A quarter of the whites live in one- or two-room apartments, compared to 15 percent of the blacks and less than 8 percent of the Spanish-speaking persons. Conversely, accommodations with five or more rooms house 12 percent of the whites, one-third of the blacks and slightly less than one-third of the Spanish-speaking respondents.

The basic problem encountered in housing welfare recipients, certainly in securing an adequate-sized accommodation, is the problem of large minority group households, who are typically ADC recipients (see Chapters 1 and 3).

EXHIBIT 4.14

LENGTH OF RESIDENCE IN PRESENT APARTMENT AND CATEGORY OF WELFARE

LENGTH OF TIME IN PRESENT APARTMENT	CATEGORY OF WELFARE BY LENGTH OF TIME IN PRESENT APARTMENT									
	CATEGORY OF WELFARE									
	Home Relief		Old Age Assistance		Aid to Disabled		Aid to Dependent Children		Total	
	No.	%	No.	%	No.	%	No.	%	No.	%
Zero to Six Months	8	10.7	3	5.5	6	10.5	27	12.0	44	10.7
Seven to 12 Months	16	21.3	5	9.1	6	10.5	36	16.0	63	15.3
13 to 24 Months	14	18.7	8	14.5	9	15.8	52	23.1	83	20.1
25 Months to Five Years	19	25.3	14	25.5	14	24.6	69	30.7	116	28.2
Six to Ten Years	14	18.7	11	20.0	10	17.5	26	11.6	61	14.8
11 to 20 Years	2	2.7	5	9.1	7	12.3	12	5.3	26	6.3
21 and Over	2	2.7	9	16.4	5	8.8	3	1.3	19	4.6
Total	75	100.0	55	100.0	57	100.0	225	100.0	412	100.0
	LENGTH OF TIME IN PRESENT APARTMENT BY CATEGORY OF WELFARE									
	No.	%	No.	%	No.	%	No.	%	No.	%
Zero to Six Months	8	18.2	3	6.8	6	13.6	27	61.4	44	100.0
Seven to 12 Months	16	25.4	5	7.9	6	9.5	36	57.1	63	100.0
13 to 24 Months	14	16.9	8	9.6	9	10.8	52	62.7	83	100.0
25 Months to Five Years	19	16.4	14	12.1	14	12.1	69	59.5	116	100.0
Six to Ten Years	14	23.0	11	18.0	10	16.4	26	42.6	61	100.0
11 to 20 Years	2	7.7	5	19.2	7	26.9	12	46.2	26	100.0
21 and Over	2	10.5	9	47.4	5	26.3	3	15.8	19	100.0
Total	75	18.2	55	13.3	57	13.8	225	54.6	412	100.0

Source: Housing of Welfare Recipients Survey, 1970.

Notice the amount of relative underutilization; for example, five of the apartments with seven or more rooms were held by families with four or fewer members of the household, and an additional six such units housed three or fewer people. These are divided between Old Age Assistance and ADC households who generally secured them with formal leases more than ten years ago—usually before going on welfare. Seven of these apartments were held by blacks, one by Spanish-speaking whites, and three by other whites.

HOUSING MOBILITY PATTERNS

What level of housing demand is generated by New York City's welfare population and how does government effort buffer it? Welfare recipients' rates of housing turnover have a significant effect on the stresses and reaction of the housing market. For example, to maintain a building on a constant level requires substantial investment by the landlord if there is a high turnover of tenants. Just moving furniture causes a fair number of bruises and scars. For this reason landlords have typically preferred long-term tenants. But one of the principal methods used by New York's landlords to secure rent increases under the rent-control law extant at the time of our survey was the 15 percent increase in rent permitted at each tenant turnover. (This was limited to one such increment every two years.)[16] The effect is to penalize good buildings, that is, those from which tenants don't want to move, and to give bonuses to poor ones with a high turnover. Obviously, moving also imposes a burden on the tenant, in terms of disruption of his life style, the costs that always attend moving, and physical and emotional strain.

Exhibit 4.14 shows by category of welfare the length of time respondents have lived in their present facilities. Fully 26 percent have lived in their present accommodations less than 13 months. Brevity of tenure was most frequent among Home Relief cases (32 percent) and ADC cases (28 percent). The most stable category was the Old Age Assistance recipients, only 14.6 percent of whom had moved within the last year, and the Aid to the Disabled category was intermediate at 21 percent. Of the individuals who have lived in their present accommodations six or more years, the Old Age Assistance group is again the least mobile at 45.5 percent. In contrast, less than one in five (18.2 percent) of the ADC cases have been in their present accommodations for six or more years, and 24.1 percent and 38.6 percent of the Home Relief and Aid to the Disabled categories fall into a similar category.

Borough Patterns

In analysis by borough, the Bronx has the highest level of mobility with no less than 30.5 percent of its present welfare recipient residents having moved within the last year. This contrasts with 23.5 in Brooklyn and 24.7 percent in Manhattan. The Queens' data, unfortunately, involve only 24 cases, six of whom had moved during the past year.

Mobility Versus Ethnicity

The several ethnic groups vary in length of residence in their present apartments. Exhibit 4.15 shows that 40.7 percent of the whites have lived in the same apartments for six or more years compared to 28.9 percent of the blacks and 16.5 percent of the Spanish-speaking individuals. Conversely, tenants who have been living in the same accommodations for less than 25 months include approximately one-third of the whites but nearly 50 percent of the blacks and Spanish-speaking individuals.[17]

EXHIBIT 4.15

LENGTH OF RESIDENCE IN PRESENT APARTMENT BY ETHNICITY

	ETHNICITY									
LENGTH OF RESIDENCE	White		Negro		Spanish Speaking		Other		Total	
	No.	%	No.	%	No.	%	No.	%	No.	%
Zero to Six Months	5	7.8	18	10.0	21	12.8	0	0.0	44	10.7
Seven to 12 Months	6	9.4	30	16.7	26	15.9	1	25.0	63	15.3
13 to 24 Months	11	17.2	38	21.1	34	20.7	0	0.0	83	20.1
25 Months to Five Years	16	25.0	42	23.3	56	34.1	2	50.0	116	28.2
Six to Ten Years	12	18.8	30	16.7	19	11.6	0	0.0	61	14.8
11 to 20 Years	5	7.8	13	7.2	8	4.9	0	0.0	26	6.3
21 Years Plus	9	14.1	9	5.0	0	0.0	1	25.0	19	4.6
Total	64	100.0	180	100.0	164	100.0	4	100.0	412	100.0

Source: Housing of Welfare Recipients Survey, 1970.

Perhaps because of their long-term residence more of the whites seem to be statutory tenants. Only 28 percent say that they have a lease, compared to 40 percent of the blacks and Spanish-speaking persons. Again, reflecting their long residence, 43 percent of the whites compared to 30 percent of the other two groups have had rent increases while in their present accommodations. Under the Rent Control Law (1970), since tenant turnover is by definition not a factor, these increases would have to have been either for hardship applications (open only to better structures) or for additional dollar inputs by the landlord. The latter would include reinvestment in the provision of additional services or major capital expenditures.

Intent to Move

Welfare recipients' future aspirations and plans will be discussed in detail in Chapter 5. It should be noted here, however, that responses

EXHIBIT 4.16

EXPECTATIONS OF LOCATION OF RESIDENCE ONE YEAR FROM NOW BY CATEGORY OF WELFARE

FUTURE LOCATION	CATEGORY OF WELFARE									
	Home Relief		Old Age Assistance		Aid to Disabled		Aid to Dependent Children		Total	
	No.	%	No.	%	No.	%	No.	%	No.	%
Same Place	45	60.0	38	69.1	36	63.2	98	43.6	217	52.7
Better Apartment	16	21.3	7	12.7	6	10.5	61	27.1	90	21.8
In Another State/Country	1	1.3	0	0.0	0	0.0	11	4.9	12	2.9
Age/Resignation	2	2.7	0	0.0	2	3.5	3	1.3	7	1.7
Other	1	1.3	2	3.6	1	1.8	13	5.8	17	4.1
Don't Know	10	13.3	8	14.5	11	19.3	39	17.3	68	16.5
No Answer	0	0.0	0	0.0	1	1.8	0	0.0	1	0.2
Total	75	100.0	55	100.0	57	100.0	225	100.0	412	100.0

Source: Housing of Welfare Recipients Survey, 1970.

EXHIBIT 4.17

APARTMENT-FINDING METHODS BY CATEGORY OF WELFARE

METHOD	CATEGORY OF WELFARE									
	Home Relief		Old Age Assistance		Aid To Disabled		Aid to Dependent Children		Total	
	No.	%	No.	%	No.	%	No.	%	No.	%
Broker	10	13.3	1	1.8	10	17.5	26	11.6	47	11.4
Newspaper	3	4.0	2	3.6	0	0.0	11	4.9	16	3.9
Relative Or Friend	41	54.7	30	54.5	26	45.6	100	44.4	197	47.8
Sign On Premises	5	6.7	5	9.1	4	7.0	15	6.7	29	7.0
Applied To Public Housing	4	5.3	3	5.5	3	5.3	18	8.0	28	6.8
Through Welfare	3	4.0	2	3.6	2	3.5	9	4.0	16	3.9
Relocation	3	4.0	2	3.6	1	1.8	8	3.6	14	3.4
Other	5	6.7	9	16.4	10	17.5	35	15.6	59	14.3
NA/DK	1	1.3	1	1.8	1	1.8	3	1.3	6	1.5
Total	75	100.0	55	100.0	57	100.0.	225	100.0	412	100.0

Source: Housing of Welfare Recipients Survey, 1970.

to the question "Where do you expect to be living one year from now?" varied greatly. Many did not expect to move—71.9 percent of the whites, 53.7 percent of Spanish-speaking individuals and 45 percent of the blacks. Perhaps old age explains the relative immobility of the whites, but the implied mobility patterns are obvious. Only 6.3 percent of the whites, but 27.2 percent and 22.0 percent respectively, of the blacks and Spanish-speaking said specifically, "A better apartment."

When asked their chances for reaching their locational goal 343 cases gave responses. The "goods" and "excellents" numbered more than a majority of each of the several groups—74.1 percent of the whites, 62.1 percent of the Spanish-speaking individuals, and 55.7 percent of the blacks.

In Exhibit 4.16 the answers are tabulated by category of welfare. The ADC cases indicate the greatest immediate mobility plans. Their implied discontent with housing and desire to move may not, however, be reconcilable within the limitations of the market.

The mean mobility data have reduced significance when one discusses a population as large and diverse as New York City's welfare recipients. There do seem to be high levels of mobility for a significant part of the welfare group, with median longevity between two and five years. If one accepts the probable average of an apartment shift every 3.5 years (which may be an understatement since it does not account for those who though discontented have sunk into apathy), the level of mobility is evident. Given approximately 350,000 households currently on welfare, one could expect a shift of 100,000 per year. And this figure only reflects the households that do move, that have found alternative accommodations despite the pervasive housing shortage.

SEARCH PATTERNS IN HOUSING

One predominant characteristic of the low-income housing market is its relative inefficiency. In research conducted in another city (Newark, New Jersey) in a period of relatively high vacancy rates, it became evident that the low-income person frequently finds his housing in a relatively hit-or-miss fashion. As a result he often pays high rents for inferior accommodations while superior ones a few blocks away go begging.[18]

Exhibit 4.17 shows the answers to the question "How did you find this apartment?" by category of welfare. Only 11.4 percent of the sample used a broker. The relative shortage of apartments in New York and their infrequent listings by owners may have contributed to this low percentage. It may also be attributed in part to the lack of an adequate referral service or inability to pay the broker's costs.

EXHIBIT 4.18

APARTMENT-FINDING METHODS BY ETHNICITY

METHOD	ETHNICITY									
	White		Negro		Spanish Speaking		Other		Total	
	No.	%	No.	%	No.	%	No.	%	No.	%
Broker	9	14.1	25	13.9	13	7.9	0	0.0	47	11.4
Newspaper	3	4.7	11	6.1	2	1.2	0	0.0	16	3.9
Relative or Friend	28	43.8	74	41.1	93	56.7	2	50.0	197	47.8
Sign on Premises	6	9.4	6	3.3	17	10.4	0	0.0	29	7.0
Applied to Public Housing	1	1.6	18	10.0	9	5.5	0	0.0	28	6.8
Through Welfare	4	6.3	7	3.9	5	3.0	0	0.0	16	3.9
Relocation	1	1.6	8	4.4	4	2.4	1	25.0	14	3.4
Other	11	17.2	27	15.0	20	12.2	1	25.0	59	14.3
NA/DK	1	1.6	4	2.2	1	0.6	0	0.0	6	1.5
Total	64	100.0	180	100.0	164	100.0	4	100.0	412	100.0

Source: Housing of Welfare Recipients Survey, 1970.

EXHIBIT 4.19

ASSESSMENT OF TREATMENT DURING SEARCH FOR HOUSING BY CATEGORY OF WELFARE

WAS TREATMENT FAIR?	CATEGORY OF WELFARE									
	Home Relief		Old Age Assistance		Aid to Disabled		Aid To Dependent Children		Total	
	No.	%	No.	%	No.	%	No.	%	No.	%
Yes	63	84.0	51	92.7	50	87.7	166	73.8	330	80.1
No	12	16.0	4	7.3	7	12.3	59	26.2	82	19.9
Total	75	100.0	55	100.0	57	100.0	225	100.0	412	100.0

Source: Housing of Welfare Recipients Survey, 1970.

When questioned about how they had found their present housing most of the respondents indicated that a relative or friend had told them of it (47.8 percent). Newspapers provided housing information to less than 4 percent, with a scattering of other patterns. Some characteristic comments were, "I found it by myself just walking around." "I lived in the same building." "I was referred to it by the landlord of the place I was living in before." "I passed by and saw it empty." "I bought it from the old tenants who worked for the former owners." "I was living downstairs, the landlord's brother told me about it."

Unfortunately, we have no adequate comparative data on middle-class housing search patterns in New York. There is no question, however, that formal hunt patterns are used by a small minority of the welfare recipients. As will be discussed in detail later, the Welfare Department rarely was named as a direct source of housing; it represented only 3.9 percent of the total responses even though at least one staff member, assigned on a part- or full-time basis to each welfare center, is a housing specialist.

Recipients of the several categories of welfare vary only slightly in their search patterns. The most significant variation is the very low use of brokers by Old Age Assistance recipients who more typically find their apartments through relatives or friends, signs on premises and one-of-a-kind methods than do the other categories.

We have emphasized the strictures of ethnicity and welfare status, yet another factor may account for part of the problem—the restrictiveness of the search process itself. While far from independent, and not infrequently reflecting the welfare recipient's vision of himself or his status and desirability in the world, it is also a unique variable in itself.

Ethnicity

Exhibit 4.18 contains the responses to the question "How did you find your apartment?" by the respondent's ethnicity. Notice the comparative similarity in the responses of the blacks and the whites compared to those who are Spanish-speaking. The latter group used brokers barely half as often as did the other two. On the other hand, Spanish-speaking persons found housing through relatives and friends substantially more often, with 56.7 percent using this approach compared to slightly over 40 percent for the other two groups.[19]

Search patterns are no doubt influenced by the welfare recipients' self-view, but they also mirror societal beliefs. The atmosphere of hopelessness that pervades some of the interviews is difficult to impart. One 68-year-old widow, born in the South, who moved up to the North to be with her children and is presently on Old Age Assistance, gives some insight into the fatalism of the poor which is parallelled in many other interviews. She lives in a one-room basement apartment in the Bedford-Stuyvesant area of Brooklyn. When asked where she stood on the Cantril Ladder, she pointed out the lowest rung for the present, the past and the future, saying, "I don't see any way out, you gotta have money." When asked how she found her apartment, she said that she pursued an ad in the Amsterdam News and the landlord ". . . knew I was old and peaceful." There were no goals expressed; she is only waiting for death.

Discrimination

Exhibit 4.19 shows the answers to the question "In searching for housing, do you feel that you were always treated fairly?" by category of welfare. Four out of five of the 412 respondents respond affirmatively. There is some variation among the several categories of welfare. The Old Age Assistance recipients are most positive in their appraisal; only 7.3 percent feel that they have been treated poorly, while 26.9 percent of the ADC cases respond negatively. The other two categories of welfare fall between these extremes, with 16 percent of the Home Relief and 12.3 percent of the "other" (the Disabled) category feeling that they have encountered prejudice in the course of their search. There is no material skew in borough responses. Clearly, the ADC cases most often feel they are discriminated against.

When the data are analyzed by ethnicity of respondent, there is substantial variation among the several ethnic groups. In the sample as a whole, for example, eight out of ten feel that they have been treated fairly. But only seven out of ten of the black respondents respond affirmatively, while the Spanish-speaking are much more positive, with only 10.4 percent feeling that they have been treated unfairly. Whites are in the middle at 14.1 percent.

Are the different evaluations of blacks and Puerto Ricans a result of variation in their levels of aspiration? Is the white response tempered by their relatively greater success in finding good housing accommodations? Unfortunately, we do not have enough information to answer these provocative questions.

When respondents are asked to specify in what way they felt they were treated unfairly, the responses vary so considerably that they are sometimes beyond the coder's ability to categorize. Some typical responses are: "People acted nasty at the realtor's office." "The rental people changed the rent fee once you had arrived at the offices and then showed very bad apartments." "Have no husband." "They're against children." "Maybe because I have no husband." "I got shoved around moving from place to place until finally I got this apartment." "People gave me the runaround. They said the apartment was vacant, the landlord said it wasn't." "No use in searching because they cut off the moving money." "Tried to get into a senior citizen's project, they turned me down, I don't know why." Rarely are the complaints personalized; rather some amorphous god from the machine is blamed—"they!"

The single most common form of discrimination mentioned by the 82 cases who reported discrimination is welfare status, with 40.2 percent of the ADC respondents giving this as the sole reason. Another 31.7 percent report racial discrimination, and "size of household" is volunteered by 25.9 percent.

Unfortunately, when analysis of discrimination by type of welfare is attempted, the subsets become very small. Only 27 percent of the ADC recipients (59) who volunteered answers indicating prejudice say that race is of prime importance, compared to 49.6 percent who give welfare status and 29.3 percent who answer size of household. The sample size in the "other" (Disabled) categories of welfare is too small for subdivision.

While perhaps more probing would have brought race to the fore, our data indicate considerable variation from the conventional wisdom, which suggests that race is the dominant factor. One-third of the 55 black respondents who report some form of discrimination indicate that it is primarily racial, while eight of the 17 Spanish-speaking respondents who say that they felt discrimination signify that race was the cause. None of the nine whites who feel discriminated against give race as the cause. The problems of welfare status are mentioned by one-third of the whites and 45 percent of the blacks, but only 30 percent of the Spanish-speaking.

When size of household as the cause of discrimination is analyzed by ethnicity, it is mentioned by three out of the nine whites who indicate some form of discrimination, 13 out of the 55 blacks and five out of the 17 Spanish-speaking respondents. Obviously, the sample is quite small, but it does provide some feeling for the range of concerns.

Race may have been given a low priority in discrimination because most welfare recipients of minority status are housed in areas where race is no longer a major concern on the part of landlords. There is, however, a strong feeling that welfare status definitely makes individuals second-class citizens within the housing market.

Security Deposit Requirements

Are patterns of prejudice exhibited by a demand for security deposits? In approximately three-fourths of the cases respondents indicate that landlords require security deposits. Significant variations occur, however, as a function of the category of welfare received. No less than

EXHIBIT 4.20

ASSISTANCE FROM THE WELFARE DEPARTMENT IN APARTMENT HUNTING BY CATEGORY OF WELFARE

RECEIVED ASSISTANCE	CATEGORY OF WELFARE									
	Home Relief		Old Age Assistance		Aid to Disabled		Aid to Dependent Children		Total	
	No.	%	No.	%	No.	%	No.	%	No.	%
Yes	13	17.3	11	20.0	12	21.1	73	32.4	109	26.5
No	48	64.0	32	58.2	35	61.4	122	54.2	237	57.5
Not on Welfare	14	18.7	12	21.8	10	17.5	30	13.3	66	16.0
Total	75	100.0	55	100.0	57	100.0	225	100.0	412	100.0

Source: Housing of Welfare Recipients Survey, 1970

EXHIBIT 4.21

POSSIBLE ASSISTANCE FROM WELFARE DEPARTMENT IN APARTMENT HUNTING BY CATEGORY OF WELFARE

POSSIBLE ASSISTANCE	CATEGORY OF WELFARE									
	Home Relief		Old Age Assistance		Aid To Disabled		Aid to Dependent Children		Total	
	No.	%	No.	%	No.	%	No.	%	No.	%
Finding Apartment	24	38.7	8	18.2	13	28.9	37	24.3	82	27.1
Financial Assistance	3	4.8	2	4.5	4	8.9	21	13.8	30	9.9
Attitude	3	4.8	2	4.5	4	8.9	8	5.3	17	5.6
More Than One of Above	2	3.2	1	2.3	0	0.0	0	0.0	3	1.0
Other	9	14.5	4	9.1	8	17.8	34	22.4	55	18.2
NA/DK	21	33.9	27	61.4	16	35.6	52	34.2	116	38.3
Total	62	100.0	44	100.0	45	100.0	152	100.0	303	100.0

Source: Housing of Welfare Recipients Survey, 1970

89.8 percent of the ADC cases live in apartments in which the landlord requires a deposit as contrasted with less than 50 percent of those in the Old Age Assistance group. For Home Relief it is 70.3 percent, while for the Aid to the Disabled categories of welfare it is 50.9 percent. Are these variations a consequence of the landlord's prejudice or the undesirability or undependability of the ADC cases in comparison to other welfare cases?

Only 45.3 percent of the whites indicate landlords insist on security deposits, compared to 72 percent of the blacks and fully 90.9 percent of the Spanish-speaking respondents. In part the type of housing used by the several groups may explain the variance—whites are in the elderly category and housed in SROs. Landlords may also be responding to tenant ethnicity and the feeling, fancied or real, that some groups are relatively transient and less reliable rent payers. While the above may explain some of the difference, it seems clear that prejudice is an important potential explanation for this differential response to tenant ethnicity.

Real Estate Brokerage Fees

Fees have been required by real estate brokers in 11.4 percent of the 412 cases. Fees are rarely demanded in the Old Age Assistance cases, where only one out of 55 respondents indicate that they have paid such brokerage fees, compared to 12 percent to 14 percent in each of the other categories. In approximately half of the cases, welfare has paid the fee in question. One in six of the blacks (16.2 percent) versus only 7.3 percent of the Spanish-speaking group and 9.4 percent of the whites claim that brokerage fees have been involved in securing their apartments.

Deposits for Utilities

Memory may not be the most reliable way of determining whether the respondents have paid deposits for utilities such as gas, electric, telephone and the like. Approximately 60 percent of the respondents, however, claim to have paid deposits on one or more utilities, and 40 percent of the cases claim two or more such payments. The highest frequency of no-deposits-at-all answers is in the Old Age Assistance group —52.7 percent. Again, this is largely a function of their more frequent use of institutional facilities or SROs without cooking arrangements. Less than one-third of the ADC group answer no deposits.

When asked whether these deposits were recovered, more than two-thirds of the cases claim that there has been neither full nor partial recovery of the utility deposit. Recipients of the several categories of welfare vary little on this point.

USE OF THE SERVICES IN HOUSING

The potential strain on the Welfare Department's real estate operations is evident. Currently less than 100 housing advisors are employed by the department. A case load of more than 1,000 for each of these individuals (given our estimate of 100,000 moves a year) would be self-defeating. But how often do welfare recipients use these city services?

There were 412 responses to the question: "Did you receive any assistance from the Welfare Department in your search for your apartment?" Barely one-fourth (26.5 percent) of the respondents say they secured assistance from welfare in finding their housing accommodations (Exhibit 4.20). In part, this low figure may be accounted for by the fact that 16 percent answer that when they found their present accommodations they were not on welfare. Still others may not be aware that these services are available.

When the data are analyzed by category of welfare assistance received, some significant deviations are revealed. For example, 21.8 percent of the 55 respondents who are on Old Age Assistance were already in their apartments at the time they went on welfare, but only 13.3 percent of ADC recipients.

Nearly one-third (32.4 percent) of the ADC recipients replied that they had received assistance from welfare in their search for apartments as compared to at least 10 percent fewer of each of the other categories of recipients. In all categories less than one-third of the welfare cases have secured help from the Welfare Department.[20]

Ethnic Patterns

More than one-fourth (26.6 percent) of the whites indicate that they found their present apartments prior to getting on welfare compared to 11.1 percent of blacks and 17.7 percent of the Spanish-speaking individuals. There is also a significant variation between the Spanish-speaking and the other groups in their use of the Welfare Department to find housing. Such aid was given to 39 percent of Spanish-speaking welfare recipients, and to whites and blacks, 18.8 percent and 17.8 percent respectively.[21] The Welfare Department is most helpful in finding a new place to live among the Spanish-speaking, with 25 percent answering positively to 14 percent for blacks and 10 percent for whites.

Type of Assistance Received

Of the 109 of the 412 respondents who received some assistance from the welfare authorities in finding their present housing, nearly three-fourths (72.5 percent) answer that it has been financial assistance, that is, the provision of landlord deposits, first rents and the like. In only 14 of the 412 cases is the Welfare Department cited as the source of an apartment. In eight additional cases the recipient has been given a list of potential landlords, one of whom ultimately provided him with a home.

Unfortunately, given the size of the sample, three-way cross-tabulations indicating those who were helped by kind of help and assistance category produce subsets too small for generalization. In the one category large enough for analysis, the 73 ADC cases who claim to have had some help from the Welfare Department, over three-fourths (76.7 percent) say that it was strictly financial.

In general, the help given by the Welfare Department is considered useful. But again, the great majority of responses reveal that the services are limited to financial support. This does not vary substantially when cross-tabulated by ethnicity.

The respondents who have not found the Welfare Department helpful in finding their present accommodations were asked: "How do you feel welfare might have been helpful in finding an apartment?" Their answers are compared by category of welfare in Exhibit 4.21. About one-fourth of the respondents (27.1 percent) say that they would have appreciated some help in finding an apartment. Slightly less than 10 percent would have liked more financial assistance, with the balance of the rest of opinions being scattered. The latter responses run the gamut from requests to "set up places for us to look over," to: "They should not have sent [a recipient's mother] to flop-houses to live." Some respondents feel that welfare "should have the power to stop discrimination," or are completely negative: "They can't be helpful, they usually put you into a worse place than you can find yourself." "They told me to find one myself." (Exhibit 4.22 shows more of these responses.) Note that 38.3 percent of the respondents cannot give any specific suggestions. Whether this indicates lack of verbal ability or apathy about the potential of the department's offerings is very difficult to determine.

There is significant variation between the categories of welfare in the type of help desired. For example, 38.7 percent of the 62 Home Relief respondents said that help in finding apartments would be of primary importance, compared to less than half of that number, 18.2 percent, of the 44 Old Age Assistance recipients. The other two categories fell in between. Among the ADC group of 152 respondents, 13.8 percent refer to additional financial assistance, but less than 7 percent of the other three categories combined desire this type of help.

SUMMARY

Of the recipients sampled 78.2 percent lived in apartments, 11.7 percent lived in public housing, 4.1 percent lived in rented or owned houses

EXHIBIT 4.22

OTHER RESPONSES TO THE QUESTION: "HOW DO YOU FEEL THE WELFARE DEPARTMENT MIGHT HAVE BEEN USEFUL IN YOUR SEARCH FOR HOUSING?"

INTERVIEW CODE NO.	HOW DO YOU FEEL THE WELFARE DEPARTMENT MIGHT HAVE BEEN USEFUL?
1-4-041	Set up places for us to look over.
2-4-236	They can't help; they find worst places for you.
2-4-202	They could tell us good places to live.
1-1-083	They should not send her to "flop houses" to live in.
3-4-407	By letting welfare recipients know of apartments available.
1-6-143	They can't help — they use their standards and find apartments in public housing or low-income areas.
3-1-475	Should have the power to stop discrimination.
3-4-515	Could provide a list of apartments available.
2-4-351	Could have helped her get into project.
1-1-124	Find out from landlord what apartments are available.
3-5-502	Help other people get in the projects.
2-4-243	Provide a list of apartments available for rent.
2-4-251	Provide names of places available.
2-4-260	Give suggestions of where to look.
2-1-304	Give suggestions of where to look.
2-1-307	Suggest places of where to look.
1-1-118	Tell people where housing is available.
2-4-249	Couldn't have helped; have to wait too long.
3-4-452	Welfare said they didn't have any places and she'd have to wait; said they wouldn't pay the fee if went to an agency.
1-4-018	Gave me a list of brokers, but those places were worse than this one, welfare wasn't a help.
2-4-237	Can't be helpful; usually put you into worse place than you can find.
3-4-403	Could have told me this was a terrible building.
2-6-273	Couldn't help me; they give only slum housing.
1-4-137	Don't think they could do anything.
1-2-097	They might have put me in a project and I wouldn't like that.
3-2-488	Don't think they could have helped.
2-4-349	Couldn't help me; couldn't find place big enough.
2-4-341	Couldn't help; always put you in undesirable location.
3-4-405	Would not have found a good neighborhood.
2-4-200	Could not help; I've asked for help.
3-6-501	Might have placed me in a similar situation, perhaps worse.
4-8-629	Went two years ago, sent me to condemned buildings; wouldn't ask again.
4-4-602	I hate them, they wouldn't help me in 1958 when my husband was sick.
3-1-464	Don't feel they could help, heard they give mouse trap places to live in, rather borrow money from a friend.
3-4-436	Don't need them because they wouldn't help me last time.
3-6-499	Find husband better-paying job.
3-4-424	Doesn't think they could have helped.
3-4-414	Don't think they could help.
3-4-525	Would do worse, welfare people get worse buildings.
2-4-217	They don't find you anything nice.
4-4-607	Probably wouldn't ask, they aren't quick enough.
2-6-287	Wasn't on welfare at that time, didn't need their help.
2-2-328	Don't expect them to help; daughter takes care.
3-4-453	They told her to find one herself.
4-4-603	Would rather find it myself.
3-4-519	Didn't need them.

EXHIBIT 4.22 cont'd.

INTERVIEW CODE NO.	How Do You feel the Welfare Department Might Have Been Useful?
2-4-221	No help, because they wouldn't pay for house.
2-1-303	Tried to get into projects, but they said I had too many children.
1-4-031	They're busy, take them a long time.
1-6-052	Tried to move, welfare wouldn't help me.
3-1-473	I would rather look myself, for welfare would send you to a place unfit to live in.
2-4-344	Rather look myself, they send you to run-down places.
3-4-425	They help but the places aren't good, I'd rather go to the projects.
2-6-280	Welfare Department could provide a list of apartments available.
1-2-125	Welfare Department could speed up her entry into senior citizen's projects.
1-4-041	Could send us up to look over decent places in decent neighborhoods.
3-4-447	Provide a list of apartments available.

while the balance typically lived in single-room occupancy facilities. The oldest housing tends to have the greatest proportion of welfare recipients. The poorest quality structures are also more frequently occupied by welfare recipients. It is very clear also that our ratings of the interior maintenance of buildings are inversely correlated to the proportion of welfare recipients in the building and directly linked to the number of building code violations. There is also evidence that housing segregation seems related to ethnicity and welfare status. Some discrimination also seems to operate against large families and families with minors. But those studied more frequently said they were discriminated against because of their welfare status than because of their race or size of household.

With the increase in the number of people on welfare in New York City in recent years, the concentration of welfare tenants has increased and has resulted in a larger number of buildings that are almost completely tenanted by welfare recipients. Welfare recipients have been moving into buildings already inhabited by welfare recipients; they have not dispersed into a larger number of buildings.

Less than half of 1 percent of all welfare recipients are housed in hotels. Many of these hotels are in poor condition, overly expensive and inadequate, particularly for large families with low incomes. This is a consistent problem encountered in housing large minority group households.

Unlike most cities, New York does not have a high concentration of welfare recipients in public housing. In September 1970, only 23.2 percent of New York's public housing was occupied by welfare recipients, but this percentage is increasing and welfare recipients tend to view public housing relatively favorably.

Over one-fourth of the welfare recipients interviewed have lived in their present accommodations less than 13 months. There is much higher mobility among blacks and Spanish-speaking welfare recipients than among white recipients. The largest group of recipients found their present housing through relatives and friends. Very few mentioned the Welfare Department as their source of finding housing. ADC recipients and Spanish-speaking recipients are more frequently required to pay security deposits.

NOTES

1. See Appendix 4.1 for details on occupants of furnished homes.

2. U.S. Department of Health, Education and Welfare, *The Role of Public Welfare in Housing*, p. 23.

3. Louis Harris and Associates, Inc., *Transition Neighborhoods in New York City* (New York, Vera Institute, 1969). It should be noted that the subject of appraising the quality of the structure is beset by pitfalls in methodology. For example, *Census Bureau Working Paper No. 25* indicates the results of some efforts at replicating the housing quality appraisals conducted during the 1960 census. Even the use of experts failed to produce consistent results.

4. Old Law structures were built before 1902. New Law structures were built from 1902 to 1929. The 50-unit-and-over category are typically in the best condition, since they date from after World War I. Post-1929 structures were constructed from 1929 to 1947 for the categories represented here. The three- and four-unit category is roughly divided between the Old Law and New Law with one dating from after 1929. See George Sternlieb, *The Urban Housing Dilemma* and Chapter 2 for more detail.

5. Note that this is based upon projection of the average number of units per building size and, therefore, there will be variations in the total number of apartments projected.

6. HEW, *op. cit.*, pp. 12-22.

7. *Ibid.*, p. 4. A 1971 study indicates a slight upward swing. For this and other national data see Abeles, Schwartz and Associates, *The Impact of the Brooke Amendment on Public Housing Tenants* (New York City, 1971).

8. *Ibid.*, p. 124.

9. This data based upon the New York City Public Housing Authority's records probably understates somewhat the actual income level. It should be noted that there was relatively little variation in the several ethnic groups that were involved. Blacks were highest at $5,794, whites were next at $5,602, and Puerto Ricans and others were lowest at $5,527.

10. All of these data are as of December 31 of the year in question. Unpublished analysis by the New York City Department of Human Resources.

11. See Appendix 5.1 for the results of the Semantic Differential using "public housing" as the stimulus word.

12. The ten buildings which are excluded were either vacant or not open to inspection.

13. At the risk of redundancy the data are presented both in terms of structures and number of apartments. Both elements are essential to projecting the costs and efforts involved in public action.

14. The exhibit gives the number of apartments by size of apartment which are overcrowded (see entries to the right of the diagonal). The data are summarized to the extreme right and to the bottom of the exhibit, respectively.

15. Some question can properly be raised as to the adequacy of one-room facilities even for one-person households. The bulk of these are occupied by elderly individuals with about one-fourth of them in some form of institution. The total number or rooms per apartment and the total number of usable rooms were asked separately in the course of the interviews. The two figures are nearly identical. Note, however, that in some of the group interviews reference is made to rooms that are not used because of heating problems or because of their poor condition.

16. For more on this point see *The Urban Housing Dilemma.* The revised New York City formula as of 1971 did away with the turnover rent increment. It also, however, permits decontrol on vacancy given certain stipulations.

17. Under the recent ruling which calls for decontrol of apartments once vacated by their present tenants, the potential of rent increases for welfare recipients is particularly evident.

18. See George Sternlieb, *The Tenement Landlord,* (New Brunswick, New Jersey: Rutgers University Press, 1969).

19. For comparative data on search patterns in job hunting by ethnicity-income level, see Jack Chernick, Bernard P. Indik and George Sternlieb, *Newark, New Jersey: Population and Labor Force* (New Brunswick, New Jersey: Rutgers University Press, 1968) p. 15.

20. In the course of a study of ADC mothers conducted from January 1 to November 10, 1966, the following question was asked: "During this year since about mid-January, did any of the investigators help you find a place to live?" Of the Puerto Ricans 23.8 percent answered in the affirmative as compared with 14.3 percent of the blacks and only 9.8 percent of the whites. A later question asked during the same interview was "During this year since January, did you want any of your investigators to help you find a place to live?" This was asked only if no help had been shown in response to the first question. Of the Puerto Ricans 46.7 percent answered yes, 40.9 percent of the Negroes similarly, and 28.5 percent of the whites. Harold Yohr and Richard Pomeroy, *Studies in Public Welfare: Effects of Eligibility* (New York: City University of New York, 1970), p. 41.

21. This is confirmed by Pomeroy's *Survey Studies in Public Welfare,* p. 13. In Pomeroy's study, based on 1966 field work, respondents were asked whether they had discussed their housing problems with agencies or professionals unaffiliated with the Department of Social Services. This was comparatively rare. In 1.1 percent of the 1,763 cases for which there were data, they had discussed housing with a professional outside of the Department of Social Services who had been suggested by the case worker; an additional 8.6 percent had discussed it with some agency or professional not suggested by the case worker. Richard Pomeroy, *Studies in Public Welfare: Reaction of Welfare Clients to Social Services* (New York: City University of New York, 1970), p. 24.

Chapter 5

THE WELFARE RECIPIENT'S ATTITUDE TOWARD HIS HOUSING AND ITS SETTING

Most literature describing the housing facilities of welfare recipients is based on the views of outsiders—the casual observer, the landlord, the social worker or the researcher. What does the welfare recipient think about his housing? In this chapter the responses to a varied series of measurements are presented.

THE PROBLEM OF STANDARDS

Many variables enter into any evaluation of consumer responses. Not the least of them, in this case, is the self-image of the welfare recipient and his opinion about his relationship to society. Furthermore, the welfare recipient's attitude toward the quality of his housing facilities may be a function of his previous experience as well as the absolute quality of the unit in question.

For example, the head of an eight-person household of gypsies views his storefront, five-room apartment, cramped though the accommodations are by most standards, as "looking like heaven to me because I used to live in Puerto Rico in a circus tent." He points out that "there are lots of rats, but I do not have any problem with them yet."

The shortcomings of machine data analysis of interviews are illustrated by another case, a mother of four children living on ADC. After complaining bitterly about problems with garbage disposal as well as the great problems with junkies and public safety, she said that she is

EXHIBIT 5.1

RELATIONSHIP BETWEEN HOUSING SATISFACTION, AND SUMMARY SCORE MEASURES OF RATED PROBLEM AREAS IN HOUSING

	NUMERICAL RATING																	
	5		7		9		12		15		18		21		24			
HOUSING SATISFACTION	Very Good				Good			Fair				Poor			Very Poor			
	6		8		11		14		17		20		23		25		Totals	
	No.	%	No.	%	No.	%	No.	%	No.	%	No.	%	No.	%	No.	%	No.	%
Very Satisfied (1)	24	70.6	14	58.3	25	30.1	11	11.8	6	6.3	0	0.0	0	0.0	0	0.0	80	19.5
Satisfied (2)	9	26.5	9	37.5	42	50.6	34	36.6	24	25.3	6	10.9	2	8.3	0	0.0	126	30.7
Undecided (3)	1	2.9	1	4.2	10	12.6	7	7.5	15	15.8	6	10.9	2	8.3	0	0.0	42	10.2
Dissatisfied (4)	0	0.0	0	0.0	6	7.2	29	31.2	31	32.6	21	38.2	8	33.3	1	33.3	96	23.4
Very Disatisfied (5)	0	0.0	0	0.0	0	0.0	12	12.9	19	20.0	22	40.0	12	50.0	2	66.7	67	16.3
Total	34	100.0	24	100.0	83	100.0	93	100.0	95	100.0	55	100.0	24	100.0	3	100.0	411	100.0

Sources: Housing of Welfare Recipients Survey, 1970.
Note: C = .59; $p < .01$; N = 411; df. = 28.

satisfied with the housing, but amplified this response by saying, "I know I can't do any better." The reader, therefore, should view the quantitative data presented in this chapter with these limitations in mind.

Three methods were used to learn about the welfare recipient's satisfaction with his housing. The first is the simple, straightforward question, "How satisfied are you with the place you are living in now?" Five alternative responses are possible: very satisfied, satisfied, undecided, dissatisfied and very dissatisfied.

A second, more complex method was suggested by the preliminary video taped group interview/discussions with recipients about their housing problems. A number of major problem areas related to housing were volunteered in these interviews, and we asked our respondents to rate their satisfaction with each of them. Among the problems included are apartment size, building maintenance, apartment maintenance, safety in the area and location. Each of these is rated on a five-point scale from "very good" (1) to "very poor" (5). A summary score for each individual is obtained by adding his responses to each of the five items. Summary scores can range from "very good" (5) to "very poor" (25).

A third measure of satisfaction was developed from the use of the semantic differential approach which was applied to the stimulus words "my apartment." (See Appendix 5.1.) This approach indicates that there are three component factors to people's attitude toward their apartments. The first dimension is a generalized favorable or unfavorable evaluation. The second is how active or passive people feel toward this area, and the third is the degree of intensity or strength of the person's attitude toward his apartment.

It is clear that the first measure of "satisfaction with housing" is clearly and significantly correlated with the second, the summary rating scale of the several problem areas (Exhibit 5.1). The correlation between the two is substantial (C = .59). It is also clear from Exhibit 5.2 that both of these two measures are significantly correlated (gamma = .72 and .52 respectively) with the evaluation factor of the semantic differential measure of "satisfaction with housing," but not at all correlated with the intensity (potency) factor or the activity factor. These latter two factors are, then, independent of all three measures of "satisfaction with housing" narrowly conceived. Evidently, the three approaches to measuring attitude toward housing are triangulating on the evaluative component of the respondents' attitudes toward housing. However, the intensity and activity factors, as defined by the semantic differential approach, are clearly different dimensions.

For ease of presentation the simplest measure of satisfaction with housing will be used in the material which follows.

EXHIBIT 5.2

RELATIONSHIPS BETWEEN HOUSING SATISFACTION AND FACTORS IN THE SEMANTIC DIFFERENTIAL MEASURE OF ATTITUDES TOWARD ONE'S APARTMENT

	Factor I Evaluation	Factor II Activity	Factor III Intensity or Potency
Housing Satisfaction	gamma = .72 (significant)	gamma = .07	gamma = −.01
	n = 412	n = 412	n = 412

RELATIONSHIPS BETWEEN THE SUMMARY SCORE MEASURE OF RATED PROBLEM AREAS IN HOUSING AND FACTORS IN THE SEMANTIC DIFFERENTIAL MEASURE OF ATTITUDES TOWARD ONE'S APARTMENT

	Factor I Evaluation	Factor II Activity	Factor III Intensity or Potency
Summary Score Measure	gamma = .57 (significant)	gamma = .02	gamma = .04
	n = 412	n = 412	n = 412

Note: Gamma is used as the measure of the amount of association; ═ means measures of covariation show statistically significant relationships.

SATISFACTION WITH PRESENT ACCOMMODATIONS

Exhibit 5.3 presents the responses to the question "How satisfied are you with the place you are living in now?" by category of welfare. Precisely half the respondents are very satisfied or satisfied, compared with 39.8 percent who are dissatisfied or very dissatisfied. Included for purposes of comparison are results of a similar question addressed to a random sample of 423 residents of Plainfield, New Jersey, a community of mixed economic character. The positive responses from Plainfield residents are more than half again the proportion secured from the New York welfare respondents. The negatives are five times as frequent in the New York welfare recipient sample.[1]

The ADC cases are least satisfied with their housing, with nearly half (48.9 percent) expressing a negative attitude versus 39.1 percent expressing a positive one. The Old Age Assistance recipients are most positive, with more than 76.4 percent either satisfied or very satisfied, versus only 16.3 percent who are negative. The other two categories are quite similar and fall between the extremes indicated.

Satisfaction Level by Ethnicity

Exhibit 5.4 contains the responses to the question of satisfaction by the respondent's ethnicity. Nearly 30 percent of the whites (29.7 per-

EXHIBIT 5.3

HOUSING SATISFACTION BY CATEGORY OF WELFARE

CATEGORY OF WELFARE	DEGREE OF SATISFACTION											
	Very Satisfied		Satisfied		Undecided		Dissatisfied		Very Dissatisfied		Total	
	No.	%	No.	%	No.	%	No.	%	No.	%	No.	%
Home Relief	18	24.0	24	32.0	6	8.0	16	21.3	11	14.7	75	100.0
Old Age Assistance	21	38.2	21	38.2	4	7.3	7	12.7	2	3.6	55	100.0
Aid to Disabled	11	19.3	23	40.4	5	8.8	11	19.3	7	12.6	57	100.0
Aid to Dependent Children	30	13.3	58	25.8	27	12.0	63	28.0	47	20.9	225	100.0
Total	80	19.4	126	30.6	42	10.2	97	23.5	67	16.3	412	100.0
Plainfield Total		56.3		28.5		6.5		5.8		2.1		100.0

Source: Housing of Welfare Recipients Survey, 1970.
Plainfield data from George Sternlieb and W.P. Beaton, *The Zone of Emergency: A Case Study of Plainfield, New Jersey.* (New Brunswick, N.J., Transaction Books, 1972).

a. 1 = very good; 2 = good; 3 = fair; 4 = poor; 5 = very poor.

b. 0.9% gave a "don't know" answer.

EXHIBIT 5.4

HOUSING SATISFACTION BY ETHNICITY

RESPONSE	ETHNICITY											
	White			Black			Spanish Speaking		Other		Total	
	No.	%	%[a]	No.	%	%[a]	No.	%	No.	%	No.	%
Very Satisfied	19	29.7	61.3	25	13.9	39.2	35	21.3	1	25.0	80	19.4
Satisfied	26	40.6	27.8	54	30.0	26.6	44	26.8	2	50.0	126	30.6
Undecided	5	7.8	5.4	20	11.1	10.1	17	10.4	0	0.0	42	10.2
Dissatisfied	7	10.9	4.2	47	26.1	12.7	42	25.6	1	25.0	97	23.5
Very Dissatisfied	7	10.9	0.6	34	18.9	8.9	26	15.9	0	0.0	67	16.3
			0.6[b]			2.5[b]						
Total	64	100.0	100.0[c]	180	100.0	100.0[d]	164	100.0	4	100.0	412	100.0

Sources: Housing of Welfare Recipients Survey, 1970.
Plainfield data from Sternlieb and Beaton, *The Zone of Emergence.*

a. Plainfield data.
b. Refers to "no answer" or "don't know."
c. N = 331.
d. N = 79.

EXHIBIT 5.5

HOUSING SATISFACTION BY BOROUGH

RESPONSE	BOROUGH											
	Manhattan		Brooklyn		Bronx		Queens		Richmond		Total	
	No.	%	No.	%	No.	%	No.	%	No.	%	No.	%
Very Satisfied	15	12.8	41	25.9	13	12.0	10	41.7	1	20.0	80	19.4
Satisfied	38	32.5	48	30.4	30	27.8	10	41.7	0	0.0	126	30.6
Undecided	18	15.4	13	8.2	9	8.3	2	8.3	0	0.0	42	10.2
Dissatisfied	27	23.1	32	20.3	36	33.3	2	8.3	0	0.0	97	23.5
Very Dissatisfied	19	16.2	24	15.2	20	18.5	0	0.0	4	80.0	67	16.3
Total	117	100.0	158	100.0	108	100.0	24	100.0	5	100.0	412	100.0

Source: Housing of Welfare Recipients Survey, 1970.

cent) are very satisfied and another 40.6 percent answer that they are "satisfied." This compares to 13.9 percent and 30 percent for the blacks and 21.3 percent and 26.8 percent for the Spanish-speaking individuals. Are these different patterns of responses a result of age, outlook, relationships with the rest of society or the actual conditions of housing? These are open questions. Some of their parameters are explored later in this chapter. However, only 21.8 percent of the whites say they are dissatisfied or very dissatisfied with their housing, compared to 41.5 percent of the Spanish-speaking respondents and 45 percent of the blacks.

Again, for comparative purposes data from the Plainfield study are shown for 331 whites and 79 blacks. While there are dramatic differences between whites and blacks, the variation between Plainfield blacks and black New York City welfare recipients also is evident.

Borough Variations

An analysis of responses was made by the respondent's borough of residence. As Exhibit 5.5 indicates, the Bronx has the most negative responses, with only 39.8 percent of welfare-receiving residents indicating satisfaction versus more than half (51.8 percent) who are dissatisfied or very dissatisfied. In Manhattan, 39.3 percent of the welfare recipients are dissatisfied or very dissatisfied, and 35.5 percent of the recipients in Brooklyn are in the same categories. The number in Queens is obviously too small for generalization but 20 of the 24 respondents are either very satisfied or satisfied.

REASONS FOR SATISFACTION OR DISSATISFACTION

Exhibit 5.6 lists the volunteered response by category of welfare of the reasons for satisfaction or dissatisfaction. Fully 29.4 percent of the total sample feel that the "bad area" in which their apartment is located is the primary negative factor. The next most important factor (20.6 percent) is felt to be the configuration of the apartment unit. Note that these negative responses are most often given by ADC recipients.

When cross-tabulated by the respondents' ethnicity, the biggest single criticism from both minority groups pertains to a "bad area," followed closely by apartment and building configuration. The number of dissatisfied whites is too small to permit generalization (Exhibit 5.7). When these data are analyzed by borough, the Bronx has the highest level of dissatisfaction with "bad area" (34.3 percent). There is little other significant variation by borough.

EXHIBIT 5.6

REASONS FOR HOUSING SATISFACTION BY CATEGORY OF WELFARE

RESPONSE	CATEGORY OF WELFARE									
	Home Relief		Old Age Assistance		Aid to Disabled		Aid to Dependent Children		Total	
	No.	%	No.	%	No.	%	No.	%	No.	%
Satisfied (No Specifics But Positive Attitude	7	9.3	17	30.9	4	7.0	13	5.8	41	10.0
Satisfied (No Specifics But Negative Attitude)	6	8.0	6	10.9	8	14.0	19	8.4	39	9.5
Apartment Configuration	15	20.0	7	12.7	13	22.8	50	22.2	85	20.6
Building Configuration	10	13.3	5	9.0	9	15.8	23	10.2	47	11.4
Good or Bad Area	19	25.3	8	14.5	11	19.3	83	36.9	121	29.4
Return to Homeland	8	10.7	5	9.0	4	7.0	9	4.0	26	6.3
Apartment and Building Configuration	6	8.0	4	7.3	0	0.0	13	5.8	23	5.6
Other	1	1.3	0	0.0	1	1.8	8	3.6	10	2.4
NA/DK	3	4.0	3	5.5	7	12.3	7	3.1	20	4.9
Total	75	100.0	55	100.0	57	100.0	225	100.0	412	100.0

Source: Housing of Welfare Recipients Survey, 1970.

EXHIBIT 5.7

REASONS FOR HOUSING SATISFACTION BY BOROUGH

RESPONSE	BOROUGH											
	Manhattan		Brooklyn		Bronx		Queens		Richmond		Total	
	No.	%	No.	%	No.	%	No.	%	No.	%	No.	%
Satisfied (Positive Attitude)	6	5.1	17	10.8	11	10.2	6	25.0	1	20.0	41	10.0
Satisfied (Negative Attitude)	17	14.5	12	7.6	8	7.4	2	8.3	0	0.0	39	9.5
Apartment Configuration (Including Furniture)	24	20.5	30	19.0	26	24.1	3	12.5	2	40.0	85	20.6
Building Configuration	14	12.0	22	13.9	9	8.3	0	0.0	2	40.0	47	11.4
Good or Bad Area (Schools, Safety, Drugs)	29	24.8	47	29.7	37	34.3	8	33.3	0	0.0	121	29.4
Return to Homeland	7	6.0	10	6.3	5	4.6	4	16.7	0	0.0	26	6.3
Apartment and Building Configuration	8	6.8	6	3.8	8	7.4	1	4.2	0	0.0	23	5.6
Other	5	4.3	2	1.3	3	2.8	0	0.0	0	0.0	10	2.4
NA/DK	7	6.0	12	7.6	1	0.9	0	0.0	0	0.0	20	4.9
Total	117	100.0	158	100.0	108	100.0	24	100.0	5	100.0	412	100.0

Source: Housing of Welfare Recipients Survey, 1970.

EXHIBIT 5.8

SATISFACTION WITH APARTMENT AMENITIES

RATING	AMENITIES															
	Apartment Size		Building Maintenance		Apartment Maintenance		Safety		Public Transportation		Location		Garbage Collection		Total Housing Satisfaction	
	No.	%	No.	%	No.	%	No.	%	No.	%	No.	%	No.	%	No.	%
Very Good	76	18.4	78	19.0	84	20.4	58	14.1	168	40.8	149	36.2	127	30.8	80	19.4
Good	114	27.7	98	23.8	108	26.2	71	17.2	143	34.7	132	32.0	142	34.5	126	30.6
Fair	127	30.8	114	27.5	106	25.7	102	24.8	80	19.4	77	18.7	90	21.8	42	10.2
Poor	70	17.0	77	18.7	68	16.5	99	24.0	14	3.4	28	6.8	31	7.5	97	23.5
Very Poor	25	6.0	45	10.9	46	11.2	82	19.9	7	1.7	26	6.3	22	5.3	67	16.3
Total	412	100.0	412	100.0	412	100.0	412	100.0	412	100.0	412	100.0	412	100.0	412	100.0
Point Rating	2.65		2.79		2.72		3.18		1.91		2.15		2.22		2.87	

Source: Housing of Welfare Recipients Survey, 1970.

a. 1 = very good; 2 = good; 3 = fair; 4 = poor; 5 = very poor.

EXHIBIT 5.9

DESIRED HOUSING IMPROVEMENTS BY CATEGORY OF WELFARE

RESPONSE	CATEGORY OF WELFARE									
	Home Relief		Old Age Assistance		Aid to Disabled		Aid to Dependent Children		Total	
	No.	%	No.	%	No.	%	No.	%	No.	%
Nothing	14	18.7	21	38.2	10	17.5	21	9.3	66	16.0
Apartment and Building Configuration	7	9.3	3	5.5	8	14.0	26	11.6	44	10.7
Apartment Configuration	15	20.0	5	9.1	10	17.5	39	17.3	69	16.7
Building Configuration	6	8.0	3	5.5	2	3.5	28	12.4	39	9.5
Good Area	15	20.0	7	12.7	8	14.0	62	27.6	92	22.3
Return to Homeland	8	10.7	4	7.3	5	8.8	12	5.3	29	7.0
Furniture/Appliances	6	8.0	3	5.5	8	14.0	26	11.6	43	10.4
Home Ownership	3	4.0	7	12.7	3	5.3	10	4.4	23	5.6
NA/DK	1	1.3	2	3.6	3	5.3	1	0.4	7	1.7
Total	75	100.0	55	100.0	57	100.0	225	100.0	412	100.0

Source: Housing of Welfare Recipients Survey, 1970.

SATISFACTION WITH APARTMENT AMENITIES

In an effort to isolate the variables that enter into consumer satisfaction, individuals were asked to rate apartment size, building maintenance, apartment maintenance, public transportation, location and garbage collection. The questions were phrased in terms of the welfare recipient's present housing accommodations. Our analysis will focus on the *relative* ranking of these amenities; then view the variables individually.

A point rating system is used for the descriptions given each of the several elements of housing. "Very satisfied" responses receive a point rating of 1, and so on down to 5—"very poor." Weighted response totals are then developed. The lower the point total, the more favorably the item is rated. Public transportation and location received the best ratings, at 1.91 and 2.15 respectively (Exhibit 5.8). These findings provide an interesting contrast to similar data gathered in surveys of other cities. A survey of the Watts area of Los Angeles, for example would show results antithetical to ours. In California lack of public transportation or its equivalent, and the location of housing facilities receive poor ratings.

Garbage collection is rated next highest in New York at 2.22 and the category rated fourth best is apartment size at 2.65. Building maintenance and apartment maintenance are both rated slightly better than poor at 2.79 and 2.72, respectively. Safety in the area has the poorest rating at 3.18. Indeed, on this latter point only 31.3 percent of the responses indicate a good or very good level of satisfaction and 43.9 percent indicate poor or very poor.

At the extreme right-hand side of the percentage distribution is shown a similar analysis of total satisfaction with housing as measured by the response to "How satisfied are you with the place you are living in now?" It should be noted that these responses are distributed along a scale from very satisfied through to very dissatisfied. Again, a similar five-point rating is used. The total satisfaction index is 2.87.

In later sections of this chapter some of these parameters will be discussed in detail. But first it is useful to view the responses of welfare recipients when asked what they want most in a place to live that they presently do not have.

ASPIRATIONS FOR BETTER HOUSING

The answers to the question "What do you want most in a place to live that you don't have now?" are shown in Exhibit 5.9. They substantially confirm reasons previously given for housing dissatisfaction. "Good area" received the single largest response (22.3 percent); apart-

EXHIBIT 5.10

OTHER RESPONSES TO THE QUESTION: "WHAT DO YOU WANT MOST IN A PLACE TO LIVE THAT YOU DON'T HAVE NOW?"

INTERVIEW CODE NO.	RESPONSE
2-4-204	I would like to own a house.
2-6-272	Like to live in public housing so I don't have to pay electric and gas, and rent is cheaper.
3-2-495	Want to live in public housing.
2-2-372	More money.
3-1-483	Washing machine and more income to better the place.
3-4-526	My own place.
2-4-224	Have a house so that she won't pay rent.
2-4-213	Would like to move to Pitkin Ave.
1-2-113	Live in a project.
3-4-401	A front porch, a yard to grow things in.
3-2-488	A landlord that makes repairs, pay less rent.
2-2-330	Have a helper around the house.
2-8-376	Want to live in public housing.
3-2-506	Food, head cooks only greasy foods which I can't eat, have to go out.
1-2-095	Want to live with Jesus, if He is ready, so am I.
2-6-277	House of our own.
2-2-373	See my family with some decent clothing.
2-6-366	Michelangelo painting on the wall.
3-1-512	Confort, proper clothing for kids.
2-4-241	My own apartment like before, I like to be independent.
3-1-476	A house of their own.
3-4-446	House of my own; be more independent.
1-6-157	I want my own home and a car.
1-4-015	Lots of hot water and heat; larger rooms (not apartment).
1-1-121	My own home somewhere out in the country (suburbia) with nice backyard.

Source: Housing of Welfare Recipients Survey, 1970.

ment configuration secured 16.7 percent; while apartment and building configuration together were noted by another 10.7 percent. Furniture/appliances secured 10.4 percent and building configuration (particularly complaints about the number of flights of stairs) 9.5 percent.

Old Age Assistance recipients give the greatest proportion (38.2 percent) of "nothing" responses, while ADC recipients feel most strongly about "good area," with only 9.3 percent indicating "nothing." However the apparent level of equanimity must be viewed with some degree of caution due to the limitations of machine coding. For example, a 60-year-old white widow recuperating from breast cancer and living alone on Aid to the Disabled, said she is satisfied with her apartment. She has lived there for seven years and it is in excellent conditon. The one thing that this respondent asked for is a shower. She has a bath but given her poor health, she is generally confined to a wheel chair and cannot make use of it. Her request is certainly modest, given her physical circumstances. Whether the welfare structure can respond to it, is unfortunately not that evident (Case No. 1-6-63).

EXHIBIT 5.11

DESIRED HOUSING IMPROVEMENTS BY ETHNICITY

RESPONSE	ETHNICITY									
	White		Black		Spanish Speaking		Other		Total	
	No.	%	No.	%	No.	%	No.	%	No.	%
Nothing (Positive Attitude)	18	28.1	25	13.9	21	12.8	2	50.0	66	16.0
Apartment and Building Configuration	10	15.6	23	12.8	11	6.7	0	0.0	44	10.7
Apartment Configuration	10	15.6	32	17.8	26	15.9	1	25.0	69	16.7
Building Configuration	2	3.1	17	9.4	20	12.2	0	0.0	39	9.5
Good Area	12	18.8	40	22.2	40	24.4	0	0.0	92	22.3
Return to Homeland	3	4.7	9	5.0	17	10.4	0	0.0	29	7.0
Furniture/Appliances	3	4.7	24	13.3	16	9.8	0	0.0	43	10.4
Home Ownership	3	4.7	10	5.0	10	6.1	0	0.0	23	5.3
NA/DK	3	4.7	0	0.0	3	1.8	1	25.0	7	1.7
Total	64	100.0	180	100.0	164	100.0	4	100.0	412	100.0

Source: Housing of Welfare Recipients Survey, 1970.

Determining the specific hopes for future housing of such individuals is a most difficult chore. The preceding respondent, when asked what she hopes for from the future, said only, "To stay alive."

Exhibit 5.10 present a random selection of responses to the question of future aspirations.

Ethnic Patterns

The question "What do you want most in a place to live that you don't have now?" calls forth substantial variation by ethnicity (Exhibit 5.11). Generally minority group members voice aspirations more often than whites. Building configuration particularly is far more important to minority group members than to whites, undoubtedly as a function of household size. The same variation holds true for furniture and appliances. The apathy toward the future which is not at all uncommon among the aged (who are largely white) may account for the discrepancy.

Computer processing sometimes gives a more positive cast to responses to inquiries such as "How satisfied are you with the place you are living in now?" than may be warranted. For example, a Puerto Rican family of eight securing supplementary benefits for an apartment in Brownsville, East New York area, responded that they are satisfied with their apartment: "We can't afford anything more." Other comments on the apartment, however, show concern with a very serious roach infestation (with the children suffering seriously from bites) as well as rats. The eight-person household has only four rooms including two bedrooms. The attitudes and standards of the family in question may play a role; in this apartment a dead rat under the kitchen sink had been there two days at the time of the interview (Case No. 5-5-555).

In another case a Puerto Rican mother living with her son who is separated from his wife and looking after their six-person household indicated that she is satisfied, "Because I live with my son and that is all that matters to me." Additional probing did not secure anything specific to add to her view of her apartment (Case No. 2-4-354).

Another case involves a 61-year-old widow living with her adopted son of 19 in a very poor structure, which according to her suffers from a number of problems in plumbing, heating, as well as roach and rat infestation. When asked how satisfied she is with the place she is living in, she said that she is satisfied. Then she volunteered, "It is the only place I know. God gave it to me, I must be satisfied" (Case No. 2-335-2).

Variations in ethnic patterns based on the unsophisticated techniques of data collection which are used here must therefore be viewed with some caution.

EXHIBIT 5.12

PLANNING COMMISSION AREA BY CATEGORY OF WELFARE

PLANNING COMMISSION AREA[1]	CATEGORY OF WELFARE									
	Home Relief		Old Age Assistance		Aid to Disabled		Aid to Dependent Children		Total	
	No.	%	No.	%	No.	%	No.	%	No.	%
Major Action	47	62.7	31	56.4	31	54.4	132	60.3	241	59.4
Protection	21	28.0	18	32.7	16	28.1	68	31.1	123	30.3
Sound	7	9.3	6	10.9	10	17.5	19	8.7	42	10.3
Total	75	100.0	55	100.0	57	100.0	219	100.0	406	100.0

Source: Housing of Welfare Recipients Survey, 1970.
[1]Department of City Planning, New York City.

EXHIBIT 5.13

PLANNING COMMISSION AREA BY ETHNICITY

PLANNING COMMISSION AREA[1]	ETHNICITY									
	White		Black		Spanish Speaking		Other		Total	
	No.	%	No.	%	No.	%	No.	%	No.	%
Major Action	17	27.4	110	62.5	110	67.1	4	100.0	241	59.4
Protection	26	41.9	55	31.3	42	25.6	0	0.0	123	30.3
Sound	19	30.6	11	6.3	12	7.3	0	0.0	42	10.3
Total	62	100.0	176	100.0	164	100.0	4	100.0	406	100.0

Source: Housing of Welfare Recipients Survey, 1970.
[1]Department of City Planning, New York City.

LOCATION OF HOUSING

The series of maps in Chapter 2 give the location of welfare recipients by category of welfare within the several boroughs. While those familiar with New York neighborhoods will easily perceive the high concentration of welfare recipients in poor areas, for others, the data may require elaboration.

Fortunately, for our purposes, the New York Planning Commission characterizes areas of housing by dividing the city into three housing categories. These are 1) Major Action areas, 2) so-called Protection areas which are in danger of becoming an area requiring significant intervention in order to be maintained and 3) Sound areas.

Exhibit 5.12 shows the planning area by category of welfare respondents based on one sample. Just under 60 percent of all welfare recipients live in Major Action areas. In part the definition of Major Action area reflects the incidence of welfare recipients, but a variety of other social factors are involved, such as police records. Major Action areas are often inhabited by ADC recipients with children; only 10.3 percent of ADC cases are in Sound areas, and 30.3 percent are in Protection areas. What pattern appears when the sample is divided by ethnicity? Only 27.4 percent of white recipients are in Major Action areas, compared to 62.5 percent of blacks and 67.1 percent of the Spanish-speaking individuals. Conversely, less than 10 percent of the blacks and Spanish-speaking and 30.6 percent of the whites live in the Sound areas. Certainly, in part, this difference is a function of the type of housing available to whites who are more often Old Age Assistance recipients, in contrast to minority groups who are more frequently in the ADC category. The results, however, speak for themselves (Exhibit 5.13).

THE LOCATION'S CONVENIENCE

New York City is serviced by a wide-ranging network of public transportation. Unlike many other cities, therefore, welfare recipients claim little difficulty with transportation. Only 13.1 percent of the total sample evaluate their apartment's location as poor or very poor. More than 36 percent say that their location, in terms of being close to things that they would like to be near, is very good. An additional 32 percent say the location is good.

Analysis by category of welfare reveals relatively little variation in the responses, but when these data are tabulated by borough, the Bronx has the greatest number of negatives, with 15.7 percent saying very poor, and an additional 4.6 percent, poor.

EXHIBIT 5.14

APARTMENT SIZE RATING BY CATEGORY OF WELFARE

RATING	CATEGORY OF WELFARE									
	Home Relief		Old Age Assistance		Aid to Disabled		Aid to Dependent Children		Total	
	No.	%	No.	%	No.	%	No.	%	No.	%
Very Good	12	16.0	21	38.2	11	19.3	32	14.2	76	18.4
Good	27	36.0	21	38.2	13	22.8	53	23.6	114	27.7
Fair	19	25.3	8	14.5	27	47.4	74	32.9	128	31.1
Poor	14	18.7	5	9.1	5	8.8	46	20.4	70	17.0
Very Poor	3	4.0	0	0.0	1	1.8	20	8.9	24	5.8
Total	75	100.0	55	100.0	57	100.0	225	100.0	412	100.0

Source: Housing of Welfare Recipients Survey, 1970.

EXHIBIT 5.15

SATISFACTION WITH APARTMENT MAINTENANCE BY CATEGORY OF WELFARE

RATING	CATEGORY OF WELFARE									
	Home Relief		Old Age Assistance		Aid to Disabled		Aid to Dependent Children		Total	
	No.	%	No.	%	No.	%	No.	%	No.	%
Very Good	13	17.3	13	23.6	12	21.1	46	20.4	84	20.4
Good	22	29.3	21	38.2	13	22.8	52	23.1	108	26.2
Fair	21	28.0	10	18.2	16	28.1	59	26.2	106	25.7
Poor	11	14.7	6	10.9	11	19.3	40	17.8	68	16.5
Very Poor	8	10.7	5	9.1	5	8.8	28	12.4	46	11.2
Total	75	100.0	55	100.0	57	100.0	225	100.0	412	100.0

Source: Housing of Welfare Recipients Survey, 1970.

Public Transportation

Most of the respondents express positive evaluations of the adequacy of public transportation. Only 1.7 percent of the 412 responses say it is very poor, while an additional 3.4 percent indicate it is poor. Nearly 41 percent say very good, with an additional 34.7 percent rating it good.

The several categories of welfare recipients vary little in their responses, with perhaps a slightly higher degree of negatives (8 percent poor or very poor) among the disabled, but none among the Home Relief respondents and only 1.8 percent among the Old Age Assistance recipients. Among the ADC recipients, 6.2 percent express negative feelings toward public transportation.

Blacks are least contented with public transportation; 8.2 percent rate it poor or very poor. By contrast, 2.4 percent of the Puerto Rican group rate transportation poor or very poor. Whites' ratings fell between the two minorities.

Apartment Size

When questioned about their apartment size, 18.4 percent of the respondents rate it very good. An additional 27.7 percent feel that it is good, with 31.1 percent indicating a fair rating. Seventeen percent give an evaluation of poor to their apartment size, and 5.8 percent give it a very poor rating.

The several categories of welfare recipients vary in their level of satisfaction: 29.3 percent of the ADC cases rate their apartment size poor or very poor and Home Relief is the second most negative at 22.7 percent. Old Age Assistance and Aid to the Disabled hover around 10 percent. The Old Age Assistance recipients are generally most satisfied, with 76.4 percent indicating the size of their present accommodation is very good or good (Exhibit 5.14).

When the data are analyzed by ethnicity, minority group members are least satisfied, with poor or very poor ratings indicated by 23.9 percent of the blacks and 25.6 percent of the Spanish-speaking individuals, compared to 12.5 percent of the whites. Unfortunately, data do not permit equalization in size of household to determine the related variables. It may be that ADC cases, which are more frequently minority group members and tend to have large families, have more difficulty accommodating themselves in the relatively small apartment units which predominate in New York. This may be complicated by prejudices based on ethnic grounds, but our sample is too small to permit any hard conclusions on this point.

BUILDING AND APARTMENT MAINTENANCE

As indicated earlier, building and apartment maintenance are rated lower than all other factors except safety in the area. In general, minority group members react much more negatively to their building maintenance than do whites: 23.1 percent of the Spanish-speaking and nearly 40 percent of the black respondents give negative responses compared to 16.2 percent of the whites.

Similar distributions are found in apartment maintenance, with 18.8 percent of the whites rating it poor or very poor compared to 40.1 percent of the blacks. Puerto Rican responses deviate quite sharply from the blacks, with only 15.8 percent rating their apartment maintenance poor or very poor. Apartment maintenance is rated good or very good by nearly six out of ten whites (59.4 percent) and by nearly the same proportion of Spanish-speaking individuals (52.5 percent) but only 36.7 percent of the black respondents.

Exhibit 5.15 analyzes apartment maintenance ratings by welfare category. ADC cases are most dissatisfied, with 30.2 percent claiming that their present apartment is maintained either in a poor or very poor condition. The Old Age Assistance group is substantially more satisfied than the other groups, with very good and good responses given by more than three out of five of the 55 respondents (61.8 percent). None of the other groups reach 50 percent of positive responses.

Garbage Disposal

Only 12.8 percent of the sample rate garbage disposal procedures as poor or very poor compared to 30.8 percent who indicate very good and 34.5 percent who say "good." The Bronx has the greatest degree of discontent at 15.7 percent, followed by Brooklyn at 14.5 percent and Manhattan at 9.4 percent.

Analysis by category of welfare recipients indicates that 15.5 percent of the 225 ADC cases rate garbage disposal poor or very poor. Old Age Assistance respondents are least negative at 5.4 percent. Despite the attention that has been focused on the garbage burnings in Brownsville and Harlem, the general response, regardless of ethnic group, tends to be quite positive. Black respondents are most negative with 16.6 percent giving a poor or very poor rating compared to half that for whites. The Spanish-speaking respondents are in between.

Sixty-five respondents show dissatisfaction with garbage disposal. Specific causes of the problem are given by 64 respondents (Exhibit 5.16). Landlords are blamed by 45.3 percent of the 64 respondents. Another 14.1 percent indicate that both landlord and tenants are responsible, and 3.1 percent mention both these, plus some other factor.

Garbage problems are blamed on tenants by 9.7 percent of the blacks and 17.9 percent of the Spanish-speaking individuals, in inverse relationship to their blaming the landlords. Two of the 31 blacks, and six

EXHIBIT 5.16

SPECIFIC PROBLEMS WITH GARBAGE DISPOSAL BY ETHNICITY

PROBLEMS	White No.	White %	Black No.	Black %	Spanish Speaking No.	Spanish Speaking %	Total[a] No.	Total[a] %
Landlord Generated	1	20.0	17	54.8	11	39.3	29	45.3
Tenant Generated	0	0.0	3	9.7	5	17.9	8	12.5
Function of Structure Limitation	1	20.0	5	16.1	2	7.1	8	12.5
Area Problem	1	20.0	4	12.9	3	10.7	8	12.5
Both Landlord and Tenant Generated	1	20.0	2	6.5	6	21.4	9	14.1
More Than Two of Above	1	20.0	0	0.0	1	3.6	2	3.1
Total	5	100.0	31	100.0	28	100.0	64	100.0

Source: Housing of Welfare Recipients Survey, 1970.

a. One case excluded due to insufficient data.

EXHIBIT 5.18

RATING OF SAFETY IN AREA BY ETHNICITY

RATING	White No.	White %	Black No.	Black %	Spanish Speaking No.	Spanish Speaking %	Other No.	Other %	Total No.	Total %
Very Good	16	25.0	11	6.1	31	18.9	0	0.0	58	14.1
Good	15	23.4	31	17.2	24	14.6	1	25.0	71	17.2
Fair	21	32.8	46	25.6	34	20.7	1	25.0	102	24.8
Poor	5	7.8	54	30.0	38	23.2	2	50.0	99	24.0
Very Poor	7	10.9	38	21.1	37	22.6	0	0.0	82	19.9
Total	64	100.0	180	100.0	164	100.0	4	100.0	412	100.0

Source: Housing of Welfare Recipients Survey, 1970.

of 28 Spanish-speaking individuals indicate problems are both landlord and tenant generated.

The sample size is quite small, and other variables may substantially affect the situation. If the data are taken at face value, however, there is some indication that Spanish-speaking recipients are more likely to feel that tenants bear responsibility for garbage problems than do blacks. Grouping the tenant generated and landlord and tenant generated responses yields a significant variation in response: 39.3 percent for Spanish-speaking versus 16.2 percent for blacks.

Rodents and Vermin

Only 10.9 percent (seven of the 64) white respondents indicate that rodent infestation is a problem in their building. More than half of the Spanish-speaking respondents (52.4 percent) and nearly as many black

EXHIBIT 5.17

RATING OF SAFETY IN AREA BY CATEGORY OF WELFARE

RATING	CATEGORY OF WELFARE									
	Home Relief		Old Age Assistance		Aid to Disabled		Aid to Dependent Children		Total	
	No.	%	No.	%	No.	%	No.	%	No.	%
Very Good	9	12.0	11	20.0	12	21.1	26	11.6	58	14.1
Good	12	16.0	14	25.5	13	22.8	32	14.2	71	17.2
Fair	22	29.3	13	23.6	11	19.3	56	24.9	102	24.8
Poor	20	26.7	7	12.7	10	17.5	62	27.6	99	24.0
Very Poor	12	16.0	10	18.2	11	19.3	49	21.8	82	19.9
Total	75	100.0	55	100.0	57	100.0	225	100.0	412	100.0

Source: Housing of Welfare Recipients Survey, 1970.

EXHIBIT 5.19

RATING OF SAFETY IN AREA BY BOROUGH

RATING	BOROUGH											
	Manhattan		Brooklyn		Bronx		Queens		Richmond		Total	
	No.	%	No.	%	No.	%	No.	%	No.	%	No.	%
Very Good	8	6.8	31	19.6	9	8.3	9	37.5	1	20.0	58	14.1
Good	22	18.8	27	17.1	17	15.7	5	20.8	0	0.0	71	17.2
Fair	40	34.2	32	20.3	25	23.1	5	20.8	0	0.0	102	24.8
Poor	29	24.8	45	28.5	19	17.6	3	12.5	3	60.0	99	24.0
Very Poor	18	15.4	23	14.6	38	35.2	2	8.3	1	20.0	82	19.9
Total	117	100.0	158	100.0	108	100.0	24	100.0	5	100.0	412	100.0

Source: Housing of Welfare Recipients Survey, 1970.

respondents (43.3 percent) indicate such difficulties. Of the 86 Spanish-speaking respondents who answer affirmatively here, 68.6 percent, compared to less than half that many in the other two groups, indicate rodents are a serious problem.

Roach infestations are listed by 46.9 percent of whites, compared to 68.3 percent of Spanish-speaking individuals and 74.4 percent of blacks. It is rated as a significant problem by 65.2 percent of Spanish-speaking individuals, 49.3 percent of blacks and 40 percent of the whites.

Exterminating Services

Approximately one-fourth of the respondents, with little variation among the several groups, complain about the lack of extermination service provided by the landlord. Perhaps tenants are unaware that landlords are supposed to provide this service (they are required to do so by New York's Health Code) but a high proportion of tenants say that they have problems requiring exterminators. Half of those who state that they have a problem with roaches volunteer that they have to spray continuously in order to maintain some level of control.

Multiple-family residences which are typical of housing in New York City, even upper-class facilities, have a continuous problem of roach infestation. But our survey indicates that the incidence of infestation is substantial and that complaints about the landlord's lack of activity are much too prevalent for complacency.

Safety

Of the seven specific housing facets for which evaluations are asked of the welfare recipients, safety is generally most negative in its rating. Less than one-third (31.3 percent) of the sample rate their areas as good or very good in safety; 19.9 percent indicate very poor safety, with an additional 24 percent rating it poor.

Exhibit 5.17 presents these data by category of welfare recipients. ADC and Home Relief respondents have the most negative evaluation of safety, at 49.4 percent and 42.7 percent respectively. But certainly there is little difference in the groups' responses. Even 30.9 percent of Old Age Assistance recipients rate their area very poor in safety.

These responses are consistent with earlier studies on the same subject. For example, in Podell's study,[2] interviews were conducted in April 1966 with 2,179 ADC households. One in four of the welfare mothers rated their neighborhoods bad or very bad. One-fifth of the ADC mothers were afraid to walk around their own neighborhood in the daytime, while two-fifths felt afraid when they went outside their immediate block.

Ratings by Ethnicity. Nearly half the whites (48.4 percent) rate safety in their areas very good or good, but only 23.3 percent of the blacks, with the Spanish-speaking individuals in the middle at 33.5 percent. Poor or very poor responses are given by less than 20 percent of the whites but more than half of the blacks and nearly that proportion of the Spanish-speaking individuals (Exhibit 5.18).

Variation by Borough. The variation in location obviously plays a role in the evaluation of safety. The Bronx has by far the most negative rating, with 52.8 percent of the welfare residents rating the areas poor or very poor (Exhibit 5.19). The sample in Queens, although too small for statistical significance, tends to indicate general levels of satisfaction, with only five of the 24 giving a negative safety rating. Barely one-fourth of the Manhattan respondents (25.6 percent) rate safety in their area positively. In Brooklyn 36.7 percent give positive ratings and in the Bronx less that one-quarter. The maps which follow illustrate the attitudes toward safety by borough and subarea (Exhibits 5.20, 5.21, 5.22, 5.23).

It is difficult to do justice to the bitterness and fear that pervades many interviews. For example, a welfare mother living in Harlem with one child, commented on the lack of safety in the area: "I carry a knife with me every time I leave the house. The cops ain't no help, they are all being paid off by racketeers. I am afraid if somethings happens to me, what will happen to my son? I want to live in a better neighborhood so that my son won't come into contact with dope or crime" (Case No. 17).

"Cleaning out those junkies and stopping robberies," comes through over and over again when respondents are asked about their hopes for the future. Fear of drug addicts and addiction among children particularly pervades the Puerto Rican responses. Frequently, the refrain is one in which the apartment basically is satisfactory; the major complaint is the problem of drug addiction in the area. One Puerto Rican mother said that she desperately wants to go back to Puerto Rico, "Because I have a daughter who is in the rehabilitation for drug addicts and I don't like her to go around with the same friends that she knows because they are drug addicts" (Case No. 2-501-1).

Another 40-year-old Puerto Rican mother of three, separated from her husband and living in the Bedford-Stuyvesant area of Brooklyn, summarized the tenor of many interviews when she said, "My fears and worries for the future of our country is to continue these things about war and drug addicts—in ten years from now the future would look terrible, you will not be able to walk the streets" (Case No. 2-308-1).

EXHIBIT 5.20
RATING OF SAFETY—MANHATTAN

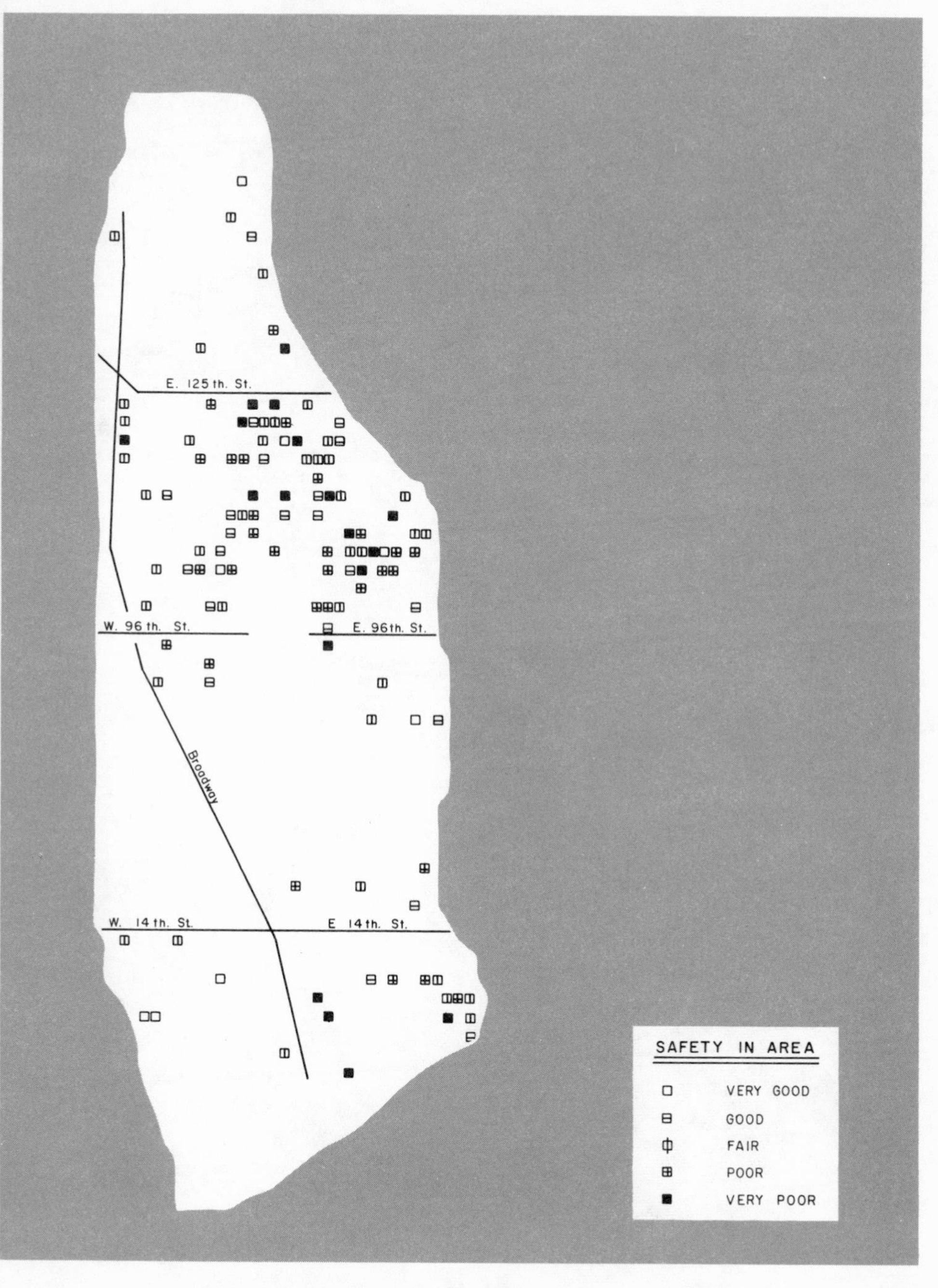

EXHIBIT 5.21
RATING OF SAFETY–BROOKLYN

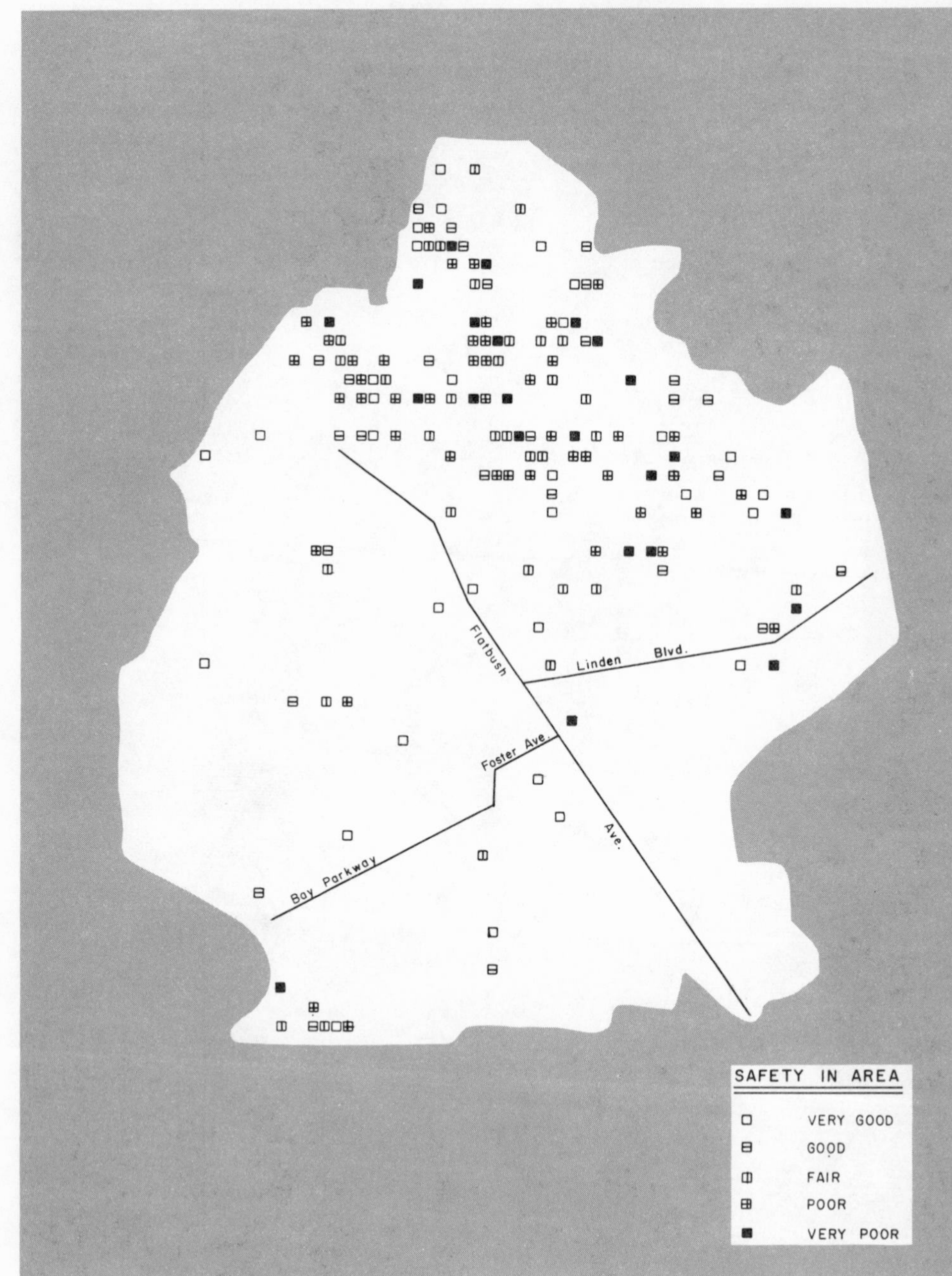

EXHIBIT 5.22
RATING OF SAFETY—BRONX

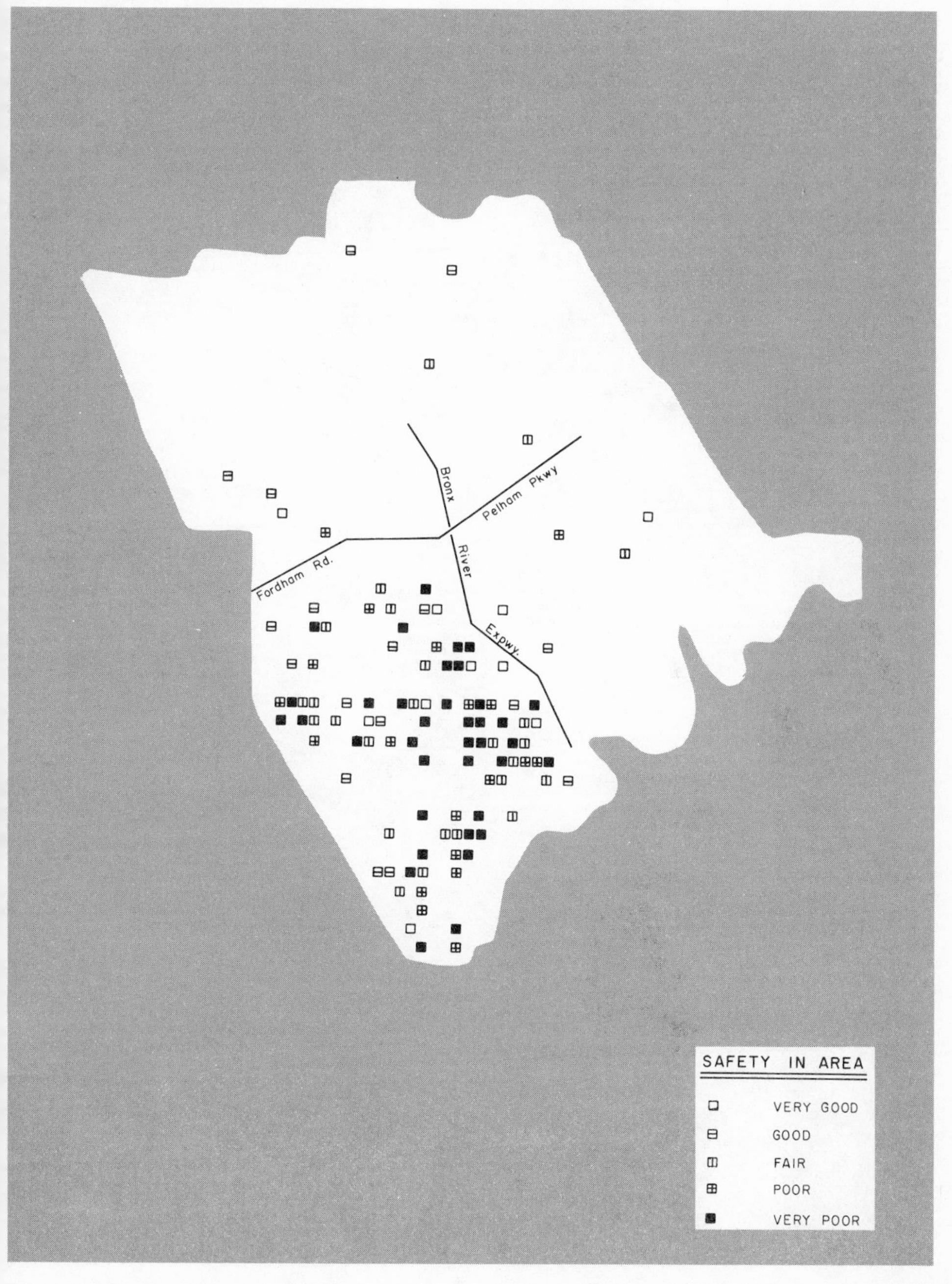

EXHIBIT 5.23

RATING OF SAFETY—QUEENS AND RICHMOND

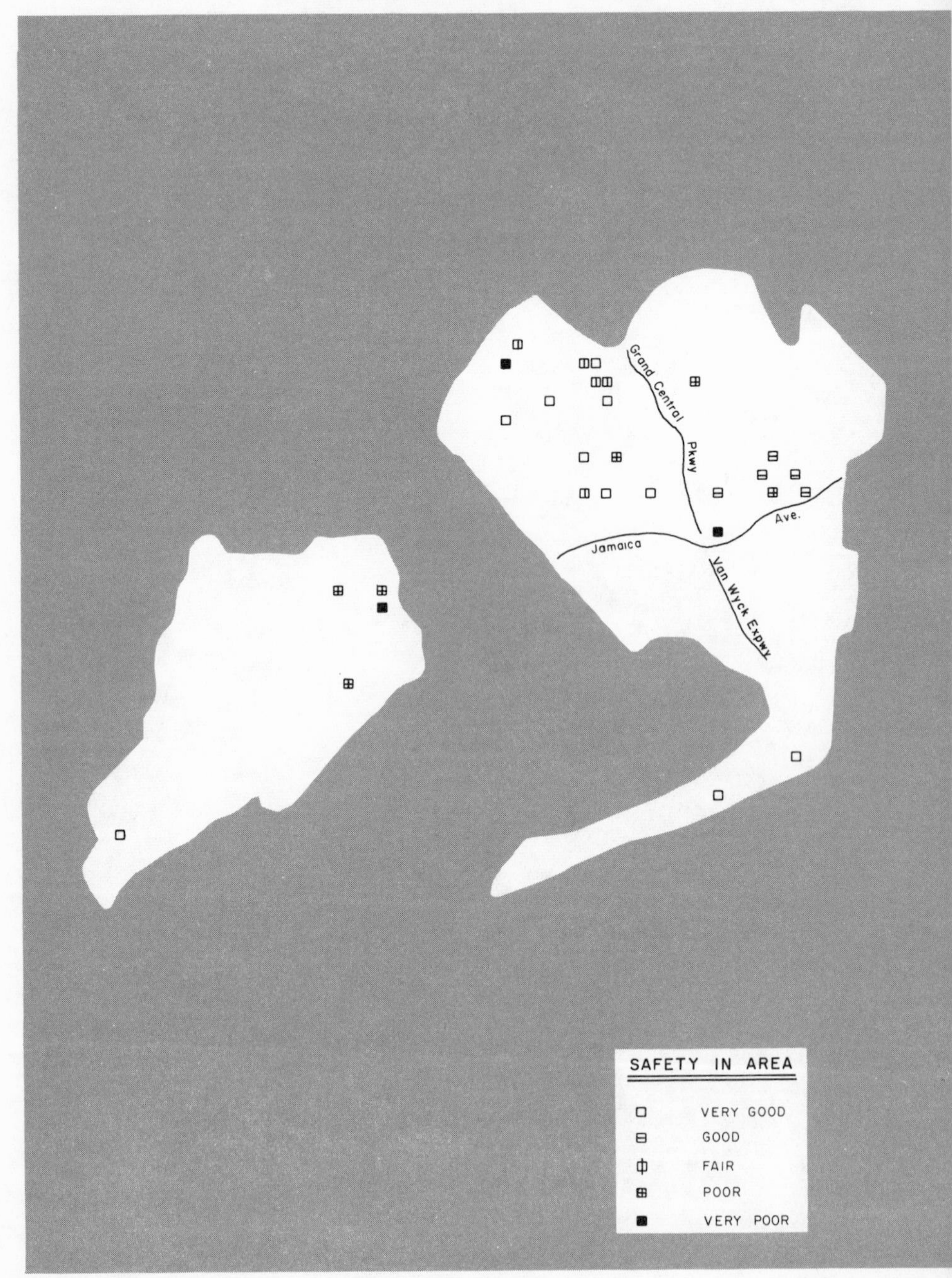

EXHIBIT 5.24

OTHER CONCERNS OF WELFARE RESPONDENTS BY ETHNICITY

CONCERN	ETHNICITY									
	White		Black		Spanish Speaking		Other[a]		Total	
	No.	%	No.	%	No.	%	No.	%	No.	%
Drugs	2	3.1	22	12.2	12	7.3	0	0.0	36	8.7
Other[a]	7	10.9	29	16.1	18	11.0	1	25.0	55	13.3
Drugs and Other	1	1.6	27	15.0	33	20.1	0	0.0	61	14.8
NA/DK	54	84.4	102	56.7	101	61.6	3	75.0	260	63.1
Total	64	100.0	180	100.0	164	100.0	4	100.0	412	100.0

Source: Housing of Welfare Recipients Survey, 1970.

a. Many of these "Other" concerns are enumerated in Exhibit 5.25.

Her words are echoed by yet another Puerto Rican mother of four small children, the oldest of whom is eight. On the question about the future of the country, she said, "Things are getting worse more and more, I don't think it is going to be easy to stop it, so in ten years from now I have no idea of how things will look like if drug addicts and war continues" (Case No. 5-555-4).

After the apartment, building and location variables were discussed in the interview, the respondents were asked about their other concerns (Exhibit 5.24). References to drugs number 36 and an additional 61 mention drugs and some other factor, typically, public safety. The other concerns typically are related to public safety. Exhibit 5.25 details these directly from the coder's transcriptions. Robberies, muggings, killings, horrendous levels of uncollected rubbish and the fear of drugs and all the things they bring with them clearly dominate. Concern about drugs is primarily expressed by minority groups. Only 4.7 percent of the whites, but 27.2 percent of the blacks and 27.4 percent of Puerto Ricans make reference to drugs.

Determining the most significant of the several reasons given for the shortcomings of a particular apartment is extremely difficult. For example, a Negro mother on ADC with three children, ages 15, 14 and 12, said, "I don't have sufficient room. I should like for my sons to have separate bedrooms. It is awful to hang things from the wall. They are weak and the plaster cracks. I can't put pictures or mirrors on the wall and I don't like the neighborhood." When asked what she would like most in a place to live, she responded, "A washing machine. I would also like to own my own kitchenette set, two sofa chairs and linoleum on the floors" (Case No. 1-40-4).

Another interview with an ADC mother of five, who is separated from her husband reveals the depth of the "housing problem." This mother's youngest child is three months old. The family lives in a one-room apartment and she feels that the landlords won't rent to her because she has too many children. She has strong feelings for the apartment's shortcomings: "Most of the furniture is falling to pieces. The hallways stay filthy. The apartment hasn't been painted and most of the time the water stays off and when it is on, it is usually cold. The toilet just got fixed after being broken for a long time. This whole building needs to be torn down." The respondent said that she was afraid to go outside. "They robbed in here twice. There is no safe place for my children to play. I don't even feel safe leaving my apartment to go to the bathroom." On the subject of police, she said, "There is never a cop around when you need one and most of them are crooked too, so they are not much help." The respondent, by the way, had completed a year of nurse's training and had come North hoping to get better wages.

EXHIBIT 5.25

OTHER CONCERNS PERTAINING TO APARTMENT AND BUILDING AMENITIES

INTERVIEW CODE NO.	CONCERNS
1-1-067	Muggers, dope addicts, unsafe after dark.
2-6-279	Junkies and drunks.
2-4-267	Drugs and robberies.
3-4-407	Drug addicts, rapists and muggers in area.
2-4-342	Drug addicts and lots of fires.
2-4-230	Drug addicts and "gangs around the area."
3-4-409	Rapes, drug addicts, muggers, etc.
1-4-028	Drug addicts, riots and violence.
3-4-408	Drug addicts, muggings and killings.
3-2-495	Drug addicts and robberies.
2-1-308	Drug addicts, robberies and fights.
1-4-130	Drug addicts and robberies.
1-1-066	Drug addicts and robberies.
2-4-240	Drug addicts, robberies and fights.
3-1-475	Ceiling keeps falling in, dope addicts around.
3-4-416	Addicts, robberies.
1-6-144	Dope addicts, muggings, robberies.
1-2-096	Dope addicts, and robberies.
3-4-404	Addicts on the roof and crime.
2-4-252	Addicts and robberies, etc.
2-4-237	Addicts shoot up in halls; bums and drunks come into hall; dope peddlers; card playing; insurance man was robbed.
3-4-421	Many robberies, muggers, drug addicts.
3-1-467	Many killings, rapes, drug addicts and muggers.
2-4-343	Drug addicts and gangs.
3-4-460	Drug addicts and robberies.
3-4-403	Drug addicts (even little children) and garbage all over the place.
3-1-480	Drug addicts sleep in halls; robberies, assaults are frequent.
1-4-034	Drug addicts and robberies.
3-4-422	Dope addicts in halls and on roof; lady was mugged.
1-1-078	Drug addicts, robbery, mugging.
4-4-610	Drug addicts, robbery, purse snatchers; need more police protection.
3-6-500	Drugs, killings, robberies, fights.
2-8-376	Drug addicts, robberies, gangs.
1-4-020	Drug addicts and robberies.
4-1-624	Drug addicts, house broken into.
4-8-629	Drug addicts, muggings, robberies.
3-1-464	Drug addicts; daughter was robbed and threatened.
3-4-436	Drug addicts, apartment broken into five times.
3-4-424	Drug addicts, robberies.
2-4-210	Drug addicts, robberies.
3-4-427	Drug addicts, robberies.
2-1-302	Junkies, thieves, criminal elements.
1-4-019	Drug addicts all over; apartment and building maintenance.
1-4-047	Drug addicts all over; apartment configuration and garbage disposal.
2-4-235	Lots of drug addicts around and lots of robberies.
1-4-005	Junkies and robberies are common.

Coders' Statement: Toward the end of the coding process the "Other Concerns" were not listed because they become repetitious—muggings, murders, rapes and robberies.

She cannot work, however, as someone must look after her children (Case No. 2-502-3).

A possible reason for Puerto Rican's frequently expressed fear of the drug problem, is that they seem to view children as insurance against the future. This was best illustrated by the comments of a middle-aged Puerto Rican couple who are presently childless. They were receiving aid for an industrial accident suffered by the head of household. When asked about their fears and worries for the future, the male head of household answered, "What worries us most is that we don't have any children. Some day my wife and I would not receive the assistance we are presently receiving and we will both be too old to work, what will come of us?" (Case No. 2-272-6).

Even when allowance is made for their neighborhoods, welfare recipients seem to be more victimized and certainly more fearful of drug addiction and plagued by security problems. In a Louis Harris study [3] of transitional neighborhoods in selected city blocks, 42 percent of the welfare recipients see drug addicts as a big problem, compared with 35 percent of the total respondents. Similarly, intruders from outside were seen as a major problem by 43 percent of the welfare recipients versus only 37 percent of the total. Security for mail boxes and entrances was seen as a major problem by welfare recipients—but involved only 39 percent of the total responses.

SUMMARY

Dissatisfaction with housing is a serious problem among welfare recipients in New York City, particularly minority group recipients: 21.8 percent of whites say they are dissatisfied or very dissatisfied with their housing, while 41.5 percent of Spanish-speaking and 45 percent of the blacks are dissatisfied or very dissatisfied. Dissatisfaction with housing is most frequent in the Bronx, and safety in the area is a particular concern. The most frequently mentioned reason for dissatisfaction is the "bad area" in which the apartment is located. Safety in the area is rated as the most serious of several negative factors including building and apartment maintenance. Apartment maintenance is more of a problem for blacks and ADC recipients. Spanish-speaking and black respondents indicate problems with rodents and roaches. Black respondents are less satisfied with the safety of the area in which they lived than are the Spanish-speaking. Whites are relatively more satisfied. Concern about drugs is primarily expressed by minority groups.

NOTES

1. These data form an interesting contrast with the results of a somewhat similar probe addressed at the same time to a probability sampling of 501 Princeton, New Jersey, residents. In this wealthy community the answers to the question "Are you satisfied with your present housing accommodations?" were "Yes," 87.6 percent; "No," 12.4 percent. See George Sternlieb et al., *The Affluent Suburb: Princeton* (New Brunswick, New Jersey: Transaction Books, 1971).

2. Lawrence Podell, *Families on Welfare in New York City* (New York: The Center for the Study of Urban Problems, Graduate Division, Bernard M. Baruch College, City University of New York, 1968), pp. 22, 52.

3. Louis Harris, *Transition Neighborhoods*, p. 56.

Chapter 6

HOPES AND FEARS OF WELFARE RECIPIENTS

Welfare recipients are often grouped as a monolithic entity in public discussion. They are *not* all alike. Part of the objective of this study is to obtain a better perspective on the attitudes and perceptions that exist among this diverse group of people. This study therefore attempts to find out the views, hopes, fears and aspirations of the broad range of people who happen to be welfare recipients in New York City.

To assess the aspirations of welfare recipients we used a technique developed by Hadley Cantril called "the Self-Anchoring Striving Scale." It provides a means of obtaining information from the respondent's own perspective. One of the additional advantages of this probe is the wealth of comparative data which is available. The Cantril scale has been implemented on a nationwide basis in the United States on at least three occasions and in 17 other countries, and has been translated and used effectively in at least 26 other languages including Spanish (Spanish was used in this study along with the original English language questions).[1]

There are four specific areas of questions: 1) wishes and hopes for your life, 2) fears and worries about your future, 3) wishes and hopes for the future of the United States and 4) fears and worries for the future of the United States. (For details on specific questions and methods see Appendix 6.1). We followed the Cantril approach to coding with some minor additional categories. Appendix 6.2 contains the complete coding formulation used in this study.

EXHIBIT 6.1

RELATIVE FREQUENCIES OF PERSONAL AND NATIONAL HOPES AND FEARS (ALL RESPONDENTS)

	QUESTIONS							
	1[a] Frequency of Personal Hopes		2[b] Frequency of Personal Fears		3[c] Frequency of National Hopes		4[d] Frequency of National Fears	
NUMBER OF HOPES AND FEARS	No.	%	No.	%	No.	%	No.	%
Zero	24	5.8	92	22.3	65	15.8	93	22.6
One	134	32.5	190	46.2	112	27.2	153	37.2
Two	166	40.4	94	22.8	117	28.4	102	24.8
Three	67	16.3	27	6.6	72	17.5	42	10.2
Four	18	4.4	7	1.7	28	6.8	16	3.9
Five	1	0.2	0	0.0	7	1.7	3	0.7
Six	0	0.0	0	0.0	5	1.2	1	0.2
Seven or More	1	0.2	1	0.2	5	1.2	1	0.2
No Response	1	0.2	1	0.2	1	0.2	1	0.2
Total Respondents	412	100.0	412	100.0	412	100.0	412	100.0
Percentage of Respondents With One or More Hopes or Fears		93.9		77.4		84.0		77.2

Source: These questions were taken from Hadley Cantril, *The Pattern of Human Concerns* (New Brunswick, New Jersey, Rutgers University Press, 1965).

a. Question No. 1: All of us want certain things out of life. When you think about what really matters in your own life, what are your wishes and hopes for the future? (personal hopes).

b. Question No. 2: Now, taking the other side of this picture, what are your fears and worries about your future? In other words, if you imagine your future in the worst possible light, what would your life look like then? Again, take your time in answering (personal fears).

c. Question No. 3: Now, what are your wishes and hopes for the future of our country? If you picture the United States in the best possible light, how would things look, let us say ten years from now? (national hopes).

d. Question No. 4: And what about your fears and worries for the future of our country? If you picture the future of the United States in the worst possible light, how would things look in about ten years? (national fears).

EXHIBIT 6.2
RELATIVE FREQUENCIES OF PERSONAL AND NATIONAL HOPES AND FEARS BY CATEGORY OF WELFARE

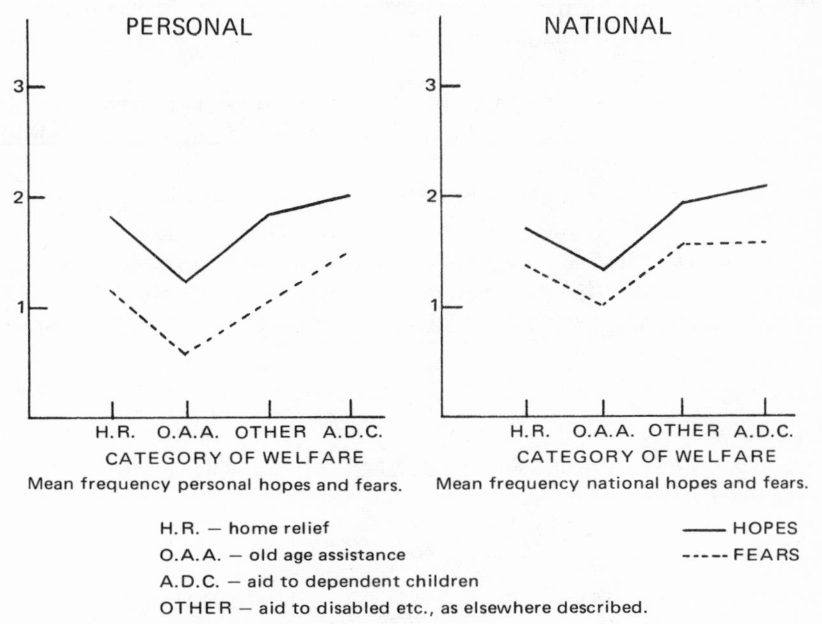

Sources: Housing of Welfare Recipients Survey, 1970.

The personal hopes and fears expressed by the respondents fall into 12 basic categories, or partitions. Analysis of the magnitude of the responses for each partition was undertaken, first of the positive responses (hopes) and then of the negative responses (fears). Where significant, subsets of the basic partitions will be discussed in detail.

The frequency of expression of personal and national hopes and fears is indicated in Exhibit 6.1. The exhibit clearly indicates that the verbal responses tend to be more positive than negative, at least in terms of frequency. For example, 93.9 percent of the respondents indicate personal hopes, compared to 77.4 percent who express personal fears; 84 percent express national hopes and 77.2 percent national fears.

Most of the respondents express three or fewer hopes or fears. Two personal hopes are given by 40.4 percent of the respondents (the largest single frequency for hopes). The largest frequency of personal fears is 46.2 percent, and only one fear is expressed by these respondents. There is slightly more dispersion for national hopes and national fears, but again the respondents tend to express more hopes than fears. In the analysis of hopes and fears which follows, the approach will be to deal with the frequencies as absolute numbers of hopes or fears. The number of responses obviously exceeds the total number of respondents (412) since one respondent may be responsible for a number of responses.

The frequency of *personal* hopes and fears is considered by category of welfare and by ethnicity of respondent. Regardless of welfare type, the frequency of personal hopes is consistently greater than the number of personal fears, and by roughly the same order of magnitude (Exhibit 6.2). The same relationship exists, with *national* hopes and fears, but the margin is clearly much narrower, with hopes just slightly more frequent than fears for each of the several categories.

The sole variation is a slightly greater separation between hopes and fears in ADC than the other categories, particularly Home Relief. ADC recipients are more optimistic about the future, both for themselves

EXHIBIT 6.3
RELATIVE FREQUENCIES OF PERSONAL AND NATIONAL HOPES AND FEARS BY ETHNICITY

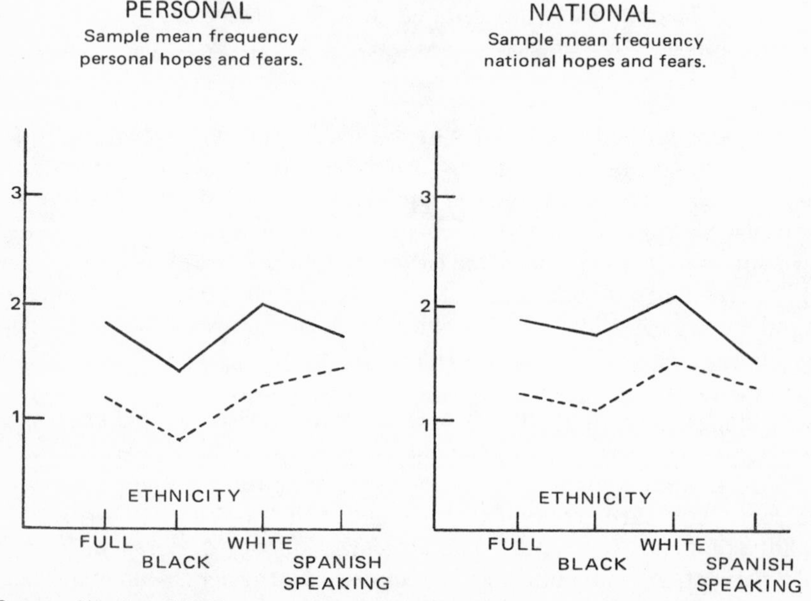

Sources: Housing of Welfare Recipients Survey, 1970.

and for the nation as a whole. Whether this reflects a generally more aspirational outlook or not is an open question. On an absolute level the number of responses, both positive and negative, given by Old Age Assistance recipients is significantly lower than it is for the other categories. This may be a measurement of lesser verbal facility on the part of the Old Age Assistance recipients, or it may indicate something of the hopelessness and apathy often felt by older people, examples of which were cited earlier. The same general findings also apply to the ethnic comparisons. Each ethnic group shows on the average more personal and national hopes than fears (Exhibit 6.3).

PERSONAL HOPES AND FEARS

The responses can be considered in a number of general categories of hopes and fears.

OWN PERSONAL CHARACTER

Hopes for oneself might include statements of the following general types: achieve emotional stability and maturity, become a normal, decent person, self-development or improvement, be accepted by others, achieve a sense of personal worth, and resolution of religious, spiritual or ethical problems. (For a fuller description, see Appendix 6.1). The fears fall into the following subsets: emotional instability, becoming

EXHIBIT 6.4

PERSONAL HOPES AND FEARS BY AREA OF CONCERN (ALL RESPONDENTS)[a]

AREA OF CONCERN	HOPES		FEARS	
	No.	%	No.	%
Own Personal Character	70	14.1	18	4.4
Personal Economic Situation	177	42.7	53	12.9
Job or Work Situation	71	17.7	11	2.7
Other References to Self	121	29.4	121	29.4
Other References to Family	207	50.2	165	40.0
Concerns About Other People in Community or Nation	3	0.7	4	1.0
Political	4	1.0	2	0.5
General Economic Situation	9	2.2	38	8.0
Social	9	2.2	0	0.0
Religion, Morality, Public Service	15	3.6	15	3.6
International and World Situation	9	2.2	55	13.4
General	24	5.8	54	13.1
NA/DK				
Total Responses	719	b	536	b

Source: Housing of Welfare Recipients Survey, 1970.

a. N = 412.

b. These figures will add up to more than 100 percent since a given respondent can have more than one hope and/or more than one fear. Non-responses are also included.

criminal or antisocial, no self-development or improvement, not being accepted by others, no sense of personal worth, being a person without character.

Seventy hopes and 18 fears for one's personal character are expressed by the respondents (Exhibit 6.4). Nearly half (34) of the hopes refer to self-development or improvement with no other especially large cluster. Six of the 18 who express a fear worry that the future holds nothing in the way of self-development or improvement. The balance of the responses are widely dispersed.

PERSONAL ECONOMIC SITUATION

The specific hopes for economic betterment include an improved or decent standard of living, to have one's own home or business, conveniences or wealth. The fears concern deterioration in or an inadequate standard of living for self or family and a variety of miscellaneous worries and fears having to do with the economic situation of self or family. Interestingly enough, 177 hopes for economic improvement are expressed, but only 53 fears. The major subgroup is 95 responses which indicate hope for an improved and/or a decent standard of living. The second largest cluster is 66 responses, which mention specific hopes for having one's own apartment, with a small additional group who hope for their own house.[2] Of the 53 personal economic fears, 40 refer to deterioration in, or a specifically inadequate, living standard of self or family.

JOB OR WORK SITUATION

The number of references to job or work situation is relatively small: only 71 hopes and a relatively trivial 11 fears. Half (36) of the 71 hopes refer to the possibility of obtaining a good job or congenial work for self or a member of the household. Another 34 simply hope for steady work for self or another member of the household. Of the few who express fear, eight of the 11 specifically mention unemployment—a lack of steady work for themselves or some other household member.

OTHER REFERENCES TO SELF

Of the categories that receive more than 100 responses, the fears equal in hopes only in this residual one; there are 121 of each. Seventy-six of the hopeful responses refer to being able to continue in good physical condition or regaining health. The balance of the hopes indicate a wide variety of aspirations, with a strong tendency among the Puerto Ricans to look forward to a return to Puerto Rico. In the 121 responses which expressed fear, most (99) are worried about ill health.

OTHER REFERENCES TO FAMILY

More responses fall into this category than any other of the personal hopes and fears, with 207 hopes and 165 fears expressed. More than half (119) express hope that their children will have adequate opportunities in their futures. Sixty-seven express hope for their family unit, sometimes referring to relatives besides those in the immediate family, and hoping that they will live up to expectations. Another 34 simply refer to a happy family life, a good marriage and good relationships within the family.

Fears of separation from their family or children, personal fears of not being able to help or take care of them or not living up to their expectations are expressed by 52 respondents. Nearly as many (50) refer specifically to their children, mentioning fears of inadequate opportunities and fears for their future happiness and success. A disturbing 47 (almost 12 percent of all respondents) express concern about family members' drug use.[3]

CONCERNS ABOUT OTHER PEOPLE, COMMUNITY OR NATION

A number of subsets fall under this heading. A number can be grouped under a "social" heading. Nine responses indicate hopes in terms of social justice and greater equality of treatment. Eighteen of the 38 who have fears are concerned specifically with addicts and pushers; another seven voice fears of criminals.

The personal responses having to do with politics are few in number as are those referring to the economic situation. Religious and morality expressions are all hopeful, but again relatively low in frequency. Personal concerns about the world situation focus on peace as a hopeful situation or war as a feared situation; each number 15 responses.

OTHER CATEGORIES

Only 24 respondents express no specific personal hopes for the future, compared to 54 who answer that they do not have or know of any fears. Another 35 respondents specifically say they have "no fears." Comparisons of all of these responses with other studies will be undertaken in a later part of this chapter. First, however, the responses to national questions will be presented and analyzed.

NATIONAL HOPES AND FEARS

Based on the questions detailed earlier, our respondents' hopes and fears in the area of national concerns were tabulated. (The coding approach utilized is detailed in Appendix 6.2; it adds to Cantril's approach

EXHIBIT 6.5

RESPONSES ON NATIONAL HOPES AND FEARS BY AREA OF CONCERN (ALL RESPONDENTS)

AREA OF CONCERN	HOPES		FEARS	
	No.	%	No.	%
Political	129	31.3	131	31.6
Economic	62	15.0	17	3.1
Social	197	47.8	130	31.6
Concerned with International Situation	207	50.2	164	39.8
International Relations, Cold War, Peace	11	2.7	17	4.1
Independence, Status and Importance of Nation				
General	27	6.6	78	18.9
NA/DK	54	13.1	64	15.5
Total Responses	687	b	601	b

Source: Housing of Welfare Recipients Survey, 1970.

a. N = 412.

b. These figures will add up to more than 100% since a given respondent can have more than one hope and/or more than one fear. Non-responses are also included.

EXHIBIT 6.6

PERCENTAGE OF RESPONDENTS SHOWING "FEAR OF COMMUNISM" IN VARIOUS PRIOR STUDIES

COUNTRY	YEAR OF STUDY	PERCENTAGE SHOWING "FEAR OF COMMUNISM"
Dominican Republic	1962	22
Panama	1962	19
Philippines	1959	17
West Germany	1957	11
Egypt	1960	8
Brazil	1960-61	7
Cuba	1960	7
India	1962	1
Yugoslavia	1962	0
Israel	1961-62	0
Nigeria	1962-63	0

Source: This chart was taken from the various studies reported in Cantril, *The Patterns of Human Concerns.*

a few additional categories which are of specific importance to this study.)

POLITICAL

Political hopes and fears are nearly in balance with 129 and 131 responses each (Exhibit 6.5). About 60 percent of those giving hopes point to an absence of tensions or antagonisms based upon religion, class or ethnicity. Another 37 refer to the maintenance of the public peace including a decrease in crime and juvenile delinquency, fair courts and penal system, and the like. (In the Cantril Coding Manual, these are grouped under the category of "law and order," but the popular implications of this phrase have recently become so mixed as to raise the question whether the grouping is appropriate for this population. For this reason they have been disaggregated here.)

The respondents were asked about their hopes for the future, but their answers may reflect the sad facts of their present life. If we turn to explicit fears for the future, 50 of the 131 responses indicate fears of lack of order or failure to maintain the public peace, an increase in crime or juvenile delinquency, poor courts, a poor juridical system and so forth. Almost as many (41) refer to fear of continued racial antagonism.

Only 4.6 percent voice fear of Communism or the threat from the Soviet Union or China. A 1971 national study found that 12 percent of all Americans voiced fear of Communism. Exhibit 6.6 shows comparable percentages of various populations that have been studied and their relative frequencies of fear of Communism.

ECONOMIC

Sixty-two respondents voice hopes about the economic situation of the nation and 17 voice fears. Of the former, 37 hope for greater national prosperity in general. Another 12 hope for no unemployment problems and jobs for eveybody. Among those who are fearful, the majority in a single sub-category refer to economic instability, inflationary prices and economic depression.

SOCIAL CONCERNS

Besides hope for international peace, which will be discussed later, social concerns received the largest single category of hopes—197. Of the social hopes, 74 (nearly 18 percent of all responses) voice hope for a decline in drug addiction.

The group which looks for an end of discrimination numbers 47. As used here, discrimination refers specifically to race and ethnicity. Another 31, without singling out ethnic discrimination, hope for increases in social justice for all elements of the population, while 25 hope for more unity within the nation in working on basic social problems. Only 22 indicate hope or concern about improved housing.[4]

Of the 130 who voice fear, 82 worry about the continuance or enlargement of the drug problem. The second largest group is the 19 who feared continued racial discrimination. While these are the two most frequent-

EXHIBIT 6.7

PERCENTAGE OF PERSONAL HOPES AND FEARS BY AREA OF CONCERN AND BY ETHNICITY

AREA OF CONCERN	HOPES			FEARS		
	White[a]	Black[b]	Spanish Speaking[c]	White	Black	Spanish Speaking
Own Personal Character	10.9%	16.7%	12.8%	3.1%	7.2%	1.8%
Personal Economic Situation	29.7	49.4	40.2	9.4	16.1	11.0
Job or Work Situation	6.2	18.9	19.5	3.1	2.8	2.4
Other References to Self	32.8	24.4	37.9	32.8	27.8	29.3
Other References to Family	39.1	48.9	66.1	23.0	45.5	70.1
Concerns About Other People, Community or Nation						
Political	0.0	1.7	0.0	0.0	1.1	1.2
General Economic Situation	1.6	1.7	0.0	0.0	1.1	0.0
Social	0.0	5.0	0.0	1.6	8.3	10.4
Religion, Morality, Public Service	0.0	3.9	1.2	0.0	0.0	0.0
International Situation	1.6	7.2	0.6	0.0	4.4	4.3
General	0.0	3.4	1.8	17.2	13.3	12.2
NA/DK	15.6	3.3	4.3	20.3	17.8	4.9

Source: Housing of Welfare Recipients Survey Semantic Differential Process, 1970.

Note: These figures will add up to more than 100% since a given respondent can have more than one hope and/or more than one fear. Non-responses are also included.

a. N = 64.
b. N = 180.
c. N = 164

ly mentioned social concerns, the responses to our probes indicate that drug concerns far outweigh concern with racial discrimination.

THE INTERNATIONAL SITUATION

The 207 positive hopes expressed are nearly exclusively concerned with the hope and desire for peace. Fear responses number 164, and again the concern is almost entirely about continuation of the war (Exhibit 6.5). This is the most frequently mentioned category of national hope and national fears and is comparable to the results obtained in Cantril and Roll's 1971 national sample.[5]

Eleven respondents voice hopes that could be categorized as concern about the United States' maintaining its position as a world power. Seventeen are concerned with the fear of Communist power or other external aggression.

GENERAL CONCERNS

Twenty-seven respondents mention general hopes and 78 general fears. Twenty-two of the former simply hope for a new and better country. The 78 fearful responses cover a broad range of topics, ranging from "something evil happening," "no future," "the country won't change," "a lot of trouble and bloodshed," "major crises in the city," to "something drastic will happen, they will blow it up."

OTHER CATEGORIES

Fifty-four gave us no positive aspirations or hopes in the national area and 64, no fears in the same sector.

HOPES AND FEARS OF ETHNIC GROUPS

The percentage of personal hopes and fears by areas of concern were explored for various ethnic groups.

Some variation in the primary area of concern is revealed when hopes are tabulated by ethnicity. The largest single area of hopeful concern of the white group (39.1 percent) is the family, and the second largest is "other references to self" at 32.8 percent and third, the job or work situation at 29.7 percent. Black respondents (49.4 percent) indicate hopeful concern for their personal economic situation; 48.9 percent express hope for their families. Spanish-speaking respondents, while expressing concern about their personal economic situation (40.2 percent) are by far more hopeful about their family, with two-thirds mentioning it (Exhibit 6.7).

"Other references to self" are a primary concern, with 32.8 percent of the white group commenting on it. Black and Spanish-speaking respondents are at 27.8 and 29.3 percent respectively. Their chief fears concern the family; 45.5 percent of the blacks and 70.1 percent of the Spanish-speaking respondents, compared to only 23 percent of the whites. Spanish-speaking respondents are particularly fearful of drugs (Exhibit 6.7).

PERSONAL HOPES AND FEARS IN THE UNITED STATES

Exhibit 6.8 presents data on hopes and fears gathered in Cantril's national sample study of August 1959. it is clear that both whites' and nonwhites' most frequent aspirations are in the area of personal economic betterment (64 percent of whites and 76 percent of nonwhites). Both of these figures are higher than the comparable figures for white and black welfare respondents in 1970.

Family concerns are also important in the 1959 study: 47 percent of the whites and 37 percent of the nonwhites listed such hopes, while in our study, 39.1 percent of whites, 48.9 percent of blacks and 66.1 percent of persons of Spanish-speaking origins indicate hopes in this area.

Whites have a higher level of health aspirations than nonwhites, with 50 percent compared to 33 percent in the 1959 United States study. The comparable percentages expressing hopes for health among the welfare

EXHIBIT 6.8

PERCENTAGES OF PERSONAL HOPES AND FEARS BY AREA OF CONCERN AND BY RACE (UNITED STATES - AUGUST 1959)

	RACE	
HOPES	White	Non-White
Values/Character	21%	13%
Economic	64	76
Job/Work	11	6
Health	50	33
Family	47	37
Political	2	3
Social	5	7
International	10	10
Status Quo	11	8
FEARS		
Values/Character	4	1
Economic	46	41
Job/Work	5	2
Health	58	32
Family	24	27
Political	5	2
Social	2	6
International	25	16
No Fears/Worries	11	14

Source: Cantril, *Pattern of Human Concerns,* p. 407.

Note: These figures will add up to more than 100% since a given respondent can have more than one hope and/or more than one fear.

EXHIBIT 6.9

RESPONSES ON NATIONAL HOPES AND FEARS BY AREA OF CONCERN AND BY ETHNICITY

AREA OF CONCERN	HOPES			FEARS		
	White[a]	Black[b]	Spanish Speaking[c]	White	Black	Spanish Speaking
Political	37.5%	38.9%	20.7%	40.6%	30.6%	29.3%
Economic	27.2	16.1	13.4	3.1	6.1	2.4
Social	39.1	53.9	45.8	12.5	29.4	41.9
Concerned with International Situation						
International Relations, Cold War, Peace	50.0	43.9	57.3	23.4	39.4	47.0
Independence, Status and Importance of Nation	4.7	1.1	3.7	1.6	6.1	3.0
General	1.6	7.8	7.3	17.2	18.3	8.5
NA/DK	12.5	14.4	11.0	23.4	15.6	11.6

Source: Housing of Welfare Recipients Survey, 1970.

Note: These figures will add up to more than 100% since a given respondent can have more than one hope and/or more than one fear. Non-responses also are included.

a. N = 64.

b. N = 180.

c. N = 160.

respondents in 1970 are 32.8 percent of whites, 24.4 percent of blacks and 37.9 percent of Spanish-speaking persons.

The incidence of fear in our study of welfare recipients is considerably different from the 1959 United States study. Whites expressed fears in 1959 as follows: 58 percent, health; 46 percent, personal economic concerns; and 24 percent, family. Our 1970 study shows 32.8 percent with health-related fears, 9.4 percent with personal economic fears and 23 percent with family-related fears (Exhibit 6.7). In the 1959 United States study nonwhites had relatively high frequencies of personal fears in all three categories: 41 percent in the economic area, 32 percent in the health area and 27 percent in the family area.

NATIONAL HOPES AND FEARS IN THE UNITED STATES

Social concerns are foremost among blacks with 53.9 percent indicating that area, particularly hopes for an end to discrimination and more social justice. Social concerns are given by 45.8 percent of the Spanish-speaking respondents and 39.1 percent of the whites (Exhibit 6.9).

Improvement in international relations, on the other hand, dominates the hopes of the whites at 50 percent, but is exceeded by the Spanish-speaking respondents at 57.3 percent. In contrast, only 43.9 percent of the blacks are concerned with international relations; typically, they hoped for peace. Relatively equal proportions of whites and blacks (approximately 37 and 39 percent) share political hopes, as do 20.7 of the Spanish-speaking respondents.

Political fears is the single largest area of responses for the whites (40.6 percent); typically these fears are of lack of law and order and disunity among the people of the nation. Blacks express less political fears (30.6 percent), as do the Spanish-speaking respondents (29.3 percent). The latter are concerned more specifically with crime than the black respondents.

Social concerns occupy 41.9 percent of Spanish-speaking individuals, less than 30 percent of the blacks and only 12.5 percent of the whites. For the Puerto Ricans these are typically fears of drug abuse, which are shared by the blacks along with a number of other fears.

International relations, expecially fear of war, dominate the Spanish-speaking responses; 47 percent mention this area as compared to 39.4 percent of the blacks but only 23.4 percent of the whites. The overall level of white responses to the question of generalized fear is 17.2 percent, split between those who have no fears or worries and those who have generalized fears and worries. For the blacks, the 18.3 percent who give fear responses focus on a general fear for the nation as a whole (Exhibit 6.9).

Exhibit 6.10 presents the findings for whites and nonwhites in the United States population in August 1959, which was a period of economic recession, and prior to the relatively turbulent urban unrest of the 1960s. The international situation was, however, unstable through the entire period of the late 1950s and 1960s.

The 1959 data show clearly that hopes for international peace were higher for whites (61 percent) than for nonwhites (37 percent). On the other hand, hopes for economic betterment were mentioned relatively equally—by 45 percent of the whites and 44 percent of the nonwhites. Both of these figures are much higher than those shown for the respondents in our study. The social aspirations percentages in the 1959 study are 32 percent for whites and 47 percent for nonwhites, and are similar to the 39.1 percent for whites and 53.9 percent for blacks gathered in the New York welfare sample.

The highest relative frequencies of national fears are expressed about the international situation (mainly reflecting fear of war) for both whites (58 percent) and nonwhites (45 percent) in the United States in 1959 (Exhibit 6.10). The roughly comparable figures for our sample are 23.4 percent and 39.4 percent, but we found more frequent mention of internal political unrest among whites (40.6).

EXHIBIT 6.10

PERCENTAGES OF NATIONAL HOPES AND FEARS BY AREA OF CONCERN AND BY RACE (UNITED STATES - AUGUST 1959)

	RACE	
HOPES	White	Non-White
Political	13%	11%
Economic	45	44
Social	32	47
International	61	37
Independent Status	4	2
Status Quo	7	2
FEARS		
Political	24	14
Economic	29	29
Social	20	26
International	58	45
Independent Status	12	6
No Fears/Worries	3	7

Source: Cantril, *Patterns of Human Concerns,* p. 407.

Note: These figures will add up to more than 100% since a given respondent can have more than one hope and/or more than one fear.

EXHIBIT 6.11
CANTRIL SELF-ANCHORING STRIVING SCALE[a]

10
9
8
7
6
5
4
3
2
1
0

Source: Cantril, *The Pattern of Human Concerns.*
a. Ladder used during interviews.

THE LADDER RATINGS

The Cantril Self-Anchoring Striving Scale[6] is used as a simple, widely applicable and adaptable technique for tapping the unique perspective of an individual and learning what his viewpoint has in common with others'. A person is asked to define, on the basis of his own assumptions, perceptions, goals and values two extremes or anchoring points on which some scale is desired—for example, he may be asked to define the "top" and "bottom," the "good" and "bad," the "best" and the "worst." This self-defined continuum is then used as our measuring device (Exhibit 6.11 and Appendix 6.1).

PERSONAL AND NATIONAL

Exhibit 6.12 shows the self-rating of New York City's welfare respondents concerning their past (five years ago), their present and their future (five years from now). They were asked to rate their personal standing and how they see the United States as a whole. The pattern that we obtained is similar to the results of other observations of our sample but is not typical of results from the studies of 13 nations re-

EXHIBIT 6.12
CANTRIL LADDER RATINGS: TOTAL SAMPLE

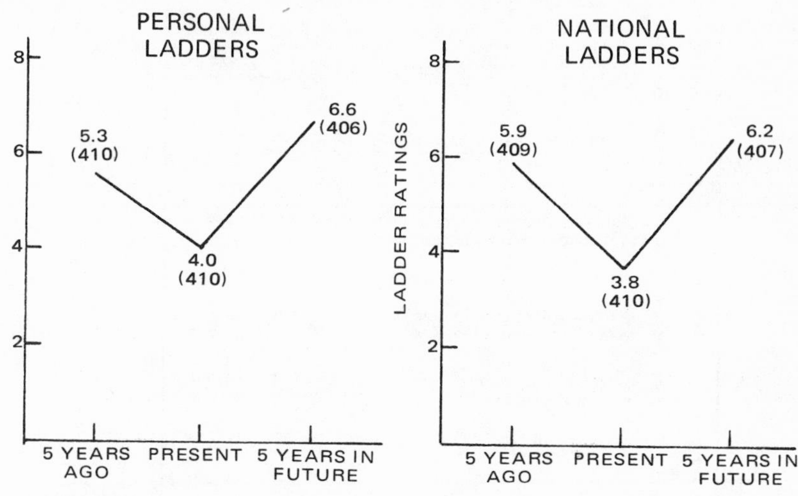

Source: Housing of Welfare Recipient Survey, Cantril Ladder Ratings, 1970.

Note: Numbers in parentheses represent the number of respondents.

ported by Cantril. The welfare respondents tend to see their personal past as better than their personal present and their personal future as considerably better than their personal present or past. The sample of welfare recipients shows a similar pattern in their national evaluations. The graph dips from past to present and then shows a rise in expectations for the future. New York's welfare recipients clearly feel negative about their present status.

The typical patterns in most of Cantril's national studies is for the respondent to rate his personal past lower than the present and the future higher than the present. For 19 of the 22 published analyses of personal ladder ratings this pattern applies, including a United States sample done in 1971.

Only in the 1959 Negro American data does the welfare sample pattern appear. In 1963 the Negro American data (Exhibit 6.13) reverted to the more typical pattern, and this continues in the nonwhite national sample of 1971.

The only other two national studies which show atypical patterns of findings occur in studies of the Dominican Republic in 1962 and the

EXHIBIT 6.13

RESULTS OF PREVIOUS STUDIES INVOLVING CANTRIL SCALE

COUNTRY	DESCRIPTIVE DATA							LADDER RATINGS					
								Personal			National		
	Date	Population (in millions)	Per Capita Income	Life Expectancy	Literacy Rate	NAW[a]	Autos Per 1000	Past	Present	Future	Past	Present	Future
U.S.	1959	177.8	$2,160	69	98%	64%	343	5.9	6.6	7.8	6.5	6.7	7.4
Negro	1959							5.9	5.3	7.3	6.6	6.3	7.2
Negro	1963							4.6	5.2	6.6	5.3	6.6	7.7
Nonwhite	1971							5.3	5.8	6.8	5.3	5.8	6.5*
White	1959							6.0	6.7	7.9	6.4	6.7	7.6
White	1963							5.7	6.3	7.5	6.3	6.7	7.3
White	1971							5.8	6.6	7.5	6.3	5.4	6.2*
U.S.	1971							5.8	6.8	7.5	6.2	5.4	6.2*
West Germany	1957	50.9	1,113	68	—	71	40	4.1	5.3	6.2	4.1	6.2	—
Yugoslavia	1962	18.5	305	57	73	18	3	4.3	5.0	6.7	4.9	6.8	8.6
Poland	1962	29.7	468	65	94	47	4	4.0	4.4	5.5	—	—	—
Japan	1962							4.6	5.2	6.2	4.2	5.3	6.4
Brazil	1960-61	70.8	268	42	49	36	8	4.1	4.6	7.3	4.9	5.1	7.6
Nigeria	1962-63	31.8	84	—	11	8	1	2.8	4.8	7.4	4.0	6.2	8.2
India	1962	440.3	70	32	17	17	1	3.4	3.7	5.1	3.5	4.9	6.7
Israel	1961-62	2.1	735	72	94	76	14	4.7	5.3	6.9	4.0	5.5	7.5
Kibbutzim	1962	.75						6.3	7.0	7.9	4.5	5.3	6.5
Egypt	1960	24.0	150	51	23	36	3	4.6	5.5	8.0	3.5	5.9	7.5
Cuba	After 1960	6.1	413	—	78	57	23	4.1	6.4	8.4	2.2	7.0	8.8
Dominican Republic	1962	3.0	251	—	66	31	4	1.6	1.6	5.8	1.7	2.7	7.0
Panama	1962	1.075	283	61	70	36	15	4.5	4.8	7.0	5.0	6.0	7.7
Philippines	1959	27.4	188	50	75	35	3	4.9	4.9	6.7	6.1	5.1	6.1

Source: Cantril, *The Pattern of Human Concerns.*
A.H. Cantril and C.W. Roll, *Hopes and Fears of the American People* (New York, Universe Books, 1971.)

[a]Not in agricultural work.

EXHIBIT 6.14

PERSONAL AND NATIONAL LADDER RATINGS FOR SPECIFIC SUB-GROUPS WITHIN VARIOUS COUNTRIES

			LADDER RATINGS					
			Personal			National		
COUNTRY	SUB-GROUP	YEAR	Past	Present	Future	Past	Present	Future
U.S.	Middle Class	1959	5.9	6.8	8.0	6.2	6.6	7.5
U.S.	Lower Class	1959	6.4	4.6	5.5	6.0	6.8	7.8
U.S.	Working Class	1959	5.8	6.3	7.5	6.5	6.7	7.4
U.S.	Non-White	1959	5.9	5.3	7.3	6.6	6.3	7.2
Israel	Middle Class	1961-62	4.9	5.7	7.2	3.9	5.5	7.4
Israel	Lower Class	1961-62	4.4	3.2	4.9	4.3	5.6	7.4
Israel	Working Class	1961-62	4.2	4.7	6.4	3.9	5.6	7.8
Brazil	Middle Class (3)	1960-61	4.1	5.3	7.8	4.8	5.2	7.7
Brazil	Lower Class (5)	1960-61	4.0	3.9	6.6	5.0	4.8	7.4
Cuba	High, Upper-Middle	1960	5.5	6.7	8.2	2.8	6.1	7.5
Cuba	Lower Middle	1960	4.1	6.4	8.3	2.2	6.7	8.6
Cuba	Low	1960	3.5	6.2	8.5	1.9	7.3	9.2
Cuba	White	1960	4.2	6.5	8.4	2.2	6.9	8.8
Cuba	Negro	1960	4.0	6.0	8.1	2.1	7.3	9.3
Nigeria	Upper Class	1962-63	4.4	5.8	8.0	4.3	5.9	7.8
Nigeria	Lower Class	1962-63	2.8	4.7	7.4	3.9	6.2	8.3

Source: Cantril, *The Pattern of Human Concerns.*

Philippines in 1959. Here the pattern of average personal ladder ratings shows that the past and present are seen as at the same level, and the future is expected (perhaps unrealistically) to be considerably improved.

Exhibit 6.13 also shows that the typical pattern on the rating of the national past, present and future is for the present to be seen as better than the past (17 of 21 studies) and the future to be better than the present (all 21 studies). In 17 of the 20 studies future expectations are also higher, and in some cases considerably higher, than evaluations of the past national situation. The data on the Philippines in 1959 showed past and future averages were the same and the present situation was slightly lower. The Philippines is, however, a special case: the national government (circa 1959) was seen to be corrupt and a short time following the Cantril study was replaced by a popular movement.

The 1959 data for Negro Americans shows a pattern parallel to the Philippines. In both, the national past was rated higher than the prescent and future expectations averaged higher than both the past and present averages. This pattern is similar to our present welfare sample data.

In contrast to our welfare sample almost all of the personal and national ladder ratings for the various countries generally showed a progression upward from past to present to future (Exhibit 6.13). A breakdown of both relatively and absolutely deprived subgroups in a number of countries shows a different pattern in which the past is seen

EXHIBIT 6.15
CANTRIL LADDER RATINGS BY ETHNICITY

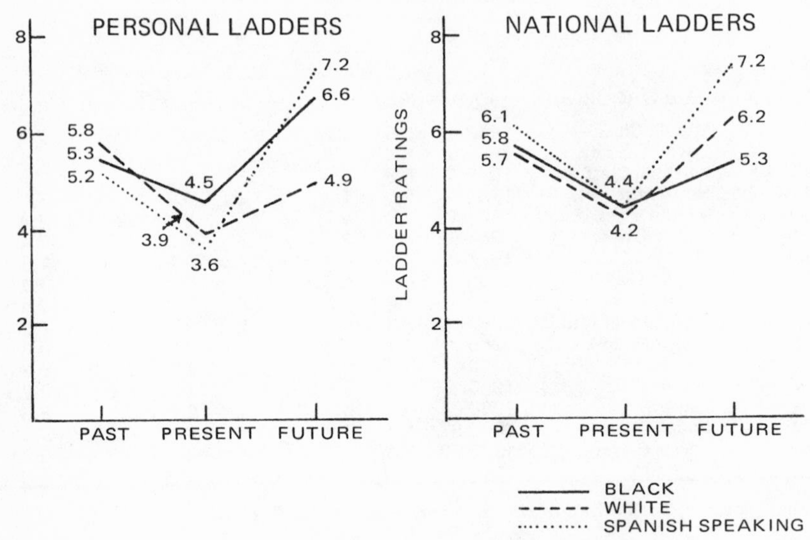

Source: Housing of Welfare Recipients Survey, Cantril Ladder Ratings, 1970.

as better than the present (Exhibit 6.14). The pattern shows up in the 1959 United States personal evaluations by the lower-class sample, in the 1959 United States nonwhite personal and national evaluations, in personal ratings by Israel's lower class and in personal and national estimates by the Brazilian lower class. All of these groups clearly felt relatively and absolutely deprived within their countries.

Cantril and Roll's 1971 United States study shows a pattern which is not evident in 1959 and 1964. In earlier national studies the pattern of past being lower than present and present being lower than future is generally true for both personal and national ladder ratings. In the 1971 study, the United States personal average ladder ratings show an upward progression from past = 5.8, to present = 6.6 and to future = 7.5; while the United States national average ladder ratings show a "plunging neckline" phenomenon, in which past = 6.2, present =5.4 and future = 6.2.

RATINGS BY ETHNICITY

Personal and national ladder ratings of past, present and future for the welfare sample by ethnicity seem to be consistent regardless of the ethnic background of the respondent (Exhibit 6.15). The similarity of personal and national ladder rating graphs is clear: In both, the present shows a decline from the past, with the decline least sharp for the blacks' ratings of their personal position.

Spanish-speaking respondents are most optimistic, both personally and nationally, about the future. They move up to a 7.2 figure—from a relatively modest present point—3.6 and 4.4 respectively. The blacks are somewhat less optimistic personally. Their ladder ratings do show higher hopes for their future than for the national future; their personal ladder shows the present at 4.5 and peaks at a 6.6 mark for the future, versus the future on the national ladder which is 5.3 rising from a present of 4.4. By contrast white expectations for the future on the personal ladder are relatively low (4.9). While they are better than the present (3.9), they are not rated as good as the past (5.8). Similar findings appear on our white sample's rating of the national past, present and future. They move from a 5.7 mean five years ago to 4.2 at present to 6.2 five years in the future.

The 1971 United States sample shows that on the personal ladder whites on the average feel they have moved up 0.8 from past to present compared to nonwhites, who feel they moved up 0.4. Whites in our welfare sample feel they have moved down 1.9 from past to present, while blacks feel they have moved down 0.8 and the Spanish-speaking welfare recipients feel they have moved down 1.6.

People over 50, those with only a grade school education and those in the lower income categories feel that they have made the least progress in the last five years.[7] Data secured in a 1970 study among the poor of three counties in northwest New Jersey provide further insight into the attitudes of different subsets of the poor. Only one-third of the respondents who qualified for welfare acknowledged receiving it at the time of the survey. The poor who said they were not on welfare felt they had moved down in the last five years an average of 1.6 while the poor who said they were on welfare felt they had moved down only slightly—0.07.[8]

Groups studied in the past generally expect that the future will be better than the past on the personal level and this is true of the United States in 1971 personal and national ratings. The overall increment in the 1971 study is 0.9 with the young most optimistic (an increase of 1.8) and those over age 50 least optimistic (an increase of 0.1). Whites show a decline in optimism of 0.9, and nonwhites an increase in optimism of 1.0 about their improvement present to future on the personal level. Although nonwhites give themselves lower ladder ratings than whites, on the key point of movement from past to present to future, the racial groups differ little in their relative perceptions.[10]

EXHIBIT 6.16

PERSONAL LADDER RATING CHANGES BY ETHNICITY

	ETHNICITY							
RATINGS	PAST TO PRESENT				PRESENT TO FUTURE			
	White[a]	Black[b]	Spanish Speaking[c]	Full Sample[d]	White[e]	Black[f]	Spanish Speaking[g]	Full Sample[h]
Percent Who See Decrease	56.2	53.9	56.1	54.9	17.2	18.3	8.5	14.3
Percent Same	29.7	16.7	13.4	17.7	40.6	14.4	11.0	17.2
Percent Who See Increase	14.1	29.4	30.5	27.4	42.2	67.3	80.5	68.5
Total	100.0	100.0	100.0	100.0	100.0	100.0	100.0	100.0

Source: Housing of Welfare Recipients Survey, 1970.

a. N = 64.
b. N = 179.
c. N = 164.
d. N = 407.
e. N = 64.
f. N = 179.
g. N = 162.
h. N = 405.

It should be noted that there are significant errors possible in judging this type of data except for the broadest of generalizations. It may be summarized simply by saying that there are variations between the several groups but the major pattern for the New York City welfare sample is one of a depressed present ladder rating with hope for the future.

Another way to look at the same phenomenon is to compare the personal ladder rating changes by ethnicity in percentages. Most respondents regardless of ethnic backgrounds see a decrease from the past to their present situation (Exhibit 6.16). There are clear-cut and significant variations as a function of ethnicity when those who see increases from past to present, versus those who see the same rating, versus those who see decreases, are compared. The whites in the sample, frequently Old Age Assistance recipients, on the personal ladder are the least likely to see an increase past to present (14.1 percent). Virtually the same percentage of black and Spanish-speaking respondents see an increase from past to present—29.4 percent and 30.5 percent respectively. On the personal ladder comparing present and future, whites again are least likely, at 42 percent, to foresee any great improvements in their future. The Spanish-speaking respondents are most optimistic of all, with 80.5 percent looking forward to improvement in the future in contrast to 67.3 percent of the blacks.

As one would expect, almost complementary results appear if we look at the percentage predicting a decline in their future ranking: 17.2 percent of whites, 18.3 percent of blacks and 8.5 percent of the Spanish-speaking responses. A remarkable 40.6 percent of whites feel that their personal future is going to remain just like the present, in contrast to the blacks (only 14.4 percent) or the Spanish-speaking (11.0). These results may well be age related.

NATIONAL RATINGS

Most of our respondents, regardless of ethnicity, see some decline in the national picture from the past to the present. This is most marked among Spanish-speaking individuals, with 80.5 percent indicating a decline from past to present compared to 57.8 percent of whites and 56.7 percent of blacks. Whites are the least optimistic about improvement at 9.4 percent. Blacks have the highest proportion who see an improvement in the national scene from past to present; 18.9 percent compared to 11.6 percent of Spanish-speaking individuals (Exhibit 6.17). In the 1971 United States data whites see a slight decline on the ladder rating of the nation, while nonwhites see an improvement, from past to present.[11]

EXHIBIT 6.17

NATIONAL LADDER RATING CHANGES BY ETHNICITY

RATINGS	ETHNICITY							
	PAST TO PRESENT				PRESENT TO FUTURE			
	White[a]	Black[b]	Spanish Speaking[c]	Full Sample[d]	White[e]	Black[f]	Spanish Speaking[g]	Full Sample[h]
Percent Who See Decrease	57.8	56.7	80.5	66.3	9.4	33.3	15.2	22.1
Percent Same	32.8	24.4	7.9	19.4	39.1	16.7	14.0	19.7
Percent Who See Increase	9.4	18.9	11.6	14.3	51.5	50.0	70.8	58.2
Total	100.0	100.0	100.0	100.0	100.0	100.0	100.0	100.0

Source: Housing of Welfare Recipients Survey, 1970.

a. N = 64.
b. N = 179.
c. N = 163.
d. N = 406.
e. N = 64.
f. N = 177.
g. N = 163.
h. N = 404.

EXHIBIT 6.18

PERSONAL LADDER RATING CHANGES BY CATEGORY OF WELFARE

RATINGS	CATEGORY OF WELFARE							
	PAST TO PRESENT				PRESENT TO FUTURE			
	Home Relief[a]	Old Age Assistance[b]	Aid To Dependent Children[c]	Aid to Disabled[d]	Home Relief[e]	Old Age Assistance[f]	Aid To Dependent Children[g]	Aid To Disabled[h]
Percent Who See Decrease	54.7	43.7	56.9	57.8	18.7	34.5	6.7	19.3
Percent Same	12.0	32.7	15.1	21.1	22.7	41.8	8.4	21.1
Percent Who See Increase	33.3	23.6	28.0	21.1	58.6	23.6	84.9	59.6
Total	100.0	100.0	100.0	100.0	100.0	100.0	100.0	100.0

Source: Housing of Welfare Recipients Survey, 1970.

a. N = 75.
b. N = 53.
c. N = 225
d. N = 57.
e. N = 75.
f. N = 51.
g. N = 223.
h. N = 57.

When national ladder rating changes for present to future are compared by ethnicity for the welfare sample, the Spanish-speaking individuals are most optimistic, with 70.8 percent seeing a better future, compared to 50 percent of the blacks and 51.5 percent of the whites. In the 1971 study both whites and non whites expect improvement from present to future of +0.8 and +0.7 respectively.

When attention is focused on the proportion who see a decrease in the national standing the contrasts are even more evident. One-third of the blacks compared to 15.2 percent of the Spanish-speaking and 9.4 percent of the white respondents project a decrease in the nation's position. (See Exhibit 6.17.)

PERSONAL RATINGS BY WELFARE TYPE

Analysis of the proportion within each welfare category who feel that the present is an improvement over past personal standing indicates some telling variations. In each of the several categories, most welfare recipients believe the present represents a decline from their past standing on the scale. The pattern in the estimates of status changes from the present to the future is quite different. Over one-third of the Old Age Assistance recipients (34.5 percent) see a decrease, but most (41.8 percent) see the situation remaining the same. Only 23.6 percent forecast a future improvement in their status. The Old Age Assistance recipients are the only group in any of the studies to show such pessimism about the future, which is, of course, supported by their other comments reported in the interviews. In contrast, the ADC recipients are quite optimistic: 6.7 percent see a decrease and 8.4 percent predict their status will be unchanged, compared to 84.9 percent who foresee an improvement. The Home Relief (58.6 percent) and the Other Disabled category (59.6 percent) also largely anticipate an improvement (Exhibit 6.18).

NATIONAL RATINGS BY CATEGORY OF WELFARE RECIPIENT

The pattern of ratings of the nation's status is consistent regardless of welfare category. All rate the past superior to the present and the future better than the present. The highest overall ratings of past, present and future are given by the disabled. (For the definition of this category see the Methodology.) The lowest single estimates given the present on the national rating is from the ADC group, but their future expectations actually show a slight improvement on their evaluations of the past value. It is interesting to compare the personal and the national ladders in this regard (Exhibit 6.19).

EXHIBIT 6.19

CANTRIL LADDER RATINGS BY CATEGORY OF WELFARE

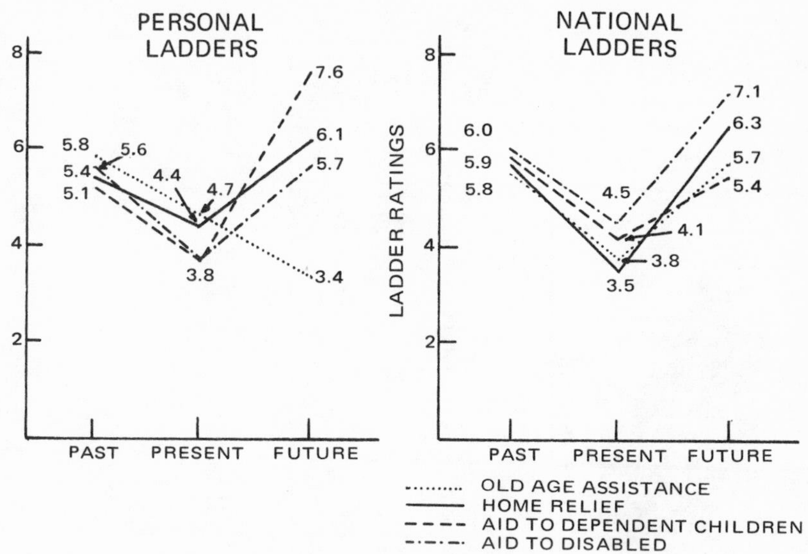

Source: Housing of Welfare Recipient Survey, Cantril Ladder Ratings, 1970.

The validity of the approach may be confirmed by the variation in the Old Age Assistance respondents to the several questions. At the personal level they see the past better than the present and the present better than the future. At the national level, they, like the other recipients, see the "plunging neckline." (Exhibit 6.19). Note the variation in ADC response between the personal ladder and the national ladder. The absolute values of the past are comparable as is true for the present. In terms of the future, however, the ratings are quite different. On a personal front a 7.6 is anticipated while on the national level the equivalent figure is 5.4 (Exhibit 6.19).

Most of the several categories of respondents see a decrease in the national status from past to present. The ADC recipients foresee the greatest future improvement in the nation's status, with 63.1 percent indicating an increase compared to only 41.8 percent of the Old Age Assistance recipients. The Home Relief and Disabled categories are intermediate at 53.3 and 61.4 percent respectively. In general it is clear that despite what some might expect, welfare recipients hold a basic belief in national improvement over time. There is, however, a feeling that the country presently has more problems and a less positive position than it did five years ago (Exhibit 6.20).

EXHIBIT 6.20

NATIONAL LADDER RATING CHANGES BY CATEGORY OF WELFARE

RATINGS	CATEGORY OF WELFARE							
	PAST TO PRESENT				PRESENT TO FUTURE			
	Home Relief[a]	Old Age Assistance[b]	Aid To Dependent Children[c]	Aid To Disabled[d]	Home Relief[e]	Old Age Assistance[f]	Aid To Dependent Children[g]	Aid To Disabled[h]
Percent Who See Decrease	68.0	56.4	69.3	61.4	26.7	20.0	23.1	14.0
Percent Same	17.3	34.5	15.6	22.8	20.0	38.2	13.8	24.6
Percent Who See Increase	14.7	9.1	15.1	15.8	53.3	41.8	63.1	61.4
Total	100.0	100.0	100.0	100.0	100.0	100.0	100.0	100.0

Source: Housing of Welfare Recipients Survey, 1970.

a. N = 75. e. N = 75.
b. N = 53. f. N = 52.
c. N = 224. g. N = 224.
d. N = 57. h. N = 56.

NORTHWEST NEW JERSEY STUDY OF THE POOR

In the unpublished New Jersey study mentioned earlier, which was done in the late summer of 1970, 512 interviews were undertaken using the ladder approach. All of the respondents fell under the poverty guidelines, i.e., a single person household had less than a $1,800 annual income, a four person household, $3,600, and a six person household, $4,800.

Approximately one-third of the respondents were on welfare and the majority were white. When asked about the ladder standing of their community now, the mean value was 4.59. Five years ago it was 4.28. Five years in the future it was projected at 4.89, i.e., a straight line progression. When asked about their own present personal status, it was placed at 4.84 for the mean; five years ago it was 4.96, and five years in the future it was projected at 5.32—the plunging neckline phenomenon again.

SUMMARY

Using the self-anchoring striving scale developed by Cantril we found that our respondents express hopes more frequently than fears at both the personal and national levels of consideration. The most frequently mentioned personal hopes have to do with their families; more than half have specific hopes for their children. The second most frequent personal hope is in the general area of personal economic improvement for themselves and/or their families. Fears with reference to their families are also the most frequently mentioned area, particularly such fears as being separated from their families or children, not being able to take care of them or not living up to their expectations, inadequate opportunities for their children's success or happiness. Forty-seven of the 165 respondents expressed concern about family member drug use.

At the national level the most frequently mentioned hope was for world peace and the most frequently mentioned fear was of war. The social concern area was the second most frequently mentioned. Hopes for the decline of drug addiction and an end to discrimination were frequently mentioned. Fears also reflected concerns in these areas. Interesting similarities and differences occur when this sample is compared with a national sample and across various ethnic groups.

In conclusion, while Cantril and Roll in their 1971 national survey find the American people personally content but deeply troubled about the state of their nation, our sample of New York City welfare recipients, while equally troubled about the nation, views their present personal situation as negative.

They evaluate their present situation as an abrupt decline from the past, while the future holds positive anticipation. The present image is a depressed one. This view of present decline in personal status is somewhat similar to the New Jersey group cited but shows a much more abrupt change. New York's welfare population views its present as an abyss between a positive past and positive future. Hope for the future is still expressed by most welfare recipients, except for the aged.

Two streams of analysis have been present in this study: one centers on the attitudes and characteristics of the welfare recipients, and the second focuses on their housing. In the next chapters the emphasis will be on housing costs and financing.

NOTES

1. Hadley Cantril, *The Pattern of Human Concerns* (New Brunswick, New Jersey: Rutgers University Press, 1965), and more recently Albert H. Cantril and Charles W. Roll, *Hopes and Fears of the American People,* (New York: Universe Books, 1971).

2. The total of 17.7 percent compared with an equivalent 11 percent response in the 1971 national sample. Albert H. Cantril and Charles W. Roll, *Hopes and Fears of the American People* (New York: Universe Books, 1971).

3. Note that specific coding for drugs is not in the original Cantril manual. It was added for the purposes of this study because of the frequency of volunteered data and fears on this point. In the Cantril 1971 study fears of drug problems in the family were given by 7 percent of the respondents. Ibid., p. 19. The comparable 1971 responses for hope on drugs was 6 percent. Ibid., p. 23.

4. The Cantril questions were administered *after* the earlier part of the questionnaire which centered on housing. If anything, this should have augmented the housing responses.

5. Cantril and Roll, op. cit., p. 23.

6. Cantril, 1959.

7. Cantril and Roll, op. cit., p. 21.

8. George Sternlieb, unpublished data.

9. Cantril and Roll, op. cit., pp. 21-22.

10. Ibid., p. 27.

Chapter 7

THE DOLLARS OF WELFARE HOUSING: RENTS, OPERATING COSTS AND PROFITS

What kinds of rent do welfare recipients pay? Are inordinate profits returned from the private operation of welfare housing? Are welfare rents high enough to support substantial rehabilitation effort? The answers to these and allied questions are essential if an effort to improve the housing accommodations of welfare recpients is to be made.

Unfortunately, the answers have more often resulted from observers' prejudices than from dispassionate analysis. The popular literature is rife with descriptions of slumlords extorting enormous rents from hard-pressed welfare departments and recipients. Many of the tenants in low-income areas believe that their landlords receive rents that yield high levels of return. In a Louis Harris study of low-income residents in New York's racially shifting areas, respondents were asked to estimate the profits landlords were making from the buildings in which the residents were located. The response "making a lot" came from 26 percent of the whites, 48 percent of the blacks and 21 percent of the Puerto Ricans. The response "making a little" was given by 9, 11 and 14 percent, respectively. "Breaking even" was guessed by 11, 4 and 7 percent, while 5, 1 and 3 percent answered that landlords were losing money. About 35 to 45 percent of each group simply said "not sure."[1]

The total amount of welfare housing expenditures often seems incongruous when compared to the quality of the amenities which it buys. There has been some demand for a better match of the amount of expenditure to the quality of the structure. For example, the report of the Joint Legislative Committee to Revive the Social Service Law of New York State notes:

> We must make a major effort to improve housing conditions for public assistance recipients. We are spending approximately 225 million dollars a year in cash outlays to clients for payment....In addition to more access to public housing, we ought to be able to generate cooperatives and rehabilitate housing out of the rent monies of public assistance clients.[2]

How much do welfare recipients pay for rent? And do they pay more than those who do not receive welfare payments?

RENT PAID BY WELFARE RECIPIENTS

The states are not consistent about the maximum rent payments they will allow welfare recipients. A recent analysis by HEW details the past range. In most jurisdictions payments are not based on the current housing market but, at best, on historical averages or on dated cost-of-rental-surveys.

The rent allowance for a family of four receiving ADC in 1968 ranged from a maximum of $125 a month in Alaska to $27 per month in Tennessee. New York, one of the more generous states, allowed $80, but was lower than New Jersey, which at the time had no statutory limit and provided an average of approximately $100 per month. The low figure, nationally, was in rural Arkansas at $12, though the average for the state as a whole was $30.

The data by no means suggest that welfare payments, assuming maximum rents are allowed, are adequate for survival. In Indiana, for example, maximum monthly payments for welfare are $80 for food, clothing, utilities and all other expenses including rents. If the recipient paid the recorded standard of $50 per month rent, he would be left with $30 for all other expenses. In Mississippi the recipient would have $10 left from a grant of $50.

While the above data are for Old Age Assistance recipients, parallel situations exist in the AFDC program. In Alabama the maximum rent for a family of four is $40, and the maximum allowable allowance for a family of four is $89 a month. In Mississippi the same family, paying the maximum allowable rent, would have $5 left.

In jurisdictions in which total housing needs are met by the state, an average of 43 percent of the recipients' income is used to pay rent. According to the HEW study: "It appears, therefore, that the higher Old Age Assistance payments provide for higher shelter costs, rather than for generally higher level of living in states meeting 100 percent of need."[3]

WELFARE RENTS IN NEW YORK

In February 1969 the average monthly rents for public assistance recipients in New York state were estimated at $74.78 per case, an average of $26.78 per person. There is wide variation based on geograph area and type of living accommodation; even within a given social services district there is no consistent pattern.[4]

As shown in Exhibit 7.1, the median rent for all welfare families in New York City is $71.47. While this is higher than upstate urban areas, which have a $67.32 median rent, it is lower than suburban New York where the equivalent rent is $109.62.

EXHIBIT 7.1

MEDIAN RENT COSTS BY FAMILY SIZE AND AREA OF THE STATE

NUMBER IN HOUSEHOLD	RENT			
	New York City	Suburban N.Y.C.[a]	Upstate Urban[b]	Rest of State
One	$ 63	$ 78	$ 56	$ 46
Two	74	103	70	52
Three	78	121	73	65
Four	82	134	78	58
Five	85	133	80	64
Six	87	134	76	70
Seven	91	145	72	58
Eight	98	153	83	70
Nine	104	174[c]	82[c]	68[c]
Ten	113			
Eleven	121			
Twelve or More	135			
Median—All Families	71.47	109.62	67.32	54.26

Source: New York State Department of Social Services, Program Brief No. 2-1970.

a. Includes the counties of Nassau, Rockland, Suffolk and Westchester.

b. Includes the counties of Albany, Erie, Monroe, Niagara, Oneida, Onondaga, Rensselaer and Schenectady.

c. Nine or more persons.

Rentals in New York City for welfare recipients vary according to the type of living accommodations and the number of individuals in the household. Public housing rents are generally cheaper than privately owned accommodations. The average rent for a family of five, for example, is $87 per month, while in project apartments it is only $79. Unfurnished apartments for a five-member family, including private dwellings which are rented expressly to house particular families, average $88. Furnished apartments are rented at $92, with the costs for homeowners (0.1 percent of the total sample) running to $133.

Rents by Size of Household

Exhibit 7.2 shows the distribution of rent costs for one-, four- and ten-person welfare households in unfurnished, private apartments in

EXHIBIT 7.2

DISTRIBUTION OF RENT COSTS
FOR ONE-, FOUR- AND TEN-PERSON HOUSEHOLDS
IN UNFURNISHED NONPROJECT APARTMENTS IN NEW YORK CITY

MONTHLY RENT COSTS	CUMULATIVE PERCENTAGE OF CASES		
	One-Person Households	Four-Person Households	Ten-Person Households
Under $ 30	3.5%	0.9%	0.4%
$ 30 to 39	8.9	2.9	1.0
40 to 49	17.2	7.6	2.5
50 to 59	28.2	15.7	7.1
60 to 69	47.4	28.1	11.2
70 to 79	64.6	47.5	19.3
80 to 89	77.7	63.9	32.9
90 to 99	85.1	75.3	40.7
100 to 109	90.1	84.4	48.4
110 to 119	92.9	90.4	54.5
120 to 129	95.7	95.8	63.9
130 to 139	97.2	97.9	72.3
140 to 149	98.0	98.9	77.4
150 to 159	98.8	99.5	86.8
160 to 169	99.1	99.7	90.7
170 to 179	99.3	99.8	95.0
180 to 189	99.4	99.9	96.2
190 to 199	99.5	99.9	96.2
200 and Over	100.0	100.0	100.0

Source: New York State Department of Social Services, *Program Brief No. 2-1970.*

New York City. Nearly half of the one-person households are housed at under $70 a month, while for four-person households the equivalent cut-off is $80. Even a great many ten-person households (48.4 percent) are in accommodations costing less than $110 a month.

At the time of our survey, New York City's municipally aided cooperative housing under the Mitchell-Lama Program, which provides the builder tax reductions of as much as 85 percent as well as tax-exempt long-term mortgaging, charged rents of approximately $60 a month *per room.* Even if a family of four could be adequately housed in a three-room apartment, this would represent a rent expenditure of $180. In February of 1969 only 0.3 percent of four-person households on welfare paid $160 or more.

Rents by Category of Welfare

Exhibit 7.3 gives, by category of welfare, the percentiles, mean values and the interquartile ranges of total monthly housing costs of welfare recipients based upon field survey data. These costs include all utilities except the telephone. The high mean is in the ADC category, with a monthly rent of $106. The average Home Relief cases receive $90 per month with the average Old Age Assistance recipients just above and

EXHIBIT 7.3

TOTAL MONTHLY COST FOR HOUSING (MINUS TELEPHONE) BY CATEGORY OF WELFARE

		TOTAL MONTHLY COST										
		Percentile										
CATEGORY OF WELFARE	Number of Cases	10	20	30	40	50	60	70	80	90	Interquartile Range (25 to 75)	Mean
Home Relief	74	$ 60	$ 66	$ 72	$ 77	$ 84	$ 88	$ 99	$110	$123	$ 68 to $105	$ 89.66
Old Age Assistance	52	50	58	61	71	76	88	93	103	128	60 to 99	83.37
Aid to Disabled	57	43	55	65	68	72	77	83	96	112	60 to 89	79.35
Aid to Dependent Children	224	70	78	86	90	97	101	108	123	140	84 to 112	106.36
Total	407											

Source: Housing of Welfare Recipients Survey, 1970.

EXHIBIT 7.4

TOTAL MONTHLY COST FOR HOUSING (MINUS TELEPHONE) BY ETHNICITY

		TOTAL MONTHLY COST										
		Percentile										
ETHNICITY[a]	Number of Cases	10	20	30	40	50	60	70	80	90	Interquartile Range (25 to 75)	Mean
White	63	$ 55	$ 61	$ 71	$ 77	$ 86	$ 92	$105	$120	$180	$ 65 to $107	$102.56
Black	178	59	68	77	87	90	98	101	110	134	72 to 105	98.99
Spanish Speaking	163	62	71	77	82	87	97	103	112	134	75 to 109	93.85
Total	404											

Source: New York City Department of Social Service Data Processing Administration, March 1968.

a. The "Other" category is excluded because of insufficient number of cases.

the average Aid to Disabled recipients just below the $80 level. As illustrated by the percentile run as well as the interquartile ranges, there is a broad span of actual shelter costs within each of the several categories. Note the variation between the means and medians; in every case the former is higher than the median (the midway point in the sample). This indicates that more than half of the sample is below the mean values shown. While this discrepancy is minor in the case of Home Relief, it is significant for all three of the other categories where the variation is close to 10 percent. In sum, more than half of the Old Age Assistance group is living with shelter costs of $76 a month or less. The equivalent figure for Aid to Disabled is $72 and for ADC cases is still under $100.

When these data are analyzed by the respondent's ethnicity, whites in general seem to have higher shelter costs than minority groups (Exhibit 7.4). The tops of the interquartile levels, however, for all three categories are comparable. Further analysis shows that a few whites are housed at very high cost, typically elderly people in institutional facilities, which somewhat distorts the mean. Overall, however, whites are generally housed at a lower cost through the sixtieth percentile.

Unfortunately, variation in the respondents' ethnicity by category of welfare is too small to permit a thoroughgoing statistical analysis. Spanish-speaking respondents, however, whose size of household tends to be larger than blacks and whose welfare categories are closely matched, appear to pay less than blacks in shelter costs, at least based upon the median and mean data. While the average Spanish-speaking household is larger than the black, fully 60 percent of them are housed in cheaper facilities. Mean rentals of Spanish-speaking households are over $5 a month less than blacks.

Rent Variation by Borough

Rents are highest in Queens at an average $112.54, with an interquartile range of $75 to $148. The next highest borough is Brooklyn at $98.05, with the interquartile range $75 to $109. The Bronx has an interquartile range from $78 to $113, with a mean value of $96.67. Manhattan, which has the bulk of the single room occupancies, is the lowest with a mean figure of $92.85 and an interquartile range of $66 to $92.

Rents Per Room by Category of Welfare

Exhibit 7.5 contains the rents per room by category of welfare. Accepting the statistical limitations in the size of subsets, it is evident that rents per room decline quite sharply as the number of rooms per apartment is increased. The extraordinarily high one-room rent, which averages $101.68, is due to institutional facilities and hotel accommo-

EXHIBIT 7.5

MONTHLY RENT PER ROOM (MEAN DATA) AND NUMBER OF ROOMS BY CATEGORY OF WELFARE

	CATEGORY OF WELFARE									
	Home Relief		Old Age Assistance		Aid to Disabled		Aid to Dependent Children		Totals	
NUMBER OF ROOMS	Number Of Cases	Rent Per Room	Number Of Cases	Rent Per Room	Number Of Cases	Rent Per Room	Number Of Cases	Rent Per Room	Number Of Cases	Rent Per Room
One	2	$54.00	12	$104.75	7	$131.71	4	$63.75	25	$101.68
Two	3	39.33	3	43.00	4	30.25	6	53.50	16	43.06
Three	14	23.71	14	22.43	14	19.07	46	26.96	88	24.47
Four	21	19.43	11	15.91	15	16.87	84	21.55	131	20.20
Five	17	17.06	5	19.60	7	16.43	56	18.29	85	17.96
Six and Over	9	14.44	6	9.33	4	10.25	25	16.68	44	14.64
Total	66	$21.00	51	$ 39.78	51	$ 33.71	221	$22.93	389	$ 25.46

Source: Housing of Welfare Recipients Survey, 1970.

dations. The latter circumstances also have significant weight in two-room costs, which have a mean of $43.06 per room. The mean value for apartments of five or more rooms is less than $20 a room per month. Again the relative paucity of the rents when contrasted with the costs of providing appropriate housing is evident.

Rent Per Room by Welfare Concentration

When rents per room are analyzed by the concentration of welfare recipients within a building, it is clear that they are inversely related to the degree of welfare tenant concentration. In buildings 33 percent or more occupied by welfare recipients, the mean figure is barely $12 a month, while in those with 1 percent to 9 percent welfare tenantry, the equivalent figure is nearly $20. The same analysis, conducted for total apartment rents and correcting for the age and size of the building, provides clear-cut evidence that buildings with significant proportions of welfare occupants (i.e., in 20 percent or more of the apartments) generally have lower rents than buildings with few welfare tenants. While this in no way means that welfare tenants are getting housing value for their rent dollar, it does indicate that relatively little money is available from rents for massive improvement of the buildings.

Rent Per Thousand Square Feet by Welfare Concentration

There is no clear-cut picture when rent per thousand feet is examined by the degree of welfare tenancy in the building. The high of $87.80 a month per thousand square feet occurs in buildings with 1 to 9 percent of their tenants on welfare. The lowest amount ($70) is for those with no welfare tenants, but for buildings with 33 to 99 percent welfare tenants rents per thousand square feet are at $72.

As a further check on the rents paid by welfare recipients, we looked at the maximum monthly controlled rents per apartment by category of structures in 1967. We based our analysis on the rent-control sample described earlier, the welfare rolls and the rent-controlled apartment data on maximum permissible rents. We found that in old law structures the rents are barely $60 a month. For categories of new law structures with less than 50 units the equivalent figure is under $70. In new law buildings with 50 units or more, the average is around $80. Only in the post-1929 structures, which have very few welfare recipients, are mean rents over $100 a month. Nearly one-fourth of the apartments occupied by welfare recipients in old law structures (built before 1901 and typically most in need of major improvement) are renting at a maximum of $40 a month. In Chapter 8 the possibility of reallocating the funds gleaned from rent payments will be considered in detail. Ob-

EXHIBIT 7.6

WELFARE RENT AS A PERCENTAGE OF RENT FOR APARTMENTS WITH NO WELFARE DATA (1967) BY BUILDING CATEGORY

	WELFARE RENT AS A PERCENTAGE OF RENT FOR APARTMENTS WITH NO WELFARE DATA											
		Percentiles									Interquartile Range	
BUILDING CATEGORY	Number of Structures	10	20	30	40	50	60	70	80	90	(25% to 75%)	Mean
Old Law Structures												
Five to 19 Units	30	79%	93%	97%	101%	113%	121%	127%	137%	156%	96% to 130%	116.0%
20 Units or more	48	80	91	96	99	103	109	117	121	129	93 to 121	108.9
New Law Structures												
Five to 19 Units	15	82	90	96	105	107	110	112	127	137	93 to 117	110.8
20 to 49 Units	65	82	90	97	103	108	110	115	123	130	95 to 118	107.6
50 Units or More	58	78	83	96	103	106	109	111	117	124	91 to 115	102.9
Structures Built After 1929												
Ten to 49 Units	25	71	79	96	104	106	106	107	109	113	92 to 108	102.5
50 Units or More	15	15	89	91	96	97	100	101	106	138	90 to 102	104.8
Small Structures												
Three and Four Units	5	83	94	141	150	247	a	a	a	a	a a	a
Total	261											

Source: Geroge Sternlieb, *The Urban Housing Dilemma*, 1970.

a. Not enough cases to complete distribution.

EXHIBIT 7.7

WELFARE RENT (1967) AS A PERCENTAGE OF RENT FOR APARTMENTS WITH NO WELFARE DATA (1955) BY BUILDING CATEGORY

BUILDING CATEGORY	WELFARE RENT AS A PERCENTAGE OF RENT FOR APARTMENTS WITH NO WELFARE DATA											
		Percentiles									Interquartile Range	
	Number of Structures	10	20	30	40	50	60	70	80	90	(25% to 75%)	Mean
Old Law Structures												
Five to 19 Units	30	84%	91%	95%	98%	101%	106%	112%	127%	132%	92% to 119%	106.8%
20 Units or More	48	85	95	96	98	101	103	110	125	133	96 to 115	108.7
New Law Structures												
Five to 19 Units	15	80	92	92	96	102	107	110	114	127	92 to 111	105.9
20 to 49 Units	65	84	88	92	95	100	102	106	113	121	90 to 107	101.4
50 Units or More	58	79	85	89	94	98	103	107	109	115	88 to 107	98.3
Structures Built After 1929												
Ten to 49 Units	25	44	79	86	91	97	99	106	110	118	83 to 109	97.9
50 Units or More	15	73	85	86	88	90	93	97	103	112	85 to 101	95.4
Small Structures												
Three and Four Units	5	93	94	104	127	132	a	a	a	a	a a	a
Total	261											

Source: Sternlieb, *The Urban Housing Dilemma*, 1970.

a. Not enough cases to complete distribution.

viously, however, unless there is a massive increase in welfare rents, the funds required for massive capital improvements cannot be secured from this source.

DO WELFARE RECIPIENTS PAY MORE?

Earlier we described the negative feelings of landlords toward accepting welfare recipients and the degree of prejudice respondents indicate they feel in their search for residences. Is this reflected in the rent they pay?

To answer this question, we compared rents in apartments occupied by welfare recipients with average rents for other apartments in the same building. This involved taking the March 1968 check tape and screening out welfare tenants in the 30,000 apartments for which we had information about rents. For half of the 1,771 welfare recipients within these buildings, we found specific apartment numbers on the check tapes which coincided with those of the rent-control records. Exhibit 7.6, based on this analysis, compares the average rents for welfare apartments as a percentage of rent for apartments in the same building with no welfare residents. This is presented by category of structure.

In every category of building the mean rents paid by welfare recipients are higher than those of other residents. Rents from welfare recipients range from 116 percent of non-welfare rents (in the 5 to 19 unit old law structures) down to 102.5 percent (in the ten to 49 unit structures built after 1929). This information is substantially confirmed by the interquartile ranges where, except for structures built after 1929, the welfare recipients on the average pay more than non-recipients. However, in every building category, a significant number of structures (at least 30 percent) have lower welfare rents than non-welfare rents.

Clearly, there is substantial variation in the desirability of units as a result of location, configuration and so forth. In order to reduce the impact of these extraneous variables, we conducted a separate analysis for the same apartments using rent control maximums as of 1955. Since these apartment rents were closer to the inception of the Rent Control Law (1943) their rents are probably more indicative of free market levels. Also there was a much lower occupancy of welfare tenancy extant in 1955 (see Chapter 1). The results of this analysis are presented in Exhibit 7.7, which shows the rent control maximums for apartments occupied by welfare recipients in 1967 compared to apartments in the same structure not occupied by welfare recipients; both of these are based on 1955 figures. It is evident that in 1955, 12 years before the 1967 data were accumulated, those apartments which later were occupied by welfare recipients were comparable in price to those occupied

EXHIBIT 7.8

DEGREE OF WELFARE TENANTRY: LANDLORD REPORT VERSUS WELFARE RECORD DATA

DEGREE OF WELFARE TENANTRY[b]	PERCENT ON WELFARE[a]											
	All Structures		0%		1% to 9%		10% to 19%		20% to 32%		33% to 99%	
	No.	%	No.	%	No.	%	No.	%	No.	%	No.	%
None	25,700	49.0	20,400	75.6	2,700	41.3	900	17.3	400	8.3	1,200	14.8
Less Than 10%	4,400	8.4	700	2.5	2,100	32.4	1,100	21.8	400	8.2	0	0.3
10% to 20%	4,000	7.6	1,400	5.2	600	9.3	600	11.5	1,100	21.7	200	2.7
20% to 50%	8,700	16.5	1,900	6.9	400	5.8	1,100	21.2	2,300	42.8	3,100	36.5
Over 50%	3,800	7.2	700	2.5	0	0.4	100	2.7	500	9.4	2,400	29.0
Some—No Breakdown	4,000	7.6	700	2.7	500	7.1	1,000	20.2	500	9.6	1,200	14.5
NA/DK	1,900	3.7	1,200	4.6	200	3.7	300	5.4	0	0.0	200	2.2
Total	52,400	100.0	27,000	100.0	6,600	100.0	5,200	100.0	5,300	100.0	8,400	100.0

Source: Sternlieb, *The Urban Housing Dilemma,* 1970.

Note: Numbers may not add precisely because of rounding.

a. Landlord estimate.
b. Check-tape data.

by non-welfare recipients. This has not been the case in more recent years.

Since the data were accumulated by welfare occupied apartments versus non-welfare occupied apartments within the same building, variables of area, building and the like have been substantially equalized. By using the same apartment rents as a base over time, other elements, assuming there have been no massive capital inputs, are similarly standardized. Thus, the rents of apartments presently occupied by welfare recipients have gone up more sharply than have the rest of the apartments within the same building, and to the degree that the 1955 data accurately reflect the market, they indicate that welfare recipients pay more for their housing than non-recipients.

In 1955 the apartments which also housed welfare recipients in 1967 were rented for from 95.4 percent to 108.7 percent of the cost of other units in the same building. In 1967 the range was 102.5 percent to 116 percent. Regardless of category, the increases are substantial—an average of 5 or 6 percent. In 1955 apartments which later housed welfare recipients were roughly comparable in rent to others in the same structure. By 1967 this was no longer the case; the welfare apartments were substantially higher in average rent levels. The number of buildings for which data could be found about welfare occupancy and specific apartment numbers which correspond to rent-control records was 261; their distribution within building groups is presented in Exhibits 7.6 and 7.7.[5]

OWNERSHIP OF WELFARE BUILDINGS

In an earlier study[6] the negative attitude of owners toward housing welfare recipients was described in detail. The use of two-party checks, that is, checks for rent issued by the Welfare Department which must be endorsed by the welfare recipient as well as the landlord, is a comparative rarity in New York. It currently involves less than 4 percent of all welfare households. Despite this, landlords seem quite aware of who is and who isn't on welfare. Exhibit 7.8 gives the comparison of the reported levels of welfare recipiency within their structures indicated by landlords in interviews conducted at the end of 1967 and in early 1968 and equivalent data secured from the Welfare Department records as of early 1968. While landlords tend to overstate the degree of welfare slightly, in general their estimates agree with Welfare Department records. Landlord awareness may be a significant factor affecting their judgement and inputs to the building.

Who are the "welfare owners"? Is there a dominant type? The conventional wisdom is that the typical welfare building is in the hands of

EXHIBIT 7.9

NUMBER OF YEARS LANDLORD HAS OWNED RENTAL REAL ESTATE BY DEGREE OF WELFARE TENANTRY WITHIN STRUCTURE

	DEGREE OF WELFARE TENANTRY WITHIN STRUCTURES															
YEARS OF OWNERSHIP	None		1% to 10%		11% to 20%		21% to 30%		31% to 40%		41% to 60%		61% to 100%		Total	
	No.	%	No.	%	No.	%	No.	%	No.	%	No.	%	No.	%	No.	%
Less Than Two Years	764	2.8	151	1.9	123	2.4	20	0.5	131	3.6	322	9.6	0	0.0	1,511	2.9
Two to Five Years	1,644	6.1	528	6.7	692	13.8	262	6.7	597	16.3	394	11.7	296	16.1	4,413	8.4
Five to Ten Years	5,233	19.4	1,228	15.5	872	17.4	897	22.9	1,099	30.0	426	12.7	288	15.7	10,043	19.1
Ten to 20 Years	6,862	25.4	1,789	22.6	1,318	26.2	801	20.4	616	16.8	1,344	40.0	937	51.1	13,667	25.9
Over 20 Years	12,348	45.7	4,068	51.4	1,667	33.2	1,939	49.5	1,226	33.4	775	23.1	314	17.1	22,337	42.4
NA/DK	147	0.5	148	1.9	352	7.0	0	0.0	0	0.0	98	2.9	0	0.0	745	1.4
Total	26,998	100.0	7,912	100.0	5,024	100.0	3,919	100.0	3,669	100.0	3,359	100.0	1,835	100.0	52,716	100.0

Source: Sternlieb, *The Urban Housing Dilemma*, 1970.

EXHIBIT 7.10

NUMBER OF YEARS LANDLORD HAS OWNED PROPERTY IN QUESTION BY DEGREE OF WELFARE TENANTRY WITHIN STRUCTURES

YEARS OF OWNERSHIP	DEGREE OF WELFARE TENANTRY WITHIN STRUCTURES															
	None		1% to 10%		11% to 20%		21% to 30%		31% to 40%		41% to 60%		61% to 100%		Total	
	No.	%	No.	%	No.	%	No.	%	No.	%	No.	%	No.	%	No.	%
Less Than One Year	919	3.4	417	5.3	466	9.3	255	6.5	165	4.5	190	5.7	0	0.0	2,412	4.6
One to Three Years	2,514	9.3	668	8.4	659	13.1	565	14.4	511	13.9	551	16.4	262	14.3	5,730	10.9
Three to Five Years	2,530	9.4	785	9.9	747	14.9	288	7.3	1,017	27.7	196	5.8	165	9.0	5,728	10.9
Five to Seven Years	2,046	7.6	605	7.6	275	5.5	184	4.7	330	9.0	177	5.3	196	10.7	3,813	7.2
Seven to Nine Years	2,949	10.9	864	10.9	811	16.1	484	12.4	621	16.9	467	13.9	157	8.6	6,353	12.1
Nine to 11 Years	1,682	6.2	350	4.4	126	2.5	682	17.4	45	1.2	428	12.7	157	8.6	3,470	6.6
11 to 15 Years	2,318	8.6	683	8.6	550	10.9	182	4.6	182	5.0	714	21.3	584	31.8	5,213	9.9
Over 15 Years	11,520	42.7	3,237	40.9	1,134	22.6	1,279	32.6	798	21.7	616	18.3	314	17.1	18,898	35.8
NA/DK	520	1.9	303	3.8	256	5.1	0	0.0	0	0.0	20	0.6	0	0.0	1,099	2.1
Total	26,998	100.0	7,912	100.0	5,024	100.0	3,919	100.0	3,669	100.0	3,359	100.0	1,835	100.0	52,716	100.0

Source: Sternlieb, *The Urban Housing Dilemma,* 1970.

major realtors or large slumlords, and thus subject to high turnover as a result of a variety of manipulations. In order to discover the actual situation, we analyzed 714 interviews secured from a structured probability sample of the owners of 963 rent-controlled buildings in New York City.[7] The responses of the building owners to a variety of questions were cross-tabulated by the degree of welfare occupancy within the building, based on the listing of all welfare recipients. The data which follow result from these analyses.

LENGTH OF TIME IN BUSINESS

Most of New York City's residential landlords are relatively seasoned property holders. Are the owners of buildings largely inhabited by welfare tenants distinctive in this respect? Are they newcomers to the real estate business or experienced operators? Exhibit 7.9 contains the pyramided results (weighted by building structure category and multiplied by the incidence of such buildings within the total universe sampled) of the answers to this question. They reveal that approximately 1,000 of the 5,400 structures with more than 40 percent of their tenants on welfare are in the hands of owners who entered the real estate market within the last five years. The owners of buildings with few or no welfare tenants, on the other hand, have the greatest longevity in the realty business.

While there is some variation among categories, most of the heavily welfare tenanted structures are held by long-term realty operators. Over 60 percent of the buildings more than 40 percent occupied by tenants on welfare are owned by individuals who have been in the business for ten or more years.

REASONS FOR PURCHASE

Recent changes in the tax law have made it more difficult for owners to secure accelerated depreciation and with it augmented tax rebates for real estate investments. This may have caused a slowdown in the high level of property turnover which was once thought to characterize the market.

Certainly, the data shown in Exhibit 7.10 do not show a particularly great number of structure transfers within recent years. While there are slightly more recent buyers (holders for less than three years) among the owners of buildings with few tenants on welfare, the great majority of the structures in all categories have been owned for long periods of time. Nearly 40 percent (39.6 percent of the 3,400 structures in the 41 percent to 60 percent welfare tenant category) have been held by the same owner for 11 or more years and the percentage of

EXHIBIT 7.11

OWNER'S REASON FOR KEEPING PROPERTY OF DEGREE OF WELFARE TENANTRY WITHIN STRUCTURES (1968)

RESPONSE	PERCENT ON WELFARE															
	None		1% to 10%		11% to 20%		21% to 30%		31% to 40%		41% to 60%		61% to 100%		Total	
	No.	%	No.	%	No.	%	No.	%	No.	%	No.	%	No.	%	No.	%
Yes (Same reason that caused purchase)	16,682	61.8	4,242	53.6	2,487	49.5	1,646	42.0	1,678	45.7	1,251	37.2	726	39.6	28,712	54.5
Want to Sell – Listed With Broker	2,562	9.5	715	9.0	1,185	23.6	643	16.4	767	20.9	249	7.4	723	39.4	6,844	13.0
Want to Sell – Not Listed With Broker	2,810	10.4	788	10.0	375	7.5	465	11.9	412	11.2	815	24.3	0	0.0	5,665	10.7
Want to Sell – No Buyer	1,872	6.9	1,554	19.6	786	15.6	903	23.0	787	21.4	879	26.2	288	15.7	7,069	13.4
Income	547	2.0	300	3.8	0	0.0	131	3.3	0	0.0	0	0.0	0	0.0	978	1.9
Land Appreciation	238	0.9	190	2.4	28	0.6	131	3.3	0	0.0	0	0.0	0	0.0	587	1.1
Tax Purposes	45	0.2	0	0.0	20	0.4	0	0.0	0	0.0	0	0.0	0	0.0	65	0.1
Other	2,045	7.6	98	1.2	123	2.4	0	0.0	25	0.7	165	4.9	98	5.3	2,554	4.8
NA/DK	197	0.7	25	0.3	20	0.4	0	0.0	0	0.0	0	0.0	0	0.0	242	0.5
Total	26,998	100.0	7,912	100.0	5,024	100.0	3,919	100.0	3,669	100.0	3,359	100.0	1,835	100.0	52,716	100.0

Sources: Sternlieb, *The Urban Housing Dilemma*, 1970.
New York City Department of Social Service Data Processing Administration, March 1968.

structures with over 60 percent of their tenants on welfare is even higher (48.9 percent). This is quite comparable to buildings with few of their tenants on welfare. The problems of the "welfare structures" as a group are therefore not directly related to high turnover in ownership.

Analysis of owners' answers to the question "Why did you buy your parcel?" shows no striking variation in responses. The proportion of welfare-building owners who buy for capital improvement is close to that of the entire group.

The one significant variation is in the proportion of welfare-building owners who secure their buildings through foreclosure. While only 1.6 percent of the weighted total of 53,000 owners acquire their buildings in this manner 260 out of the 1,800 buildings with 61 percent to 99 percent of the tenants on welfare and 123 out of 3,400 (3.7 percent) of the structures with 41 percent to 60 percent of their tenants on welfare had done so. The next highest category was the buildings with 31 percent to 40 percent of their tenants on welfare in which 2.7 percent of the 3,700 had acquired their buildings through foreclosure. In no other category was the incidence over 2 percent.

There are any number of reasons why a high level of foreclosures occurs in buildings with a large number of residents on welfare. Not the least among them is the practice of owners in poor areas who, unable to find cash buyers or institutional financing and anxious to get rid of their parcels because of housing violations and/or other problems, sell them to local residents and sometimes even tenants. This is usually accompanied by inflated purchase money mortgages, i.e., mortgages granted by the seller. The heavy debt service charges involved frequently result in default on the mortgage and the reacquisition of the parcel by the seller.[8]

Regardless of the reasons, however, a significant number of structures are in the hands of their owners not by design but by default. It is difficult to envision any substantial capital investment resulting from this situation.

REASONS FOR KEEPING THE PROPERTY

Exhibit 7.11 shows owners' attitudes toward keeping their buildings. As the proportion of welfare tenants in their buildings increases, the owners' level of satisfaction with the possession of the structure quite abruptly declines. More than three out of five of the owners of structures without welfare residents retain the motivation which they possessed at the time of purchase. The proportion that retains a desire to keep the building decreases, however, as the level of welfare tenancy increases until, for buildings more than 40 percent inhabited by welfare

EXHIBIT 7.12

SCALE OF OWNERS' HOLDINGS BY DEGREE OF WELFARE TENANTRY WITHIN STRUCTURES

SIZE OF HOLDINGS	DEGREE OF WELFARE TENANTRY WITHIN STRUCTURES															
	None		1% to 10%		11% to 20%		21% to 30%		31% to 40%		41% to 60%		61% to 100%		Total	
	No.	%	No.	%	No.	%	No.	%	No.	%	No.	%	No.	%	No.	%
No Other	12,602	46.7	1,452	18.4	1,213	24.1	1,233	31.5	1,570	42.8	1,827	54.4	618	33.7	20,515	38.9
Other—Not Resident	453	1.7	60	0.8	177	3.5	0	0.0	0	0.0	0	0.0	0	0.0	690	1.3
One to Two More	5,808	21.5	1,105	14.0	1,226	24.4	1,252	31.9	766	20.9	759	22.6	543	29.6	11,459	21.7
Three to Six More	3,100	11.5	1,507	19.0	949	18.9	303	7.7	275	7.5	328	9.8	0	0.0	6,462	12.3
Seven to 12 More	1,788	6.6	616	7.8	460	9.2	406	10.4	347	9.5	229	6.8	288	15.7	4,134	7.8
13 to 25 More	583	2.2	928	11.7	25	0.5	288	7.3	123	3.4	60	1.8	0	0.0	2,007	3.8
26 and Over	984	3.6	886	11.2	550	10.9	299	7.6	411	11.2	156	4.6	386	21.0	3,672	7.0
Other	1,490	5.5	1,283	16.2	267	5.3	138	3.5	177	4.8	0	0.0	0	0.0	3,355	6.4
NA/DK	190	0.7	75	0.9	157	3.1	0	0.0	0	0.0	0	0.0	0	0.0	422	0.8
Total	26,998	100.0	7,912	100.0	5,024	100.0	3,919	100.0	3,669	100.0	3,359	100.0	1,835	100.0	52,716	100.0

Source: Sternlieb, *The Urban Housing Dilemma*, 1970.

tenants, the "constant interest" responses are two out of five. Conversely, those who indicate a desire to sell are generally found to be owners of heavily welfare-tenanted buildings.

If those landlords who want to sell and who are listed with brokers, and those who are not listed with brokers and want to sell but have no buyer are grouped together, they represent slightly over one out of four of the buildings with no welfare tenants. Close to 50 percent of the landlords of buildings with a great number of welfare tenants are ready to sell. The number of those who want to sell but have no buyer varies from only 6.9 percent for the "no welfare tenant" structures to more than double that in each of the other categories.

In essence, these are owners by default, owners looking forward to the sale of their building or wanting to sell, or worse yet, owners who feel that they are trapped for lack of purchasers. Their interest in improving the structures is clearly limited. Could it be reactivated? Or is an alternate, institutional form of holding the answer? We will turn to these questions in a later chapter.

SCALE OF HOLDINGS

Most buildings which house a great many welfare tenants are in the hands of small-scale owners who have, at most, one or two additional parcels. More than three out of four of the structures with 40 percent to 60 percent welfare tenants and nearly as many (63.3 percent) of those with 61 percent to 99 percent of the residents on welfare are owned by small owners. The very large owners, on the other hand, who hold 26 or more parcels, account for 21 percent of the buildings most heavily tenanted by welfare recipients (Exhibit 7.12) compared with 7 percent for the weighted projection as a whole. Nevertheless there is little statistical linkage between large-scale owners' holdings and a high level of welfare tenancy. Most of the parcels are in the hands of relatively modest owners.

This is further corroborated when owner occupation is considered. About 30 percent of the total weighted sample structures is in the hands of professional real estate operators with an additional 3.2 percent in the hands of lawyers, many of whom are essentially working full time in real estate. Structures with over 60 percent of their tenants on welfare are 29.6 percent owned by professional real estate operators with no lawyers represented. In structures with 41 percent to 60 percent of their tenants on welfare, the equivalent figures are 12.3 and 8.8 percent. The professional landlord plays a major role in structures with only a few tenants on welfare (less than 10 percent); more than half of these buildings (52.7 percent) are held by professionals, with an additional 6.1 percent in the hands of lawyers.

EXHIBIT 7.13

PROPORTION OF INCOME FROM REALTY HOLDINGS BY DEGREE OF WELFARE TENANTRY WITHIN STRUCTURES

PROPORTION OF INCOME FROM REAL ESTATE	DEGREE OF WELFARE TENANTRY WITHIN STRUCTURES															
	None		1% to 10%		11% to 20%		21% to 30%		31% to 40%		41% to 60%		61% to 100%		Total	
	No.	%	No.	%	No.	%	No.	%	No.	%	No.	%	No.	%	No.	%
Full Time Real Estate Owner (3/4 of Income or More)	5,869	21.7	3,832	48.4	1,354	27.0	1,352	34.5	948	25.8	445	13.2	543	29.6	14,343	27.2
Substantial (1/3 to 3/4)	3,702	13.7	1,892	23.9	564	11.2	336	8.6	325	8.9	700	20.8	255	13.9	7,774	14.7
Minor Supplement	15,639	57.9	1,881	23.8	2,843	56.6	2,074	52.9	2,396	65.3	1,775	52.8	906	49.4	27,514	52.2
No Income, Self-sustaining	803	3.0	282	3.6	8	0.2	157	4.0	0	0.0	0	0.0	131	7.1	1,381	2.6
Claims No Loss on Operation	846	3.1	0	0.0	255	5.1	0	0.0	0	0.0	439	13.1	0	0.0	1,540	2.9
NA/DK	139	0.5	25	0.3	0	0.0	0	0.0	0	0.0	0	0.0	0	0.0	164	0.3
Total	26,998	100.0	7,912	100.0	5,024	100.0	3,919	100.0	3,669	100.0	3,359	100.0	1,835	100.0	52,716	100.0

Source: Sternlieb, *The Urban Housing Dilemma*, 1970.

Who then owns heavily welfare-tenanted buildings? House skill oriented craftsmen (plumbers, electricians, carpenters and so on) own 20.9 percent of the 41 percent to 60 percent welfare tenanted structures and nearly the same proportion of the 31 percent to 40 percent structures, but none of the very heavily welfare-tenanted structures with 61 percent to 99 percent of their tenants on welfare. In the latter category 16.1 percent of the owners hold other professional and managerial occupations. Between 25 and 30 percent are owned by non-house skill oriented craftsmen of one kind or another and an additional 12 or 13 percent are owned by retired or unemployed individuals. In sum, there is little to corroborate the assumption that buildings largely tenanted by welfare recipients are more frequently owned by large-scale professional landlords than are other structures.*

To confirm this finding, owners were asked what proportions of their income came from their realty holdings. In general, buildings with a substantial number of tenants on welfare have about as many owners whose incomes are completely derived from realty as do those with only a few such residents. In none of the building categories with a high proportion of welfare tenants does this type of owner account for more than 30 percent.

The full-time/full-income operators are most predominant in buildings with only 1 percent to 10 percent of their tenants on welfare. This is also true of those who secure a substantial part of their incomes (33 percent to 75 percent) from rentals (Exhibit 7.13). For about half of the owners of the buildings largely inhabited by welfare tenants, realty holdings represented simply a minor income supplement. Later, the actual incomes derived from the operation of the buildings will be analyzed in detail. First, however, we will analyze patterns of owner ethnicity.

OWNER ETHNICITY

Exhibit 7.14 is a weighted projection of the sample universe of 53,000 structures and their degree of welfare tenantry by owner ethnicity. In New York City most housing, regardless of welfare occupancy, is owned by whites. It is evident, however, that minority owned structures tend to be concentrated in buildings largely occupied by welfare tenants. Of the structures in the category with over 60 percent of their tenants on welfare for which data on the owner's ethnicity are available, 35 percent are minority group owned. The same is true of a nearly equal pro-

* The city both in the course of urban renewal and as the "owner of last resort" of parcels abandoned by their owners operated over 2,000 multiple dwelling structures in 1970. Many of these were inhabited by welfare recipients.

EXHIBIT 7.14

ETHNICITY OF OWNER BY DEGREE OF WELFARE TENANTRY WITHIN STRUCTURES

OWNER'S ETHNICITY	DEGREE OF WELFARE TENANTRY WITHIN STRUCTURES															
	None		1% to 10%		11% to 20%		21% to 30%		31% to 40%		41% to 60%		60% to 100%		Total	
	No.	%	No.	%	No.	%	No.	%	No.	%	No.	%	No.	%	No.	%
White	23,288	86.3	7,371	93.2	4,121	82.0	3,394	86.6	2,094	57.1	2,195	65.3	1,060	57.8	43,523	82.6
Spanish Speaking	757	2.8	0	0.0	275	5.5	0	0.0	314	8.6	683	20.3	322	17.5	2,351	4.5
Negro	2,463	9.1	419	5.3	353	7.0	517	13.2	922	25.1	481	14.3	322	17.5	5,477	10.4
NA/DK	490	1.8	122	1.5	275	5.5	8	0.2	339	9.2	0	0.0	131	7.1	1,365	2.6
Total	26,998	100.0	7,912	100.0	5,024	100.0	3,919	100.0	3,669	100.0	3,359	100.0	1,835	100.0	52,716	100.0

Source: Sternlieb, *The Urban Housing Dilemma,* 1970.

EXHIBIT 7.15

EXPENSES AS A PERCENTAGE OF NET RENT RECEIVED BY PERCENT OF NEW YORK CITY WELFARE (1968)

PERCENT ON WELFARE	EXPENSES AS A PERCENTAGE OF NET RENT RECEIVED											
	Total Structures	Percentiles 10	20	30	40	50	60	70	80	90	Interquartile Range (25% to 75%)	Mean
None	26,921	40%	46%	50%	52%	54%	57%	61%	69%	82%	47% to 65%	60.5%
1% to 10%	8,350	46	49	53	55	58	60	63	67	81	51 to 65	60.5
11% to 20%	5,042	47	52	57	60	62	66	71	78	86	53 to 76	68.7
21% to 30%	3,746	45	46	49	51	54	57	62	66	72	47 to 62	57.3
31% to 40%	3,757	41	42	52	53	56	58	61	68	87	49 to 68	59.6
41% to 60%	3,393	44	53	54	58	63	66	71	80	87	53 to 73	66.7
61% to 100%	1,630	44	53	55	65	66	69	75	81	91	53 to 81	67.1
Total	52,839											

Source: Sternlieb, *The Urban Housing Dilemma,* 1970.

portion of the 41 percent to 60 percent welfare tenanted structures. The contrast is obvious when we focus on buildings with 1 percent to 10 percent welfare tenants; the total number of apartments in such buildings owned by minority group operators is only 1.4 percent. Despite the dominance of white ownership, minority group owners play a fairly significant role in the housing of welfare recipients.

How can these data best be summed up? Certainly, it is difficult to discern a "welfare landlord" type which is discrete and singular from the balance of the market. The most salient and striking feature of the "welfare landlord" is that he is more likely to be a member of a minority group than is the non-welfare landlord. Certainly in terms of the scale of operation, occupational level and income received, there is little evidence that large-scale professionalism is the dominant form of ownership in welfare tenanted buildings.

The owners' degree of professionalism and occupations are all essential factors in investment behavior. Even more central, however, are the actual costs of operating welfare structures—their profits and losses.

PROFITABILITY OF WELFARE HOUSING

Are operating profits secured from welfare buildings competitive with other forms of investment? Could they support an even higher level of capital investment?

Earlier in this chapter we discussed the actual rents paid by welfare recipients compared to others in the same structure. Our information indicates that welfare recipients do pay more, and that, based upon historical analysis of the rent levels within these particular apartments, these rents are somewhat higher than those for equivalent accommodations. Further analysis of the actual rents paid by recipients shows them to be relatively modest.

But the modesty of the rent payment must be measured by the level of amenity that it secures. Does a pattern of low expenditures and poor repairs characterize the housing occupied by welfare recipients and, in turn, yield substantial operating profits? In the following section we will focus on this question.

The analysis will undertake initially to examine the *expenses* of operating welfare buildings. The definition of expense used here is a relatively limited one. It includes management,[9] legal and accounting costs, wages, taxes, insurance, rubbish and garbage removal, fuel, electricity, water and sewer, janitorial, exterminator and furnishing. Repair costs include: plumbing, electrical, masonry, glazing and other costs more specifically a function of wear and tear. The full definition of repair costs includes: painting, elevator, roofing, plumbing, heating and air conditioning, masonry, glass, floor work and grounds.

When expenses and repair costs are deducted from the rent, the remainder is the *operating profit*—the contribution to debt service, if any, depreciation and ultimately to profits. The third part of this analysis will examine this key variable.

Most residential realty has some form of *debt financing* involved in its acquisition. This subject is of such consequence that it is reserved for a later chapter.

A fourth part of this analysis will concern *cash flow.* This is a key variable in landlord decision-making. It involves the measurement of actual amounts of cash dollars produced by the operations of buildings after debt service is taken into account. It does not, however, include depreciation, i.e., the decline in capital value of the building as a function of its aging. From a cash flow point of view (and often in terms of the actual market value of the structure) depreciation is strictly a "bookkeeping" figure. The building which for tax purposes may show a decline in value of 3 percent a year, in terms of the actual market, may not have altered in value at all. Depreciation does, however, provide a significant tax shield, that is, a tax shelter income for owners, typically those in higher tax brackets. Depreciation, both in terms of present levels and its potential as a source of funds for rehabilitation, will be discussed in the next chapter.

The final item is *net taxable income.* This differs from cash flow in that the amortization of the mortgage on the parcel, if any, is included as part of the income of the building. As an offset, however, amortization is allowed as a deduction. Since it incorporates all the vagaries of debt structure and depreciation practice, net taxable income is perhaps the weakest measure of profitability.

EXPENSES

As mentioned earlier, the term "expenses" as used here attempts to segregate most of the elements involved in the operations of structures which essentially are fixed either by the requirements of the structure or by law or both.

The first question is whether expenses as a percentage of net rent received vary with the proportion of the building's occupants who are on welfare. Exhibit 7.15 projects results of the data secured during the course of the rent control study on expenses as a percentage of net rent received by the percentage of residents on welfare.

The pattern is far from one-sided. Certainly, at a minimum, the expenses in buildings which house a greater proportion of welfare tenants

EXHIBIT 7.16

ANNUAL EXPENSE PER APARTMENT BY DEGREE OF WELFARE TENANTRY (1968)

PERCENT ON WELFARE	ANNUAL EXPENSES PER APARTMENT											
	Number of Structures	Percentiles 10	20	30	40	50	60	70	80	90	Interquartile Range (25% to 75%)	Mean
None	26,921	$336	$397	$433	$480	$519	$563	$640	$730	$845	$415 to $682	$576
1% to 10%	8,350	357	412	432	466	491	539	579	613	693	419 to 591	525
11% to 20%	5,042	276	303	365	426	461	503	551	583	627	363 to 562	455
21% to 30%	3,746	324	344	381	449	486	496	542	638	647	356 to 607	486
31% to 40%	3,757	333	395	425	438	480	536	554	588	635	399 to 583	488
41% to 60%	3,393	244	308	407	495	521	527	615	815	1182	398 to 815	598
61% to 100%	1,630	444	449	449	454	493	532	532	561	618	449 to 561	520
Total	52,839											

Sources: Sternlieb, *The Urban Housing Dilemma,* 1970.
New York City Department of Social Service Data Processing Administration, March 1968.

EXHIBIT 7.17

ANNUAL EXPENSES PER ROOM (1967) BY DEGREE OF WELFARE TENANTRY WITHIN STRUCTURE (1968)

PERCENT ON WELFARE	ANNUAL EXPENSES PER ROOM											
	Number of Structures	Percentiles 10	20	30	40	50	60	70	80	90	Interquartile Range (25% to 75%)	Mean
None	25,224	$71	$80	$91	$107	$118	$133	$147	$166	$188	$86 to $155	$125.71
1% to 10%	7,378	86	106	117	131	140	146	157	175	199	112 to 168	143.23
11% to 20%	4,634	69	85	92	101	107	114	120	145	162	90 to 131	118.61
21% to 30%	3,510	73	80	95	98	101	108	116	123	159	94 to 119	106.04
31% to 40%	3,467	80	86	97	99	104	109	112	116	133	86 to 114	104.74
41% to 60%	3,103	47	61	84	87	93	95	115	128	165	71 to 124	99.64
61% to 100%	1,630	73	88	105	111	112	112	114	114	154	102 to 114	111.11
Total	48,946											

Sources: Sternlieb, *The Urban Housing Dilemma,* 1970.
New York City Department of Social Service Data Processing Administration, March 1968.

are typically as much, and in a significant number of cases more, than they are in buildings with few or no apartments housing welfare recipients. Note, particularly, the upper quartile figures for the structures with 41 percent to 60 percent and 61 percent to 100 percent of their tenants on welfare. For one-fourth of each of those cases the expenses as a percentage of net rent received are 73 percent and 81 percent of the total rent dollars, respectively. This figure is significantly higher than that for the buildings under 10 percent occupied by welfare tenants: in these expenses are 65 percent of rents. This indicates that the buildings welfare recipients live in often have few cash resources from the property with which to service other expenditures.

But, as has already been seen, rent levels differ significantly as a function of the degree of welfare tenantry. What are the dollar data?

Annual expense costs per apartment by the degree of welfare tenantry are shown in Exhibit 7.16. While expenses are somewhat lower generally in welfare structures, our information does not imply that substantial low expense windfalls result from a high level of welfare tenantry.

Analysis of annual expenses per room is shown in Exhibit 7.17. The fact that buildings with a large number of welfare tenants have a relatively large number of rooms per apartment influences the data somewhat. But, if the structures with the highest level of welfare—with more than 60 percent of their tenants on welfare—are excluded, there is a reasonably clear-cut gradient: the low figure is 41 percent to 60 percent welfare residents with a mean expense of slightly under $100 per room. The figures ascend to a high of $143 for structures with from 1 percent to 10 percent of the tenants on welfare.

In sum, therefore, the relatively fixed expenditures grouped as expenses do not vary significantly as a consequence of the resident being on welfare, when measured as a percentage of net rents received. This is also true in terms of annual costs per apartment. When analyzed by expenditures per room, however, there is a significant correlation between welfare status and low expenditures. This correlation shows up because welfare recipients generally live in larger apartments than non-recipients. Are less repairs done in apartments occupied by welfare recipients?

REPAIR COSTS

Repair costs take up a larger proportion of the rent dollar in buildings with a high proportion of welfare tenants than in those with few or no tenants on welfare. The lowest repair expenditures as a percentage of rents are in buildings with 1 percent to 10 percent welfare

EXHIBIT 7.18

ANNUAL REPAIR COSTS AS A PERCENTAGE OF NET RENT RECEIVED BY DEGREE OF WELFARE TENANTRY (1968)

PERCENT ON WELFARE	Number of Structures	ANNUAL REPAIR COSTS AS A PERCENTAGE OF NET RENT										
		Percentiles 10	20	30	40	50	60	70	80	90	Interquartile Range (25% to 75%)	Mean
None	26,060	4%	6%	9%	11%	12%	14%	17%	21%	27%	8% to 19%	15.6%
1% to 10%	8,185	5	7	8	9	11	12	13	15	17	7 to 14	11.0
11% to 20%	5,042	7	8	10	13	17	19	21	26	33	9 to 25	18.0
21% to 30%	3,746	5	7	10	13	13	16	18	20	22	8 to 18	14.2
31% to 40%	3,757	8	10	12	13	15	19	20	30	34	11 to 28	18.1
41% to 60%	3,393	5	7	10	14	15	17	20	22	29	9 to 21	16.5
61% to 100%	1,630	8	18	19	19	19	20	24	33	34	18 to 33	20.0
Total	51,813											

Sources: Sternlieb, *The Urban Housing Dilemma,* 1970.
New York City Department of Social Service Data Processing Administration, March 1968.

EXHIBIT 7.19

ANNUAL REPAIR COSTS PER APARTMENT BY DEGREE OF WELFARE TENANTRY (1968)

PERCENT ON WELFARE	Number of Structures	ANNUAL REPAIR COSTS PER APARTMENT										
		Percentiles 10	20	30	40	50	60	70	80	90	Interquartile Range (25% to 75%)	Mean
None	26,060	$48	$ 66	$ 86	$100	$113	$138	$166	$207	$288	$ 78 to $183	$144.50
1% to 10%	8,185	49	60	69	78	100	105	117	129	154	63 to 122	98.87
11% to 20%	5,042	42	67	74	85	114	128	131	150	208	70 to 137	115.51
21% to 30%	3,746	46	73	81	85	88	136	144	170	194	75 to 159	118.17
31% to 40%	3,757	66	91	100	111	130	144	178	217	244	97 to 211	155.53
41% to 60%	3,393	41	57	75	100	126	143	178	225	300	59 to 207	145.08
61% to 100%	1,630	46	121	127	155	161	205	207	394	398	121 to 394	235.54
Total	51,813											

Sources: Sternlieb, *The Urban Housing Dilemma,* 1970.
New York City Department of Social Service Data Processing Administration, March 1968.

EXHIBIT 7.20

ANNUAL REPAIR COSTS PER ROOM BY DEGREE OF WELFARE TENANTRY (1968)

PERCENT ON WELFARE	Number of Structures	ANNUAL REPAIR COSTS PER ROOM										
		Percentiles									Interquartile Range (25% to 75%)	Mean
		10	20	30	40	50	60	70	80	90		
None	24,363	$ 9	$15	$19	$23	$26	$31	$36	$44	$60	$16 to $40	$31.33
1% to 10%	7,213	13	15	19	22	24	30	32	37	45	18 to 34	26.68
11% to 20%	4,634	11	13	14	23	26	34	41	46	54	13 to 45	30.02
21% to 30%	3,510	10	15	18	21	23	28	35	38	43	15 to 38	26.33
31% to 40%	3,467	13	16	18	22	25	32	40	42	58	16 to 41	32.31
41% to 60%	3,103	6	8	10	18	23	35	37	43	49	10 to 43	27.29
61% to 100%	1,630	11	24	25	31	37	41	51	54	91	24 to 54	40.11
Total	49,920											

Sources: Sternlieb, *The Urban Housing Dilemma,* 1970.
New York City Department of Social Service Data Processing Administration, March 1968.

tenants. The next lowest is 14.2 percent of the rent dollar which is consumed in repairs for buildings with 21 percent to 30 percent of their tenants on welfare. However, the percentage of the rent dollar going toward repairs is somewhat higher (15.6 percent) for buildings with no welfare tenants (Exhibit 7.18). Generally, though, actual repair costs take more of the rent dollar in buildings with a large number of welfare tenants than they do in other buildings.

What does this mean in terms of absolute costs? Exhibit 7.19 examines the crucial data for the over 50,000 structures represented in the sample. Again, the pattern is very mixed with some indication that buildings with a high proportion of welfare tenants have higher absolute dollar repair costs per apartment. Those structures with over 30 percent of their tenants on welfare have average repair costs in excess of $155 a year per apartment. This is significantly higher than any of the categories with fewer tenants on welfare. Certainly, there is no evidence from our sample that repair costs in welfare buildings are lower than those in non-welfare tenanted buildings. Buildings with many welfare tenants may be in poorer condition than those with fewer welfare tenants. This does not, however, seem to result from low repair expenditures per apartment.

In Exhibit 7.20 these data are analyzed in terms of annual repair costs per room. The pattern is more mixed here, but the basic finding holds—variation in repair expenditures is not a function of the proportion of welfare tenants in a building.

OPERATING PROFIT

What is the operating profit, that is, the contribution to debt payment, depreciation and profit based on rents that results from welfare property? There is little reason, based on the data shown in Exhibit 7.21 to believe that welfare buildings are more "profitable" in terms of operating profits than are buildings which do not house welfare tenants.

The mean operating profits for the non-welfare structures is 22.5 percent; for those with 1 percent to 10 percent of the tenants on welfare, it is 27.4 percent. By contrast, structures with 31 percent to 40 percent welfare tenants have a 20.9 percent operating profit, while those with 41 percent to 60 percent of their tenants on welfare contribute a 15.6 percent operating profit. Again there are significant variations in the interquartile ranges, with operating profits more consistent in structures with few or no tenants on welfare. Twenty-five percent of the parcels with 41 percent to 60 percent of their tenants on welfare have operating profits of 5 percent or less, with an even more dismal operating profitability for those buildings with over 60 percent of their tenants on welfare.

EXHIBIT 7.21

DEBT, DEPRECIATION AND PROFIT AS A PERCENTAGE OF NET RENT RECEIVED BY DEGREE OF WELFARE TENANTRY WITHIN STRUCTURES (1968)

PERCENT ON WELFARE	DEBT, DEPRECIATION AND PROFIT AS A PERCENTAGE OF NET RENT RECEIVED											
	Total Structures	Percentiles 10	20	30	40	50	60	70	80	90	Interquartile Range (25% to 75%)	Mean
None	26,921	– 5%	12%	21%	27%	31%	35%	37%	44%	48%	17% to 41%	22.5%
1% to 10%	8,350	6	18	24	26	30	32	36	40	47	22 to 36	27.4
11% to 20%	5,042	–11	1	8	11	16	20	28	34	45	6 to 29	12.1
21% to 30%	3,746	7	20	24	30	32	35	39	40	44	24 to 40	27.1
31% to 40%	3,757	–16	8	15	22	27	29	30	36	52	12 to 32	20.9
41% to 60%	3,393	–27	4	5	16	20	29	29	35	46	5 to 31	15.6
61% to 100%	1,630	–10	1	10	10	14	16	22	26	27	1 to 22	2.1
Total	52,837											

Sources: Sternlieb, *The Urban Housing Dilemma,* 1970.
New York City Department of Social Service Data Processing Administration, March 1968.

EXHIBIT 7.22

NET CASH FLOW AS A PERCENTAGE OF NET RENT RECEIVED BY DEGREE OF WELFARE TENANTRY WITHIN STRUCTURES (1968)

		NET CASH FLOW AS A PERCENTAGE OF NET RENT RECEIVED										
		Percentiles										
PERCENT ON WELFARE	Total Structures	10	20	30	40	50	60	70	80	90	Interquartile Range (25% to 75%)	Mean[a]
None	26,921	– 27%	– 8%	1%	6%	12%	20%	27%	33%	41%	– 3% to 30%	4.8%
1% to 10%	8,350	– 10	– 2	5	8	11	14	20	23	32	1 to 22	3.3
11% to 20%	5,042	– 37	–18	–10	– 5	– 1	9	16	23	29	–16 to 17	– 4.2
21% to 30%	3,746	– 27	5	8	20	22	23	25	28	35	6 to 26	12.9
31% to 40%	3,757	– 27	–23	–14	– 3	3	8	10	23	29	–16 to 13	– 5.6
41% to 60%	3,393	– 66	–23	–21	–13	9	16	27	31	36	–22 to 29	– 3.2
61% to 100%	1,630	–221	–29	2	4	4	10	10	14	16	–29 to 14	–31.3
Total	53,839											

Sources: Sternlieb, *The Urban Housing Dilemma,* 1970.
New York City Department of Social Service Data Processing Administration, March 1968.

[a]Note that there is a substantial variation between the means and the medians because of a few large losers in every category.

It should be noted that these calculations do not take into account debt service or depreciation. They do attempt to measure the funds available after operating costs which, assuming no debt service, might be available for capital improvements or increased expenditures on maintenance. After debt service even smaller operating profits are probably available to pay the costs of new major capital improvements.

CASH FLOW

What are the levels of cash flow in buildings with a large number of welfare tenants? The results of our extrapolations appear in Exhibit 7.22. For each of the building categories with over 30 percent of the tenants on welfare, the mean cash flow is negative; the landlord is taking in less cash than is going out as a result of the operational costs and debt service on his specific parcel. While the cash flow in the 21 percent to 30 percent welfare-occupied buildings is positive, poor cash flow is also evident in the 11 percent to 20 percent welfare-occupied buildings.

Part of this negative cash flow undoubtedly can be attributed to paying back debt out of profit, but in any case, cash flow is essential for immediate capital improvement rather than taxable income or operating profits *per se.* Given the shape of the institutional mortgage market, as will be discussed in detail later, possibilities of recapturing amortization through refinancing the mortgage are dim.

Our information reveals a paucity of means available for welfare buildings to bootstrap their own rehabilitation. More than 40 percent of the 3,700 structures with 31 percent to 40 percent of their tenants on welfare have cash flows of minus 3 percent or more, while the same proportion of the 41 percent to 60 percent category have cash flows of minus 13 percent or more. The sample size is very small in the category of buildings with more than 60 percent of the residents on welfare, but at least one-fourth are running in the red by 29 percent or more of the net rents received.

Contrast the cash flow results for structures that have no welfare tenants. Here the bottom 25 percent of buildings has a negative cash flow of minus 3 percent. In structures with 1 percent to 10 percent of their tenants on welfare, the bottom 25 percent of buildings has a cash flow of plus 1 percent. Certainly, even the top quarter of the buildings do not present particularly sanguine operating yields. Projecting an approximate cash flow average for the top 25 percent of the more heavily welfare-tenanted structures as about 20 percent indicates a mean of approximately $16 a month profit per apartment. This does not take into account landlord profits, depreciation, or indirectly charged but significant landlord inputs for services.

EXHIBIT 7.23

NET TAXABLE INCOME AS A PERCENTAGE OF NET RENT RECEIVED BY DEGREE OF WELFARE TENANTRY WITHIN STRUCTURES (1968)

		NET TAXABLE INCOME AS A PERCENTAGE OF NET RENT RECEIVED										
		Percentiles										
PERCENT ON WELFARE	Total Structures	10	20	30	40	50	60	70	80	90	Interquartile Range (25% to 75%)	Mean
None	26,921	−32%	−13%	− 5%	2%	9%	15%	21%	29%	35%	− 9% to 26%	.2%
1% to 10%	8,350	−15	− 5	− 1	2	5	7	10	14	24	− 2 to 12	4.0
11% to 20%	5,042	−30	−16	−12	− 6	− 3	− 1	6	17	22	−14 to 14	− 8.5
21% to 30%	3,746	−21	− 3	7	11	16	20	22	24	29	5 to 23	8.9
31% to 40%	3,757	−39	− 8	− 2	1	3	10	15	16	28	− 6 to 16	− 3.1
41% to 60%	3,393	−62	−30	−13	−12	4	10	19	22	23	−27 to 22	− 9.0
61% to 100%	1,630	−39	−20	−16	− 2	4	7	9	11	14	−20 to 11	−12.9
Total	52,839											

Source: Sternlieb, *The Urban Housing Dilemma*, 1970.

Even if $16 a month were available for improvements, there is some question of the total amounts that would be available for this investment. Given a twenty-year, 3.5 percent self-amortizing base, the above cash flow would buy, at most, $2,000 a year in capital investment. On a ten-year base, it would buy barely $1,500. This subject is discussed in detail in Chapter 8.

Negative cash flows are far from unique to heavily welfare-tenanted structures. To the degree, however, that welfare buildings bear the stigma of location in poor areas and, even more significantly (as will be discussed later), poor financing and poor prospects, the pressure on the landlord to forego even essential replacements is great.

NET TAXABLE INCOME

Net taxable income, as earlier discussed, is perhaps the weakest measure of operating yield, incorporating, as it does, the vagaries of debt service and depreciation policy. Exhibit 7.23 presents net taxable income as a percentage of net rent received by the percentage of the buildings' apartments which house welfare tenants. There is little indication from the data shown that, based on this criterion of net taxable income, welfare structures are securing extraordinarily high yields based upon rents.

The minimum conclusions called for by these data are that, if welfare-tenant structures are to secure significant amounts of capital investment, more cash flow than is presently generated by current rent levels will be required. Where is the money to come from?

SUMMARY

Many low income residents, particularly among blacks in New York City, feel that landlords are making a large profit on housing for the relatively poor. While the median monthly rental for an average welfare case in New York City is $71.47, it varies considerably depending on the type of accommodation and the number of individuals in the household. Public housing is, on the average, cheaper than private housing. The average housing cost also varies considerably by category of recipient. ADC cases are on the average highest, Home Relief cases are next, followed by Old Age Assistance cases and Aid to Disabled recipients. There is significant variation in housing costs associated with borough. Queens is highest followed by Brooklyn, the Bronx and Manhattan. When rents per room are analyzed by the concentration of welfare recipients within a building they are inversely related to the degree of welfare tenant concentration. It is clear that in every category of building studied the mean rents paid by welfare recipients are higher, on the average, than those of residents who are not welfare recipients but live in comparable housing.

Expenses of landlords in buildings which house greater proportions of welfare tenants are typically as high and in significant numbers higher than in buildings with few or no welfare tenants housed there. This, however, seems to be related to the tendency of welfare recipients to have somewhat larger apartments. Repair costs take up a larger proportion of the rent dollar in buildings with a high proportion of tenants on welfare. There is little reason to believe that buildings with welfare tenants are by any means more "profitable" in terms of operating profit than are buildings that do not house welfare tenants. Present rents are not an adequate source of financing either a major renovation program or a building program. It also seems to be true that buildings largely tenanted by welfare recipients are not more frequently owned by large-scale professional landlords. In New York City, most housing is owned by whites, while minority-group members own buildings largely occupied by welfare tenants.

Given the clear need for major renovations and new construction, where is the money to come from? Several possibilities have been explored in this chapter and found deficient. The next chapter explores some more hopeful prospects.

NOTES

1. Louis Harris and Associates, Inc., *Transition Neighborhoods in New York City* (New York: Vera Institute, 1969) p. 72 and following.

2. Joint Legislative Committee, p. 28.

3. U.S. Department of Health Education and Welfare *The Role of Public Welfare in Housing*, p. 42 and appendices. Note that this is a constantly evolving scene. For some of the recent changes in attitudes on rents see Chapter 8.

4. The New York state data presented here are based upon Program Brief No. 2-1970, February 1970, New York State Department of Social Services.

5. As earlier noted, historically one of the principal means of rent increase under New York's rent-control law was the 15 percent increment obtainable on the turnover of an apartment. Given the high mobility of welfare tenants their rents obviously have been impacted by this proviso.

6. George Sternlieb, *The Urban Housing Dilemma* (New York: Housing Development Administration, 1970). See the second half of the study.

7. For an analysis of the methodology and a comparison between the respondents and non-respondents, see George Sternlieb, *op. cit.*, Chapter 2.

8. For more on this pattern of transfer see George Sternlieb, *op. cit.* and his *The Tenement Landlord* (New Brunswick, N.J.: Rutgers University, 1966).

9. Charges under this heading were limited to actual out of pocket payments for this purpose to management firms on an arms' length relationship base. In no case were management fees included which were over the prevailing fee schedules. No provision is made here for landlord services per se. The data therefore *understate* the actual management costs involved. See George Sternlieb, *The Urban Housing Dilemma* for fuller details of the accounting approaches used.

Chapter 8

FINANCING THE REHABILITATION OF WELFARE HOUSING

In Chapter 7 we considered the basic costs of operating welfare structures. It is evident that there is little basis for the belief that welfare structures are significantly more profitable, in terms of their operating percentages, than buildings housing few or no welfare recipients. Where, then, can funds be found within the operating income in order to provide the means for rehabilitation? This chapter analyzes the operating statement and gives some rough orders of magnitude for each of the major elements.

Leaving aside the question of total gross income for the moment, the first entry on the conventional operating statement is deductions for vacancies, allowances and nonpayment of rent. These are finite elements which are within the purview of the Department of Social Services. The largest single expense (and perhaps the only one with significant potential for change from an overall societal point of view) is taxes. For this reason the potential savings in this area will be considered separately. Expense items for repairs and maintenance are, as has been noted earlier, fully as high in welfare structures as in nonwelfare structures. There is, therefore, little promise of dollar savings here, though certainly the potential savings from centralized repair facilities and the like might provide better use of the landlord's dollars.

The major potential lies in other financial areas. For this reason we will discuss debt service with specific reference to amortization and to interest. The availability of mortgaging especially is a major determinant of landlord ability to maintain the property. This discussion, therefore, will be coupled with an analysis of the "mortgageability" of welfare structures as well as landlords' belief in their mortgageability, which may be as significant as the reality itself. The final item which will be discussed is the possibility of using income tax credits derived from depreciation to provide funds for rehabilitation.

THE GAP BETWEEN GROSS RENTS AND NET RENTS

Landlords who house welfare tenants voice frequent complaints about the problems of rent collections, loss of rent occasioned by turnover and, despite the current housing shortage, vacancies. These problems typically account for the gap between gross rents and net rents received. Other items which lower the landlord's gross rents typically occur in a softer housing market and/or high-rent structures as some form of allowance to tenants who sign leases, for example, a month's concession for each year of the lease. These concessions play a very small role in welfare recipient housing.

Several approaches can be taken to minimize landlord problems with rent collection and the like. Typically the use of two-party checks—a check made out to and which must be endorsed by both landlord and tenant—has been frowned on by federal welfare authorities because it emphasizes the variation in status between welfare recipients and more fortunate individuals. However, New York City welfare authorities have found that the use of two-party checks minimizes nonpayment of rents and have therefore expanded the practice in certain limited cases. Much more important, however, is the wider use of long-term leasing of apartments directly by municipal authorities. The potential of this approach has not yet been fully realized.

As significant as this juridical arrangement in minimizing the gaps between the gross rents and net rents received, is the potential capacity it provides of a bankable lease. Commercial real estate developers have long used lessee's credit to finance real estate development. Shopping centers are typically financed by the developer's securing long-term leases from first-class tenants; these in turn are used as collateral for raising funds to build the center itself.

Can long-term leases by the city's welfare authorities be used as collateral for improvement loans in whole or in part? A positive answer depends on there being enough rent money over and above the immediate needs of the building to make this endeavor worthwhile to the owner. Furthermore, the standards set by the welfare department must be enforced so as to insure that this is reflected in improving the building. There are serious problems in administering this type of program and

EXHIBIT 8.1

TOTAL REAL ESTATE TAX ASSESSMENT PER APARTMENT BY DEGREE OF WELFARE TENANTRY

PERCENT ON WELFARE	Number of Structures[a]	TOTAL REAL ESTATE TAX ASSESSMENT PER APARTMENT										
		Percentiles									Interquartile Range (25% to 75%)	Mean
		10	20	30	40	50	60	70	80	90		
None	28,490	$2,000	$2,500	$2,900	$3,200	$3,500	$3,900	$4,400	$5,000	$6,700	$2,800 to $4,700	$4,100
1% to 10%	7,330	1,900	2,500	3,100	3,500	3,900	4,300	4,500	5,200	6,000	2,800 to 4,800	4,200
11% to 20%	5,400	1,600	1,800	2,200	2,300	2,500	2,700	3,100	3,400	4,800	1,900 to 3,200	2,900
21% to 30%	3,950	1,700	1,900	2,100	2,200	2,400	2,700	3,200	3,800	4,500	2,000 to 3,400	2,800
31% to 40%	3,650	1,700	1,800	2,000	2,100	2,200	2,700	3,500	4,000	4,700	2,000 to 4,000	3,300
41% to 60%	2,850	1,400	1,500	1,900	2,100	2,500	2,600	3,600	4,500	7,000	1,700 to 4,200	3,100
61% to 100%	1,530	2,000	2,200	2,300	2,500	2,600	2,600	2,900	4,000	4,500	2,300 to 2,900	2,800
Total	53,200											

Source: Sternlieb, *The Urban Housing Dilemma*, 1970.

[a]Weighted number of structures.

insuring quality control of repairs and improvements. Nevertheless, more attention should be turned here.

In the meantime, if success is achieved in minimizing or eliminating the gap between gross rents and net rents received, through the selective application of the two-party check system as well as the local welfare department guaranteeing long-term leases and, thus, occupancy of the apartment, the landlord's attitude toward welfare recipients might be perceptibly changed. Given an average rent of $100 a month, however, the cash flow difference probably would be only approximately $5 a month, or $60 a year.[1]

USING CURRENT REAL ESTATE TAXES

To ask any of our older major cities to reduce their tax basis substantially in order to provide funds for rehabilitation is perhaps impossible, given the municipal financial crises which are currently prevalent. The poor cannot afford to bootstrap the poor.

New York City, however, has given very substantial tax subsidies to middle-income housing. Under the Mitchell-Lama Program, for example, buildings frequently housing people with incomes in excess of $20,000 a year are receiving tax reductions of as much as 85 percent. Certainly the level of assessment and of actual taxation per unit is of substantial consequence to operating costs. The single largest expenditure item in the operations of residential realty in New York City is real estate taxes.

In Exhibit 8.1 total assessment per apartment is indicated to the nearest hundred dollars. (The level of assessment per apartment is the total value of the structure including land divided by the number of housing units.) In general, buildings with a high proportion of welfare residents have lower assessments per apartment than do those with few or no tenants on welfare. The mean values run from approximately $3,000 in the former cases to $4,000 or more in the latter.

Given a tax rate of approximately 6 percent, this indicates a current tax level of about $180 per dwelling unit for structures which have significant numbers of their apartments tenanted by welfare recipients. On a 20-year base at a 3.5 percent tax rate, such funds will service slightly under $3,000 in total capital improvements; computed on a ten-year base it will yield a little more than half that, perhaps $1,500.[2] Of the several items examined here, this has perhaps the most potential consequence.

Comparatively little municipal income is derived directly from housing welfare recipients. If the rough computation of $180 a year is compared to the needs and aspirations of welfare recipients described in

Chapters 5 and 6, it would be obvious that the city's resources are hardly sufficient. New York City has a broader range of taxes than does any other city in the United States, but real estate taxes still provide approximately 40 percent of its total municipal revenue. Marking them, therefore, for capital improvements in housing is a step which must be taken very carefully.

MORTGAGEABILITY AND DEBT SERVICE

The mortgageability of real estate plays a major role in landlord decision-making. Without the benefit of a bank, savings and loan or other institutional source of financing, it is extremely difficult to sell a building. Few potential buyers are capable of making an "all cash" purchase. Unless there is an institution willing to give a mortgage on the structure, the potential seller must take back a mortgage, that is, a purchase money mortgage. Instead of receiving cash for his equity and profit in the structure, the seller may secure only a nominal amount of real dollars plus a mortgage which may involve payments over a lengthy period of time.

Let us consider the hypothetical case of a building that had a bank mortgage upon its purchase some years ago. Perhaps the dilemma of the owner may thus be made more clear. A good part of the owner's operating profit is expended in paying back that mortgage over a period of years. Assuming that the original purchase cost was $15,000 and the buyer put up $5,000 in cash, the first mortgage secured from the bank would be $10,000. Over the period of mortgage, the latter is paid back to the bank. The owner now has a $15,000 equity in the structure. He attempts to recover this equity through sale. If a new bank mortgage cannot be secured, however, and a potential buyer once again has only $5,000, the owner discovers that this is all the cash that he can take out of the parcel (and often not even that much) and the balance is secured to him only through a stream of payments from the purchaser. The owner's responsibilities for the structure are relatively unaltered. His only collateral is the building itself. If sold to a faulty operator or someone who decides to desert the building, the earlier owner may be faced with the return of a completely vandalized structure. Obviously, therefore, his incentives to make capital improvements in a limited resale market are minimal.

A somewhat similar observation applies if a structure which has had a substantially amortized mortgage is examined. Rather than selling the structure (and having to pay capital gains tax on the difference between the sale price and the depreciated "book" value) owners will frequently remortgage in order to recover the "excess" equity which has been stored away in the building through a paid-down mortgage. If the bank is not willing to "roll over" the mortgage, that is, grant a new mortgage absorbing the old one for a higher face amount, the amortization, rather than being an annuity, a nest egg stored away for future needs, becomes merely a reflection of the degeneration of the market value of the parcel.

Most real estate sales *are* attended by some form of debt service. Is this also true of welfare structures?

DEBT SERVICE

Exhibit 8.2 indicates the proportion of mortgaged structures by welfare densities. The majority of every case has some form of debt service obligation. The sources of the first mortgage, however, vary as a function of welfare tenancy. While buildings with less than 11 percent of their tenants on welfare have relatively few mortgages from private individuals (12.4 percent for those with no welfare tenants; 11.0 percent for those with 1 percent to 10 percent) there is an abrupt upward shift when buildings with significant proportions of welfare tenants are considered. This shift is on the order of double the earlier incidence. The importance of this finding will be discussed in a later part of this chapter when owner attitudes about the availability of institutional financing are examined. In any case, typically this type of private financing is a tribute to the weakness of the market. Our focus here will be on the size of the obligations involved.

EXHIBIT 8.2

PROPORTION OF STRUCTURES WITH MORTGAGES BY WELFARE DENSITIES

PERCENT ON WELFARE	NUMBER OF STRUCTURES WITH MORTGAGES	TOTAL NUMBER OF STRUCTURES	PERCENT OF STRUCTURES WITH MORTGAGES
None	15,000	27,000	55.6%
1% to 10%	5,700	7,900	72.2
11% to 20%	3,300	5,000	66.0
21% to 30%	2,200	3,900	56.4
31% to 40%	2,600	3,700	70.3
41% to 60%	1,900	3,400	55.9
61% to 100%	1,200	1,500	80.0
Total	31,900	52,400	61.1

Source: Sternlieb, *The Urban Housing Dilemma,* 1970.

Are welfare-tenanted structures highly leveraged, involving the buildings in overly high interest and amortization charges? Is one of the problems in securing good maintenance the high level of debt service?

EXHIBIT 8.3

DEBT SERVICE AS A PERCENTAGE OF NET RENT RECEIVED BY DEGREE OF WELFARE TENANTRY (1968)

PERCENT ON WELFARE	Number of Structures	DEBT SERVICE AS A PERCENTAGE OF NET RENT RECEIVED: Percentiles 10	20	30	40	50	60	70	80	90	Interquartile Range (25% to 75%)	Mean
None	15,038	10%	13%	19%	24%	27%	32%	35%	41%	57%	16% to 37%	31.01%
1% to 10%	5,700	10	14	17	20	24	26	33	38	43	14 to 35	35.08
11% to 20%	3,292	6	11	15	21	22	29	34	37	39	15 to 37	24.68
21% to 30%	2,215	8	13	19	19	20	23	23	47	55	14 to 25	25.35
31% to 40%	2,640	10	13	19	29	30	43	45	54	64	16 to 46	37.52
41% to 60%	1,944	6	14	18	24	27	38	43	43	65	18 to 43	32.66
61% to 100%	1,164	6	7	8	11	22	28	30	210	—	— —	45.93
Total	31,993											

Sources: Sternlieb, *The Urban Housing Dilemma,* 1970.
New York City Department of Social Service Data Processing Administration, March 1968.

If debt service were obliterated through refinancing would there be a substantial flow of funds available for capital improvements?

Exhibit 8.3 indicates debt service as a percentage of net rent received by the percentage of welfare tenants within the building. The data are pyramided for the approximately 32,000 structures represented by the sample which do have mortgages. Debt service as a percentage of net rent received does not seem to be intimately linked to the degree of welfare tenantry except that structures with 60 percent or more of their tenants on welfare have the highest mean debt service (45.93 percent), in part because a few structures in this group have little rent income. The median figure might well be the more appropriate measurement here. It does not seem to be much out of line with the others, which run between 20 percent and 30 percent. In the categories with 31 percent to 60 percent of the tenants on welfare, more than 30 percent of the 4,500 structures in this group have substantially more than 40 percent of their net rents applied toward debt service. If the mean data for these categories are used, it indicates that, given an average rent of approximately $80 per month, about $35 of it would go for debt service.

On a 3.5 percent interest level, assuming 20-year amortization, this flow of funds could support $6,000 in investment. At a ten-year payback period, which might well be realistic for cosmetic rehabilitation, the equivalent figure would be approximately $3,500. This assumes that there would be appropriate governmental programs which permit repairs at these low market interest rates, for periods of ten years.

Such federal housing finance programs as 236 and the 312 housing provisos involve generous financing. For the latter, there is a 3.5 percent interest rate; in the case of the former, it is even lower. These long-term loans at the above interest rates are dependent upon securing improvements which measure up to FHA standards. There is some question whether the capital investment levels suggested here would be adequate.[3] In any case, use of the present debt service would assume that somehow it could be wiped off the boards, which is highly questionable. The cash flow left after refinancing extant mortgages, even at a lower rate, would obviously be lower.

The costs of debt service are a function not only of interest rates but also of the longevity of the indentures in question. In addition, as an earlier study of New York City rental realty indicated, there is great variation in amortization. Not uncommonly, mortgages that have been written for relatively short terms have very limited payback provisions during their lifetime. Subject to this limitation, however, the very lengthening out of a mortgage, even given equivalent interest rates, has significant impact upon the debt service required to maintain the mortgage. Purchase money mortgages, for example, typically

EXHIBIT 8.4

AVAILABILITY OF ADEQUATE INSTITUTIONAL FINANCING AT TIME OF PURCHASE BY DEGREE OF WELFARE TENANTRY WITHIN STRUCTURE

AVAILABILITY OF FINANCING	PERCENT ON WELFARE															
	None		1% to 10%		11% to 20%		21% to 30%		31% to 40%		41% to 60%		61% to 100%		Total	
	No.	%	No.	%	No.	%	No.	%	No.	%	No.	%	No.	%	No.	%
Yes	20,300	75.1	6,400	81.3	2,600	52.7	2,500	63.9	2,600	71.2	1,800	54.1	1,000	64.7	37,300	71.1
Partly – Had To Be Supplemented	300	1.1	300	3.2	0	0.0	0	0.0	0	0.0	200	4.9	0	0.0	700	1.3
No – Substantially Purchase Money	1,600	5.8	400	5.2	400	7.4	100	3.3	100	3.6	500	14.3	100	6.4	3,200	6.1
No	2,200	8.0	400	4.4	900	17.6	700	17.7	700	18.2	600	17.3	200	10.2	5,500	10.5
NA/DK	2,700	9.9	500	5.9	1,100	22.3	600	15.1	300	7.0	300	9.3	300	18.7	5,700	10.8
Total	27,000	100.0	7,900	100.0	5,000	100.0	3,900	100.0	3,700	100.0	3,400	100.0	1,500	100.0	52,400	100.0

Sources: Sternlieb, *The Urban Housing Dilemma,* 1970.
New York City Department of Social Service Data Processing Administration, March 1968.

EXHIBIT 8.5

LANDLORDS' RESPONSES TO QUESTION: "IF YOU WERE SELLING NOW, WOULD IT BE POSSIBLE TO GET A MORTGAGE FROM A LENDING INSTITUTION?" BY DEGREE OF WELFARE TENANTRY (1968)

RESPONSE	PERCENT ON WELFARE															
	None		1% to 10%		11% to 20%		21% to 30%		31% to 40%		41% to 60%		61% to 100%		Total	
	No.	%	No.	%	No.	%	No.	%	No.	%	No.	%	No.	%	No.	%
Yes	11,800	43.8	2,600	33.2	1,500	29.3	600	15.3	1,100	30.0	500	13.5	200	10.7	18,200	34.8
No	9,700	36.1	4,200	52.7	3,000	59.3	2,400	60.1	2,200	60.3	2,300	69.2	1,200	79.1	25,000	47.7
NA/DK	5,400	20.2	1,100	14.1	600	11.4	1,000	24.6	400	9.7	600	17.3	200	10.2	9,200	17.5
Total	27,000	100.0	7,900	100.0	5,000	100.0	3,900	100.0	3,700	100.0	3,400	100.0	1,500	100.0	52,400	100.0

Sources: Sternlieb, *The Urban Housing Dilemma,* 1970.
New York City Department of Social Service Data Processing Administration, March 1968.

may be for only ten to 15 years at 6 percent. In terms of straight-line amortization, these involve $11.10 or $8.44 per month per $1,000. On a 20-year base the equivalent figure is $7.16, while at a 25-year base the cash flow reduction is $2 per $1,000 per month or more than 20 percent.

Interestingly enough, the lower interest rates are not quite so significant with a 20-year mortgage at 6 percent involving a debt service of $7.16 per month per $1,000 versus $5.80 at 3.5 percent. Assuming that 3.5 percent of the money is available for recasting of mortgages on a 20-year base, there is a potential saving in debt service of somewhere on the order of 15 to 25 percent.[4] This could support perhaps $1,500 per apartment in capital investment. While this is far from trivial, there is still the question of whether this could be effectively used, given the difficulties of administering cosmetic repair and the poor condition of much of the aged housing stock which is typically inhabited by welfare recipients.

ADEQUACY OF INSTITUTIONAL FINANCING

The major problem with welfare structures may not be their heavy levels of debt service but rather the financing institutions' lack of interest in getting involved with them at all.

Owners who cannot secure institutional financing are going to have serious difficulties in either selling their structures or in using mortgaging or remortgaging as a significant source of funds for capital improvements. In either case the effect on the level of inputs into the structure needs no amplification. Paying off an old mortgage through amortization, or example, will represent not a nest egg which can ultimately be cashed in through resale or a new mortgage, but rather an unhappy mirror of the decline in the structure's value. How does welfare tenantry affect financibility?

Exhibit 8.4 shows that simple affirmative answers to the question of whether adequate institutional financing was available when the present owner bought his building are given by 71.1 percent of the pyramided sample. There is, however, some skew in distribution: 75 percent of owners of structures having no tenants on welfare give affirmative answers as do 81.3 percent with one to ten percent welfare tenants. Landlords of buildings with many welfare tenants give significantly fewer affirmative answers. The relationship is by no means perfect, but indicates that even at the time of purchase (which may have been long ago) institutional financing, with its relatively low cash flow requirements, was rarer in welfare structures than in those which on the whole had few or no tenants on welfare.

Opinions about the current possibilities of financing welfare structures are indicated in Exhibit 8.5, which presents the responses of owners to the question of whether they would be able to secure institutional mortgages if they were selling now. The rate of positive answers tends to be inversely related to the degree of welfare recipiency. While in general the responses are negative in tone, with only 43.8 percent of the non-welfare landlords giving an unequivocal "yes"; the answers are even more dismaying as the degree of welfare residency increases. One-third of the structures with 1 percent to 10 percent welfare residents had owners who believed they could get institutional financing on a current sale; the responses for structures housing more than that percentage of welfare recipients are generally more negative. Less than one-sixth of the 21 percent to 30 percent welfare-tenanted structures and barely 13 percent of those with over 40 percent welfare tenants give positive answers. Over 70 percent of the latter category answer unequivocally no, nearly double the proportion in the no-welfare cases. While there is some variation in the 31 percent to 40 percent welfare category, welfare building owners more frequently feel that their properties are not financeable.

Is this simply a tribute to the age and size of the structures or is it specifically related to welfare tenancy *per se*? Certainly the two are related. In the earlier study, we analyzed this point at some length, using interviews not only with owners but also with lending institutions. There is no question that when both groups say that building in "bad areas" are not financeable, they tend to include within this definition the degree of welfare tenancy. Outright comments on this point were secured from a number of owners during the survey.

A substantial proportion of the structures which presently have welfare recipients are not of interest to the private enterprise financing institutions. This isolation has significant meaning to the landlord's willingness to make capital repairs, and even more impact on his financial ability, assuming a positive attitude on his part.

DEPRECIATION

What is the meaning of depreciation? Nominally it represents the Internal Revenue Department's decision about the lifetime of a structure. If a building of a particular configuration and fabric, for example, is projected as having a 30-year lifetime, then in terms of its use for any one year of that lifetime, an average of 3.333 percent of the total value of the improvements may be deducted as an expense.

Analysis of variations in actual depreciation policies used by landlords shows a great range of variation—from 2 percent per year to as much as 4 percent. There are a number of permissible formulas for accelerated depreciation, though these are substantially limited by recent tax legislation. To a high tax bracket owner, an individual paying a 50

EXHIBIT 8.6

DEPRECIATION AS A PERCENTAGE OF NET RENT RECEIVED (1967) BY DEGREE OF WELFARE TENANTRY

	DEPRECIATION AS A PERCENTAGE OF NET RENT RECEIVED											
		Percentiles										
PERCENT ON WELFARE	Number of Structures	10	20	30	40	50	60	70	80	90	Interquartile Range (25% to 75%)	Mean
None	273	7%	8%	10%	11%	13%	14%	16%	19%	24%	9% to 17%	14.36%
1% to 10%	173	7	8	9	10	12	13	15	17	21	9 to 15	13.09
11% to 20%	47	6	8	9	11	12	14	15	18	21	9 to 17	13.02
21% to 30%	36	5	7	8	9	10	10	14	16	21	7 to 15	11.81
31% to 40%	31	5	7	8	8	9	11	13	15	18	7 to 14	11.52
41% to 60%	28	6	7	10	12	12	13	15	17	23	8 to 16	13.25
61% to 100%	10	4	6	7	8	10	11	12	14	24	6 to 12	9.90
Total	598											

Source: Sternlieb, *The Urban Housing Dilemma*, 1970.

percent tax rate (including state, local and municipal income taxes) on his marginal income, a depreciation allowance of 12 percent of the net rents received is equivalent to securing a 6 percent tax-free income from the structure in question.

In theory, assuming fully taxable alternative investments were available at a 6 percent yield or 16.666 times their cost, the owner should be willing to pay double that, or 33.33 times the flow of funds for a tax-sheltered flow of earnings. In actuality there seems to be some variation in this equation. Tax-exempt bonds do not sell for precisely half the yield of equivalent coupons, fully taxable indentures, but rather seem to be hovering at around 60 percent.

To the degree that the individual's marginal tax rate is even higher than 50 percent, the tax-free investment is worth even more; to the degree that it is under 50 percent, it is worth less. When welfare-tenant structures are held by people of relatively low incomes, the tax cover may be worth very little. If there is no taxable income whatsoever with which to use depreciation as a shelter, it is worth nothing.

Furthermore, these calculations assume that the depreciation entry is completely nonfunctional, that is, it does not reflect in any way the decline in value or the necessity for replacing capital equipment in order to maintain a building's value as it grows older. This is far from the reality in the case of some buildings. In some buildings, particularly those in poor areas, depreciation lags behind the real decline in market value.

Exhibit 8.6 shows the actual depreciation as a percentage of the net rents in 1967 by the level of welfare tenancy within the structures projected for the sample universe. There is a rather wide range of depreciation. In a number of cases, for example, no depreciation is taken. These not uncommonly are structures which have been owned for so long as to exhaust the potential depreciation. The mean values with the exception of the most heavily welfare-tenanted structures run around 10 percent to 14 percent with some indication that depreciation tends to be smallest in structures that have a higher proportion of welfare tenants.

Accepting depreciation completely as a tax cover element and further accepting a mean net taxable income of somewhere on the order of 4 percent or 5 percent of all the rents paid, the composite with depreciation would yield a mean of somewhere on the order of 14 percent to 20 percent of the rents. How much would a corporation paying approximately 50 percent of its profits in taxes pay for such a covered investment? The answer is probably not very much more than three times the rent roll. Given a post-tax income of 2 percent or 3 percent on the profit and with nontaxable depreciation of 10 percent to 16 percent, post-tax income would be 12 percent to 19 percent of the total rent roll. If the purchaser paid three times the rent roll, his post-tax yield would be 4 percent to slightly over 6 percent.

Limited partnerships are currently available in commerical realty occupied by first-class tenants with close to comparable yields. At the time of this study, BAA rated (lower medium grade) industrial bonds were selling at close to 9 percent yields, and New York City's tax-exempt bonds hovered near 7 percent. Considering the relative lack of entrepreneurial input required for the latter, and their relative safety, the rates of return on structures with a high proportion of welfare tenants are clearly far from enticing.

There is comparatively little gain through depreciation, therefore, to serve as a considerable inducement for new groups of investors unless the operating performance is completely recast.

NOTES

1. See George Sternlieb, *The Urban Housing Dilemma* (New York: Housing Development Administration, 1970) pp. 145-147 for the amounts involved.

2. A reduction to a 1 percent interest level (available in the Federal Rent Subsidy Programs 235-236) increases the debt servicing capacity only slightly. On a ten-year base, the figure would be $1,700; on a 20-year base, $3,250.

3. Frank Kristof, *Working Paper No. 14* (New York: Housing Development Agency, 1967). This is an excellent analysis of the costs and problems of rehabilitating various housing types in New York City.

4. The 6 percent interest rate mentioned here obviously refers to mortgages written before the wave of increased costs of borrowing moved rates to their current levels of 8 percent plus. Clearly, the higher the mortgage rate, the greater the potential impact of refunding.

Chapter 9

POLICY IMPLICATIONS

How can we best optimize the relationship between the funds available for the maintenance of welfare recipients and their effective use? Housing is only one of many potential inputs. Compared with inputs into health facilities, better schools, or improved clothing allowances, however, housing has several advantages. It is easily counted and administered. Its sheer physical existence makes it easier to define than so many other necessities of the good life.

But would X dollars in housing be of more significance to welfare recipients than an equivalent investment in public safety or in recreation facilities? We can hardly provide a definitive answer to that important question. Certainly, as the materials presented earlier indicate, housing must be viewed in the context of an environment which drastically needs improvement, particularly in the broad area of public safety.

Housing's importance as a measuring stick of societal concern, on the other hand, should not be underestimated. The wit and folklore of the good life in America have replaced the cartoons having to do with automobiles, with those of the suburban homeowner, the reluctant grass cutter, the overcrowded garage. The homogeneity of the tract house is at one and the same time a mocked but affectionate symbol. Does the improvement of existing structures or their replacement with new multifamilied structures which the space limitations of the city make mandatory fulfill the need to partake of this vital symbol of affluence?

EXHIBIT 9.1

INTERVIEWER'S INTERIOR MAINTENANCE RATING BY RESPONDENT'S EVALUATIVE FACTOR SCORE (MY APARTMENT)

INTERIOR MAINTENANCE RATING	EVALUATIVE FACTOR SCORE[a]															
	Low Evaluation 25 to 34		35 to 43		44 to 48		49 to 51		52 to 56		High Evaluation 57 to 65		66 to 75		Total	
	No.	%	No.	%	No.	%	No.	%	No.	%	No.	%	No.	%	No.	%
20	18	45.0	18	29.0	9	15.0	8	14.0	7	9.9	8	6.8	0	0.0	68	16.5
40	13	32.5	14	22.6	11	18.3	10	17.5	12	16.9	9	7.7	0	0.0	69	16.7
60	6	15.0	22	35.5	23	38.3	16	28.1	21	29.6	26	22.2	2	40.0	116	28.2
80	3	7.5	7	11.3	13	21.7	15	26.3	25	35.2	34	29.1	0	0.0	97	23.5
100	0	0.0	1	1.6	4	6.7	8	14.0	6	8.5	40	34.2	3	60.0	62	15.0
Total	40	100.0	62	100.0	60	100.0	57	100.0	71	100.0	117	100.0	5	100.0	412	100.0

Source: Housing of Welfare Recipients Survey, 1970.

[a]Gamma = 0.474.

As pointed out earlier, surprisingly little research has been done on the secondary implications of housing improvement. The material presented here does not so much focus on the effects of housing quality *per se,* but rather on the thinking and mindset of respondents in relation to the degree of housing satisfaction which they indicated to our interviewers.

Can some salient attitudes and characteristics of New York City's welfare population be related to variations in housing conditions? In the first part of this chapter, we shall present some findings on this point. The latter part of the chapter is reserved for an analysis of alternate policy approaches.

EVALUATION OF APARTMENT QUALITY

A comparison of the interviewers' interior maintenance rating with the evaluative factor score on the semantic differential method using the stimulus words "my apartment" (a non-obvious measure of his attitude toward his housing)[1] shows a strong correlation (Exhibit 9.1). The interviewers' evaluation of apartment quality is clearly significantly related to the respondents' evaluation score secured through the semantic differential measure (gamma = 0.474). Satisfaction with housing and the actual condition of housing are clearly linked. This evaluative factor and those for overall housing satisfaction and for the several specific physical elements which were appraised during the course of the interview are discussed in Chapter 5 and are clearly positively intercorrelated.

How would society benefit from better housing for its welfare recipients? Even if there is a strong statistical linkage between poor housing and a variety of other social ills, this does not necessarily prove that improving the former will influence the latter. Unfortunately, as noted before, we have very little information on this key variable, and much more research on this question must be done before definitive answers can be given.[3] However, we did analyze ladder ratings on the Cantril Scale from past to present, present to future status by degree of housing quality and housing satisfaction. There did not seem to be any definitive relationships found.

Housing defined broadly to include area and safety within the household, freedom from drugs and their victims, are the key concerns of welfare recipients. The Cantril probes and the earlier open-end interviewing or the later structured parts show no equivocation on this point. At the very least, housing is a necessary and essential, if not sufficient condition, for the material upgrading of life styles, hopes and aspirations of New York City welfare recipients.

Improving the physical amenities of welfare housing may not be sufficient to enhance recipients' outlook and life styles but it is probably an essential requisite. How is better housing to be secured? Where are the financial and operational resources to come from?

There are no easy answers to these questions. We have shown that little in the present operating expenses of the typical welfare residence and rent pattern will permit massive changes in housing facilities without tapping the public purse. While this may be viewed as a negative finding, it may be very important if we are ever to deal realistically with the housing market. There has probably been too much energy expended in pursuit of individual profiteers, of ineffectual landlords, of individuals and institutions who are slumlords in the worst sense. This statment is by no means intended as a defense of these groups. However, such efforts have probably absorbed more reformist energies than is justified by results produced.

A much more systematic approach to the housing dilemma is required. It is essential to acknowledge that more money is going to be needed. With the one exception of more active use of long-term leasing, as suggested in Chapter 8, there is little that can be optimized within the present rent structure. Regardless of whether the subsidies are hidden in the form of tax rebates, or more obvious in the form of large, direct rent subsidies, it must be if there is to be any material change in the condition of housing. Clearly, financial support cannot end with improving the physical parameters of the dwelling unit. Area characteristics are euphemisms for congeries of ills that require attention—public safety issues as well as public expenditures on other aspects of the social infrastructure. These requirements are beyond the limits of this study, but they are central to any successful overall strategy.

The thesis has been advanced that the absolute conditions of housing for the poor in the central city have improved over time. Certainly, if we keep in mind the hideous conditions of the slums of a generation or two ago, the lack of even the basic amenities, the tremendous overcrowding, we must admit that much has been done. There are, however, counter tendencies at work which must threaten our complacency.[4]

Basic among them is the increasing residential segregation of welfare recipients. This is a function not only of the sheer growth in their number but, as was pointed out in Chapters 3 and 4, of their increasing concentration within what for lack of a better term must be referred to as welfare buildings, welfare blocks and welfare neighborhoods. The population density of classic poverty areas is being reduced; the middle class and aspirants to that group, and those who are mobile in general, are moving out. Left behind are those who cannot make it. Their exclusion

EXHIBIT 9.2

ANSWERS TO THE QUESTION: "IF YOU HAVE PLANS FOR THE FUTURE, IN ABOUT HOW LONG DO YOU HOPE THEY WILL BE ACHIEVED?" BY DEGREE OF HOUSING SATISFACTION

	DEGREE OF HOUSING SATISFACTION											
RESPONSE	Very Satisfied		Satisfied		Undecided		Dissatisfied		Very Dissatisfied		Total	
	No.	%	No.	%	No.	%	No.	%	No.	%	No.	%
One Month or Less	2	6.9	3	5.8	1	4.0	2	3.7	5	12.2	13	6.5
Two to Six Months	3	10.3	6	11.5	0	0.0	6	11.1	8	19.5	23	11.4
Six Months to One Year	4	13.8	7	13.5	7	28.0	15	27.8	9	22.0	42	20.9
One to Three Years	10	34.5	16	30.8	10	40.0	17	31.5	7	17.1	60	29.9
Four Years or More	9	31.0	13	25.0	6	24.0	13	24.1	10	24.4	51	25.4
NA/DK	1	3.4	7	13.5	1	4.0	1	1.9	2	4.9	12	6.0
Total	29	100.0	52	100.0	25	100.0	54	100.0	41	100.0	201	100.0

Source: Housing of Welfare Recipients Survey, 1970;
Note: C=.320; X^2=22.94; df=20; $p < .30$.

EXHIBIT 9.3

ANSWERS TO THE QUESTION: "DO YOU FEEL THE ACHIEVEMENT OF THESE PLANS WILL BE WORTH THE EFFORT ON YOUR PART?" BY DEGREE OF HOUSING SATISFACTION

	DEGREE OF HOUSING SATISFACTION											
RESPONSE	Very Satisfied		Satisfied		Undecided		Dissatisfied		Very Dissatisfied		Total	
	No.	%	No.	%	No.	%	No.	%	No.	%	No.	%
Well Worth it	24	82.8	31	59.6	16	64.0	43	79.6	30	71.6	144	71.6
Worth it	4	13.8	15	28.8	8	32.0	8	14.8	10	24.4	45	22.4
Undecided	1	3.4	0	0.0	1	4.0	2	3.7	1	2.4	5	2.5
NA/DK	0	0.0	6	11.5	0	0.0	1	1.9	0	0.0	7	3.5
Total	29	100.0	52	100.0	25	100.0	54	100.0	41	100.0	201	100.0

Source: Housing of Welfare Recipients Survey, 1970.
Note: C=.314; X^2=22.03; df=12; $p < .05$.

EXHIBIT 9.4

ANSWERS TO THE QUESTION: "WHERE DO YOU EXPECT TO BE LIVING ONE YEAR FROM NEW?" BY DEGREE OF HOUSING SATISFACTION

	DEGREE OF HOUSING SATISFACTION											
RESPONSE	Very Satisfied		Satisfied		Undecided		Dissatisfied		Very Dissatisfied		Total	
	No.	%	No.	%	No.	%	No.	%	No.	%	No.	%
Same Place	63	78.8	96	76.2	18	42.9	27	27.8	13	19.4	217	52.7
Better Apartment	5	6.3	6	4.8	8	19.0	37	38.1	34	50.7	90	21.8
Another State/City	0	0.0	3	2.4	3	7.1	6	6.2	0	0.0	12	2.9
Age/Resignation	0	0.0	1	0.8	1	2.4	2	2.1	3	4.5	7	1.7
Other	1	1.3	2	1.6	3	7.1	5	5.2	6	9.0	17	4.1
DK	11	13.8	18	14.3	9	21.4	19	19.6	11	16.4	68	16.5
NA	0	0.0	0	0.0	0	0.0	1	1.0	0	0.0	1	0.2
Total	80	100.0	126	100.0	42	100.0	97	100.0	67	100.0	412	100.0

Source: Housing of Welfare Recipients Survey, 1970.

Note: C=.507; X^2=142.53; df=24; p⟨.001.

EXHIBIT 9.5

CHANCES OF REACHING THIS HOUSING GOAL BY DEGREE OF HOUSING SATISFACTION

	DEGREE OF HOUSING SATISFACTION											
RESPONSE	Very Satisfied		Satisfied		Undecided		Dissatisfied		Very Dissatisfied		Total	
	No.	%	No.	%	No.	%	No.	%	No.	%	No.	%
Excellent	32	46.4	27	25.0	6	18.2	13	16.9	7	12.5	85	24.8
Good	22	31.9	56	51.9	10	30.3	23	29.9	14	25.0	125	36.4
Fair	10	14.5	18	16.7	10	30.3	19	24.7	20	35.7	77	22.4
Poor	1	1.4	2	1.9	4	12.1	13	16.9	8	14.3	28	8.2
Very Poor	0	0.0	0	0.0	1	3.0	6	7.8	4	7.1	11	3.2
NA/DK	4	5.8	5	4.6	2	6.1	3	3.9	3	5.4	17	5.0
Total	69	100.0	108	100.0	33	100.0	77	100.0	56	100.0	343	100.0

Source: Housing of Welfare Recipients Survey, 1970.

Note: C=.416; X^2=71.92; df=20; p⟨.001.

from the rest of society imposes enormous physical and emotional strains upon them.

We know too little about upward mobility, but certainly one of its keystones is to have front runners—people and families who set an example for the balance of the neighborhood, who show that regardless of skin color, language disabilities and all the other difficulties of the poor, there is a path up and out. But these very examples are leaving the areas inhabited by welfare recipients. The concentration of welfare recipients indicated by the maps in an earlier chapter may eventually generate a microcosmic welfare society.

PLANS FOR THE FUTURE AND HOUSING SATISFACTION

There is a definite relationship between plans for the future and levels of housing dissatisfaction.[2] While only 36 percent of those who are very satisfied with their housing have plans for the future, this rose to 41 percent for those who are merely satisfied, to 59.5 percent for those who are undecided, slightly less than that (55.7 percent) for those who are dissatisfied, and reaches its peak at 61 percent for those who are very dissatisfied. ($C = .192, P < .01, X^2 = 15.79, df = 4$). The degree of dissatisfaction also seems to influence the immediacy of planning, that is, the less satisfaction, the more immediate are the plans for action (Exhibit 9.2).

Judging the vigor of future anticipations is far from foolproof. The respondents, therefore, were asked in this context whether their plans would be worthwhile. The results of this probe are shown in Exhibit 9.3. The size of the subsets is relatively small, but there seems to be a U-shaped relationship: 82.8 percent of the very satisfied indicate their future plans are well worthwhile, but there is a decided drop in the satisfied and undecided levels at 59.6 percent and 64 percent respectively, and an increase in positive anticipation among the dissatisfied and very dissatisfied at 79.6 percent and 71.6 percent respectively.

When these data are analyzed by the level of housing satisfaction they clearly parallel the resonses to another question in the interview: "Where do you expect to be living one year from now?" The results of this probe are shown in Exhibit 9.4 To the degree that plans for moving correlate with actual moves, housing dissatisfaction clearly is a factor in the high level of mobility which has been noted among welfare recipients. Fully half of the very dissatisfied indicate that they plan to be in a better apartment within the year compared to less than one-seventh of the very satisfied and satisfied.

How hopeful are welfare recipients of achieving their goals? Exhibit 9.5 analyzes the response to the question "What are your chances of

EXHIBIT 9.6

OTHER PLANS FOR THE FUTURE AND DEGREE OF HOUSING SATISFACTION

RESPONSE	Very Satisfied No.	Very Satisfied %	Satisfied No.	Satisfied %	Undecided No.	Undecided %	Dissatisfied No.	Dissatisfied %	Very Dissatisfied No.	Very Dissatisfied %	Total No.	Total %
DEGREE OF HOUSING SATISFACTION BY FUTURE PLANS												
Back to School	3	10.3	8	15.4	6	24.0	8	14.8	8	19.5	33	16.4
Work	5	17.2	9	17.3	6	24.0	10	18.5	12	29.3	42	20.9
Move to New Place	5	17.2	5	9.6	5	20.0	15	27.8	7	17.1	37	18.4
Get Off Welfare	2	6.9	0	0.0	0	0.0	0	0.0	1	2.4	3	1.5
Get Off Welfare Plus Additional Response	2	6.9	3	5.8	1	4.0	2	3.7	2	4.9	10	5.0
Work Plus Additional Response	0	0.0	10	19.2	3	12.0	11	20.4	2	4.9	26	12.9
Other	12	41.4	17	32.7	4	16.0	5	9.3	9	22.0	47	23.4
DK	0	0.0	0	0.0	0	0.0	2	3.7	0	0.0	2	1.0
NA	0	0.0	0	0.0	0	0.0	1	1.9	0	0.0	1	0.5
Total	29	100.0	52	100.0	25	100.0	54	100.0	41	100.0	201	100.0
FUTURE PLANS BY DEGREE OF HOUSING SATISFACTION												
	No.	%	No.	%	No.	%	No.	%	No.	%	No.	%
Back to School	3	9.1	8	24.2	6	18.2	8	24.2	8	24.2	33	100.0
Work	5	11.9	9	21.4	6	14.3	10	23.8	12	28.6	42	100.0
Move to New Place	5	13.5	5	13.5	5	13.5	15	40.5	7	18.9	37	100.0
Get Off Welfare	2	66.7	0	0.0	0	0.0	0	0.0	1	33.3	3	100.0
Get Off Welfare Plus Additional Response	2	20.0	3	30.0	1	10.0	2	20.0	2	20.0	10	100.0
Work Plus Additional Response	0	0.0	10	38.5	3	11.5	11	42.3	2	7.7	26	100.0
Other	12	25.5	17	36.2	4	8.5	5	10.6	9	19.1	47	100.0
DK	0	0.0	0	0.0	0	0.0	2	100.0	0	0.0	2	100.0
NA	0	0.0	0	0.0	0	0.0	1	100.0	0	0.0	1	100.0
Total	29	14.4	52	25.9	25	12.4	54	26.9	41	20.4	201	100.0

Source: Housing of Welfare Recipients Survey, 1970.

Note: X^2=46.32; df=32; p$\langle$.05.

reaching this goal?" by the degree of satisfaction with housing. These data have a troublesome import. While those dissatisfied with housing are more likely to have future plans, they are far from secure in evaluating whether they are achievable. The excellent and good responses among those very satisfied and satisfied together total more than three-fourths of each group. Of those dissatisfied 46.8 percent think they are likely to succeed in their future plans, while for those very dissatisfied, the figure is only 37.5 percent. The housing need and desire are there. The feeling that the plans are worthwhile is there. But the majority of those who are most dissatisfied and most in need are least optimistic about their capacity to secure the housing amenities that they desire. Furthermore, it seems likely that their evaluation of the present situation is realistic.

Leaving moving plans aside, do respondents have other plans for the future as a function of housing satisfaction? In general, housing dissatisfaction is linked with plans for the future over and above those just for moving. More than 60 percent (61.2 percent) of those who are very dissatisfied with their housing have other plans compared to 36.3 percent of those who are very satisfied. In Exhibit 9.6 plans for the future are analyzed by category as a function of housing satisfaction. It is clear that even though the question was phrased to exclude housing, 37 respondents still indicate their prime desire is moving to another place. The largest single response is the 42 out of the 201 (20.9 percent) who indicate they hope to go to work. In addition, 26 (13 percent) refer to work as well as some other plan. Moving to another place is most significant for those who are dissatisfied or very dissatisfied with their housing.

In general, the better the housing, the greater the probability that the repondent feels confident of attaining his goals. Is this because people who answer that they are satisfied with their housing have minimal levels of aspiration and are thus satisfied with relatively easily attainable ends? Do those who indicate a great deal of housing dissatisfaction and who voice plans for the future also lack confidence in their realization? In the light of the interviewer's relatively objective appraisal of the housing quality and its correlation with the evaluation of respondents, this would not seem to be the case.

Welfare recipients rate housing highly negatively. In an earlier chapter, we analyzed their responses using the same methodology as in two other cities, one with a mixed economic group (Plainfield), and the other much more affluent (Princeton). There is a markedly negative distinction between the ratings given their accommodations by our New York City respondents compared to the others. And again, ratings given by occupants are substantially in accord with those secured from our own observations.

At the same time, the private market, which still dominates the housing of welfare recipients, is retreating from these areas. The private operator is influenced not only by current yield but by future expectations of yield. What will the building be worth over the next ten or 15 or 20 years? Will the owner be able to find somebody to finance a resale? Will he be able to increase the rent roll if he makes improvements? Or does he just play an end game, minimizing capital inputs, maximizing current yield and if the building or the health inspector or the tenants give too much trouble, essentially abandoning it? The answers to the first such questions play a large part in his decisions regarding the property, but the "end game" strategy is beginning to make substantial inroads among landlords. The rate of abandonment in New York City has been gauged at around 30,000 housing units per year; this in a city faced with a dreadful housing shortage. It is paralleled in a number of older core areas in other cities.[5]

While we hold no brief for the private operator of welfare structures, it should be clear that a workable alternative pattern has yet to be evolved. Low income co-ops and condominiums are much talked of but little experience has been accumulated with them. Nonprofit corporations and charitable institutions that have operated poverty housing have been more frequently burned by the deed than enhanced by it. Their contribution so far is relatively small. Even if one were willing to accept the basic parameters of the current market as satisfactory, a policy of inaction is not possible. The market is slipping, the parameters eroding and the necessity for action becoming more obvious every day.

It is too late to raise serious questions about whether the agrarian migration which was experienced a generation ago could have been diverted with less cost to the public and to its participants. While the New Deal did much to industrialize the South and aid its large-scale farmers, little thought was given to poor displacees from the land. Regardless of what potential efforts to develop migration policy might have had, most welfare recipients in New York City are either born in the city or are long-term residents there. New York has the incongruity of being the world's wealthiest city and the nation's major repository of the poor and helpless, of being a city whose housing stock is substantially designed for small families, affluent youth and office workers, while it serves as a major center for large households with many children. One can wish that the incongruity of the city's needs and its resources had generated more public action earlier, but it did not; yet this is the basic area in which policy must be optimized.

In the meantime, as the problem deepens it generates short-run resolutions which may be costly and deleterious in the long run. An area of potential danger is the question of tenant mix in public housing. Faced with desperate problems in finding housing for its welfare recipients, New York has adopted a policy of giving them priority in public housing. The question of the secondary impact of such a decision—of making public housing units the equivalent of welfare buildings, of compounding all of the problems that many of the recipients face by concentrating them—has not been properly weighed.

There is no question that previous relocation efforts have been scandalously inadequate. Old flophouses have masqueraded as hotels for large families, buildings about to be torn down have been used for relocation; such revelations have generated political discontent. They will not be resolved, however, by another Pruitt-Igoe development. What is the magic number? What is the correct proportion of welfare families in a building both in terms of the betterment of their lives and the perpetuation of the housing project as a livable mode of accommodation? These questions remain to be resolved. Depending upon the families under consideration, however, in all probability less than 100 percent welfare recipients, substantially less, is desirable; unfortunately 100 percent seems to be the direction of present policies.

New York City has some underutilized land occupied presently by police stations, by low-rise schools, by parking lots and the like. Much of this is suitable for private development. Whether the city should reserve part of the residential accommodations which could be generated under long-term leases for welfare recipients, or whether the city's return from the sale of compound building sites in very high-cost, high-value areas should be earmarked for construction in less desirable sites is a simple question of dollars and cents.

Reformers must realize that the city's capacity to deliver social services is substantially a function of its own wealth, of its capacity to generate new ratables in excess of the cost attendant to their construction. The optimization of facilities for the rich is inextricably tied to the capacity to provide for the poor. They are not antithetical goals, they are essentially complementary; every new ratable should be viewed as a victory rather than a defeat for the social reformer. Given the high costs attendant to maintaining the poor in big northern cities in general, and in New York City particularly, there is little hope that national policies or national support will ever adequately resolve the city's singular problems. The economic vigor of the city itself is essential to any degree of continuing social progress.

But any new housing policy must be developed with an understanding that the housing shortage has been a dominant characteristic of New York life for so long as to question whether it is not a chronic fact of life. However, the average size of the New York City household is decreasing sharply; the enormous number of new units constructed since World War II—estimated at about a half million units (in excess of demolitions)—have not been accompanied by increases in population but by a diminishing household size. This process may now be stabilizing as more suburbs open up to affluent minority groups, and the potential for bettering the housing and physical setting of the poor should increase. But this poses a problem in and of itself unless a stable middle class can be assumed. There is little point to a policy of dispersion of welfare recipients that produces a segregated situation through the dynamic of non-welfare recipients moving out. The ecology of the city is a most delicate one; what is required is a full-scale systematic analysis rather than short-run expedient actions.

The costs of failure are so great that much more experimentation should be tried than has been the case up to now. Building rehabilitation in New York City, for example, has not been generally successful, but this lack of success may be a consequence of lack of experience; as the learning curve is extrapolated much more in the way of expertise may be acquired on the part of contractors and administrators; the end results may well be satisfactory. The costs of experimental dollars must be weighed against the magnitude of the problem; from this perspective all past efforts in this direction have been trivial indeed. Furthermore, given present costs of new construction and the slow administrative process which characterizes it, there is no substitute for rehabilitation. It can be made to work, but it will require much harder-nosed political decision-making, a much more modest vision of the aesthetics, and a much more realistic view of the longevity of the improvements than has been the case in previous ventures.

New or updated building units within the environmental context described by the welfare recipients interviewed in this study cannot survive. Nor can the morale of the occupants. The fear of personal danger and of drug addiction must be erased. Building owners and their welfare tenants share one characteristic in common—a feeling that they are trapped in a hopeless struggle. If this pessimism and its underlying causes can be reversed, then progress can be made. If they cannot, then we will be left with a world that only science fiction writers at their most morbid have envisioned.

NOTES

1. For more data on the methodology which secured the latter see Chapter 2 and Appendix 5.1.

2. Helpful preliminary work on the material reported on in this section was done by Glen E. Margo, "A Social-Psychological Study of the Relationship of Satisfaction With Housing to Goal Planning and Achievement Motivation of Welfare Recipients," unpublished paper (New Brunswick, New Jersey: Rutgers University Graduate School of Social Work, December 1970).

3. See Charles W. Barr, *Housing-Health Relationships: An Annotated Bibliography* (Monticello, Illinois, Council of Planning Libraries, May 1969).

4. See Edward C. Banfield, *The Unheavenly City: The Nature and Future of Our Urban Crisis* (Boston: Little, Brown & Co., 1970), and Frank S. Kristof, "Housing: Economic Facets of New York City's Problems," pp. 297-348 in *Agenda for a City: Issues Confronting New York*, edited by Lyle C. Fitch and Annmarie Hauck Walsh (Beverly Hills, California: Sage Publications, 1970).

5. See George Sternlieb, *Some Aspects of the Abandoned House Problem* (New Brunswick, N.J.: Rutgers, 1970) and *Abandonment and Rehabilitation*, paper submitted to the House of Representatives Subcommittee on Housing of the Committee on Banking and Currency, Washington, D.C., January 1971.

Appendix 1.1

MEMORANDUM ON TRENDS IN AFDC BENEFIT LEVELS

TO: The Under Secretary   Date: July 2, 1971
Through: OS/ES _______
FROM: Department of Health, Education, and Welfare
Office of the Secretary
Assistant Secretary for
Community and Field Services

SUBJECT: Trends in AFDC Benefit Levels—Summary Memorandum

1. States which have reduced AFDC benefits during the past year, the amount of the reduction and the effect on a family of four with no income.

Alabama: Change in method of determining eligibility caused 6,000 of 30,000 families to be dropped from AFDC. *Effect on a family of four with no income:* For those who remained eligible, there was no change in benefits.

Georgia: Administrative changes resulted in a 2 percent drop in the payment per person, from $28.69 to $28.13 per month.

Maine: Legislative action. AFDC program for unemployed fathers discontinued.

New Jersey: Legislative action. AFDC unemployed fathers program eliminated and replaced by "Assistance to the Working Poor" program. The payment level is set at two-thirds of the AFDC standard.

New Mexico: Administrative action. Two percent ratable reduction from 90 percent to 88 percent. *Effect on a family of four with no income:*

Maximum monthly payment reduced from $183 to $179 ($4 per month reduction).

New York: Legislative action. Ten percent ratable reduction on the basic New York City standard in AFDC and Home Relief (the reduction does not apply to shelter, fuel for heating or special circumstance items). Thus, actual reductions occurred in New York City and in the seven metropolitan areas in which the New York City standard was in effect. This represents approximately 85 percent of all families receiving AFDC in the state. *Effect on a family of four with no income:* In eight Upstate counties, the statewide standard increased from $203 per month to $208 per month; In 42 Upstate counties, the statewide standard increased from $207 per month to $208 per month; In New York City and seven metropolitan areas, the Statewide standard decreased from $231 per month to $208 per month.

South Dakota: 10 percent reduction. *Effect on a family of four with no income:* $30 per month reduction.

2. States that have legislation pending to reduce AFDC benefits, and states that have had proposals for reductions that were defeated.

California: Legislation is pending which includes closed end appropriations and other measures that would reduce benefits or restrict eligibility.

Kansas: Legislation to reduce AFDC benefits considered in recent sessions but not passed.

Nebraska: Legislation to reduce AFDC benefits considered but not passed.

Nevada: Legislation to reduce AFDC benefits and legislation to eliminate AFDC defeated.

Rhode Island: Legislation to eliminate two specific benefit items (indebtedness and household furnishings and equipment) enacted, but has not been implemented due to pending court case.

Texas: A constitutional amendment to place a $55 million limit on AFDC was defeated in May 1971. The current constitutional limit is $80 million.

3. States that are anticipating changes in AFDC levels either by administrative action or through recommendations to the legislature.

Arizona: Closed end appropriation will result in a ratable reduction if program exceeds budget expectations.

Connecticut: Though the state welfare commissioner has the administrative authority to make a ratable reduction in assistance payments, he will request legislative action.

Delaware: Reduction by administrative action in response to legislative recommendations anticipated.

Georgia: Administrative changes resulted in slight increases overall effective July 1, 1971, though some families with considerable resources in addition to AFDC payments will experience slight decreases.

Hawaii: Three percent "cost of living" increase has been granted effective July 1, 1971.

Idaho: Minor reductions in benefits may be necessary if AFDC case loads continue to rise.

Illinois: Administrative action to adopt a ratable reduction possible later in the year if costs exceed expectations.

Kansas: Administrative action to reduce AFDC and all adult programs by 20 percent is to take effect September 1, 1971.

Maryland: Upward increase by administrative action in response to legislative recommendations likely.

Minnesota: Ratable reduction may be necessary before the end of the fiscal year due to $18 million cut in state agency AFDC request.

Mississippi: Effective March 1971, increased the percentage of the deficit met from 30 percent to 40 percent. The average payment increased from $12.07 to $13.97 per person per month.

Nebraska: Administrative action to reduce AFDC by 10 percent is planned to take effect August 1, 1971.

Nevada: Effective July 1, will increase benefits for a family of four with no income from $144 per month to $176 per month.

New Hampshire: Failure of the state legislature to approve the $13 million welfare budget for the next two years would result in a 48 percent reduction in all categories by August 15, 1971.

Ohio: Upward increase, but amount not yet determined. State currently pays 62 percent of its standard in AFDC cases.

Oklahoma: Effective June 1, 1971, AFDC payments raised $1 per person per month.

Oregon: There is the possibility of reductions in AFDC benefits if additional federal help is not forthcoming.

Pennsylvania: Reduction similar to that imposed in New York being considered.

Texas: Administrative action to reduce AFDC payments if case loads continue to rise.

Vermont: Administrative action to apply a ratable reduction of payments to AFDC recipients is likely in fiscal year 1972 if current trend of rising cost and case loads continues.

Washington, D.C.: Upward increase from 75 percent to 85 percent of standard (February 1970 level).

Wisconsin: Governor has requested funds from the legislature to raise AFDC from 82 percent to 90 percent of need.

4. States anticipating no changes in AFDC benefits: Arkansas, Colorado, Florida, Guam, Indiana, Iowa, Kentucky, Louisiana, Massachusetts, Michigan, Missouri, Montana, North Dakota, Puerto Rico, South Carolina, Tennessee, Utah, Virgin Islands, Virginia, Wyoming.

Appendix 1.2

CATEGORIES OF WELFARE

In New York City welfare recipients are granted aid under five basic public assistance categories:

1. *Aid to Families of Dependent Children.* This major category includes Aid to Families of Dependent Children (ADC) and Temporary Aid to Dependent Children (TADC). In May 1967 these two classifications incorporated three of every four welfare recipients in New York City. There were 506,269 recipients of ADC (inclusive of TADC) and of these, 368,937 were children under age 18. By February 1970 there were 737,957 persons receiving ADC and TADC and, if the ADC Unemployed Parent Category is added as a very close relative, the total number of recipients in this category is 778,397, or over three-fourths of the total of 1,049,386 persons receiving assistance in February 1970.[1]

2. *General Assistance.* In New York City General Assistance is known as Home Relief, and is granted to persons and families not eligible for aid under the other existing categories of public assistance. The Home Relief category of aid is the only one to which the federal government makes no contribution. As a result, local authorities tend to shift recipients from this category into programs which receive federal aid whenever permissible. For example, in 1960 there were 60,000 Home Relief recipients in New York City. In 1961 there were 50,500 and in 1962 there were 43,000. This decline was due to the introduction of TADC as a new

1. *Monthly Statistical Report,* the City of New York, Department of Social Services, April, 1970.

EXHIBIT APPENDIX 1.1.1

NATIONAL PUBLIC ASSISTANCE: AVERAGE MONTHLY PAYMENT BY CATEGORY OF WELFARE

YEAR	CATEGORY OF WELFARE								
	OAA	Aid to Blind	APTD[a]	AFDC (Family)	AFDC (Recipient)	General Assistance (Case)	General Assistance (Recipient)	EAF[b]	Inst. Serv. Inter. Care Fac.[c]
1960	$58.90	$ 67.45	$56.15	$108.35	$28.35	$ 71.60	$24.85	—	—
1961	57.60	68.05	57.05	114.65	29.45	67.95	26.15	—	—
1962	61.55	71.95	58.50	119.10	29.30	66.80	26.30	—	—
1963	62.80	73.95	59.85	122.40	29.70	67.95	27.45	—	—
1964	63.65	76.15	62.25	131.30	31.50	68.60	30.50	—	—
1965	63.10	81.35	66.50	136.95	32.85	68.95	31.65	—	—
1966	68.05	86.85	74.75	150.10	36.25	80.40	36.20	—	—
1967	70.15	90.45	80.60	161.70	39.50	87.65	39.40	—	—
1968	69.55	92.15	82.65	168.15	42.05	94.45	44.70	—	$153.05
1969	73.95	98.75	90.20	176.05	45.15	101.65	50.05	$113.00	246.80
1970 (Feb.)	75.20	100.30	91.30	178.00	45.75	104.75	50.95	109.00	238.60

Source: *Social Security Bulletin* (Vol. 34, No. 1, U.S. Department of Health, Education, and Welfare, Jan. 1971, Table M-24, p. 58).

[a]Aid to Persons Totally Disabled.

[b]Emergency Assistance Fund (excludes New York City).

[c]Institutional Service in Internal Care Facility (Social and Rehabilitation Service).

EXHIBIT APPENDIX 1.1.2
Part 1

NATIONAL PUBLIC ASSISTANCE MONEY PAYMENTS

	CATEGORY OF WELFARE								
	AFDC					GA[c]			
YEAR	Number of Families[b]	Number of Recipients Total	Number of Recipients Children	Total Payments	Average Monthly Payment[d]	Number of Recipients	Total Payments	Average Monthly Payment[d]
1960	803	3,073	2,370	$ 994,425	$28.35	1,244	$319,521	$24.85
1961	916	3,566	2,753	1,148,838	29.45	1,069	351,395	26.15
1962	932	3,789	2,844	1,289,824	29.30	900	289,538	26.30
1963	954	3,930	2,951	1,355,538	29.70	872	277,432	27.45
1964	1,012	4,219	3,170	1,496,525	31.50	779	270,260	30.50
1965	1,054	4,396	3,316	1,644,096	32.85	677	260,612	31.65
1966	1,127	4,666	3,526	1,849,886	36.25	663	251,877	36.20
1967	1,297	5,309	3,986	2,249,673	39.50	782	323,060	39.40
1968	1,522	6,086	4,555	2,823,841	42.05	826	419,514	44.70
1969	1,875	7,313	5,413	3,533,281	45.15	857	474,418	50.05
1970 (Feb.)	1,973	7,676	5,664		45.75	919		50.95

Source: Social and Rehabilitation Service, U.S. Department of Health, Education and Welfare in *Social Security Bulletin* (Vol. 33, No. 12, December 1970).

[a] In thousands.
[b] In thousands.
[c] Date incomplete.
[d] Amounts to recipient only. (Separate data for AFDC families; separate data for GA cases.)

EXHIBIT APPENDIX 1.1.2
Part 2

NATIONAL PUBLIC ASSISTANCE MONEY PAYMENTS

	CATEGORY OF WELFARE									
		OAA			AB			APTD		
YEAR	Total Amounts[a]	Number of Recipients[b]	Total Payments	Average Monthly Payment	Number of Recipients[b]	Total Payments	Average Monthly Payment	Number of Recipients[b]	Total Payments	Average Monthly Payment
1960	$3,262,769	2,305	$1,626,021	$58.90	106.9	86,080	67.45	369	$236,402	$56.15
1961	3,410,548	2,229	1,568,987	57.60	102.7	84,506	68.05	389	255,645	57.05
1962	3,512,128	2,183	1,566,121	61.55	98.7	83,856	71.95	428	281,117	58.50
1963	3,647,906	2,152	1,610,310	62.80	96.9	85,122	73.95	464	317,656	59.85
1964	3,817,446	2,120	1,606,561	63.65	95.5	86,189	76.15	509	355,643	62.25
1965	3,995,907	2,087	1,594,183	63.10	85.1	77,308	81.35	557	416,765	66.50
1966	4,305,507	2,073	1,630,131	68.05	83.7	84,708	86.85	588	487,212	74.75
1967	4,931,681	2,073	1,698,145	70.15	82.7	86,950	90.45	646	573,575	80.60
1968	5,672,143	2,027	1,673,191	69.55	80.7	87,828	92.15	702	655,792	82.65
1969	6,866,372	2,077	1,746,714	73.95	80.5	91,390	98.75	803	786,757	90.20
1970 (Feb.)		2,062		75.20	80.3		100.30	819		91.30

category of public assistance in May 1961, and many eligible Home Relief recipients were reclassified. By 1965, however, there was a total of 67,300 persons in the Home Relief category. In October 1970 the number of Home Relief recipients had grown to 70,954.

3. *Old Age Assistance.* According to the Social Security Act, needy persons age 65 or over are entitled to Old Age Assistance. In 1960, 41,900 persons were recipients of this type of assistance in New York City. The number declined in 1961 and 1962 when some aged recipients were separated and placed into a new category, Medical Assistance to the Aged. However, by February 1970 this category had grown to 63,932 persons.

4. *Aid to the Disabled.* According to the Social Security Act Amendments of 1950, aid was given if a needy person was at least 18 years old and permanently and totally disabled. In New York City in 1960 there were 24,700 recipients in this category, in 1965 there were 21,500, while in February 1970 there were 53,370.

5. *Aid to the Blind.* The federal statutory requirements of Aid to the Blind are similar to requirements for Old Age Assistance except that there is no age requirement. The states have the responsibility to define blindness. This group is clearly small and has been rather stable in number over the last ten years. In 1960 there were 2,500 recipients and in 1965 there were 2,100 persons in this category. In February 1970 there were 2,380.

Exhibits Appendix 1.1.1 and 1.1.2 contain data on New York and national welfare costs respectively.

In the analysis which follows the categories of welfare have been grouped as follows: 1) ADC including TADC; 2) Home Relief; 3) Old Age Assistance; 4) Other Disabled—all other forms of disability related welfare.

Appendix 2.1

INTERVIEW FORMS

1. Interview Number
2. Health Area
3. Serial Number of Housing Unit
4. Identification Number of Interviewer
5. Address
6. Apartment Number

6A. Borough

Note Classification Change: (That is if assignment identified respondent to have one type of welfare and interviewer finds respondent the recipient of another type.)

Note: Has respondent ever lived in public housing? How long has respondent been on welfare?

7. Who is the head of this household? (Enter response on Line 1 of Table 2.1.1.)
8. Who are the other family members living in this apartment? (Enter names below Line 1 of Table 2.1.1 and complete columns about each one.)
9. Does anyone else besides your immediate family live in this apartment? (Enter names in remaining spaces in Table 2.1.1.)

   Is there anyone who usually lives here but is temporarily away on business? at school? in hospital or on a visit or vacation?

TABLE 2.1.1

Line Number (Circle Line Number of Respondent)	Name (Last Name First)	Relationship to Household Head	Household Member	Sex	Age Last Birthday	Color or Ethnic Group	If 16 Years or Over		
							Marital Status	Education Completed	In School Now
	List all persons staying here and all persons who usually live here who are absent. Be sure to include infants under 1 year of age.	Examples: head, wife, son, daughter-in-law, partner, lodger, lodger's wife, etc.	Circle Y for yes Circle N for no	Circle M (male) Circle F (female)	Enter year. If under one year enter "0"	White Negro Puerto Rican Cuban Other (specify)	Is now married widowed divorced separated single	Enter code from below.	Circle Y for yes Circle N for no
1.			Y N	M F					Y N
2.			Y N	M F					Y N
3.			Y N	M F					Y N
4.			Y N	M F					Y N
5.			Y N	M F					Y N
6.			Y N	M F					Y N
7.			Y N	M F					Y N
8.			Y N	M F					Y N

Codes for education completed: None – 00; Elementary – 01-08; High School – 09-12; College (Academic) – 13-18; Other – explain.

Is there anyone who usually lives here but is temporarily away on business? at school? in hospital or on a visit or vacation?

TABLE 2.1.2

Type of Housing (Excluding hallways, bath, foyer)

10A. Housing	10B. Number of Rooms	10C. Number of rooms for sleeping	10D. Number of rooms used
1. House			
2. Apartment			
3. Public Housing			
4. Other (explain)			

TABLE 2.1.3

FACILITIES	LANDLORD	RESPONDENT	SHARED	NOT IN BUILDING
Furnished dwellings				
Unfurnished dwellings				
Cold running water				
Hot running water				
Flush toilet				
Bath/shower (specify number)				
Stove (cooking equipment)				
Refrigerator				
Superintendent in building				
Washing machine				
Clothes dryer				
Exterminating service				
Other (specify)				

11. With reference to where you are now living, check one of the following:
    1. Own it
    2. Pay full rent
    3. Share the rent
    4. Superintendent*
       * (Amount of rent reduction for service)
    5. Other (explain)

11A. If rent is shared, by whom?
    1. With another family
    2. With member of the household

12. How long have you lived in your present apartment?
    1. Number of years
    2. Number of months

13A. Do you have a lease for your present apartment?
    1. Yes If yes, for how long?
    2. No

13B. Have there been any increases in your rent since you moved in?
   1. Yes If yes, how many times?
      From_____ to ______
      For what services? (explain)
   2. No If no, how much do you presently pay?
13C. Are there any additional payments made?
14. How did you find this apartment?
14A. In searching for housing, do you feel you were always treated fairly?
   1. Yes
   2. No
14B. If no, in what way do you feel you were treated unfairly?
15. Did you receive any assistance from the Welfare Department in your search for this apartment? (Probe: any other apartment?)
   1. Yes
   2. No
15A. If "Yes," what kind of assistance did you receive?
15B. Did you find the assistance useful? (Probe)
15C. If "No," how do you feel the Welfare Department might have been helpful? (Probe)
16. Which of the following items are included in your rent?
   Note: Check columns in Table 2.1.3 for person responsible.

Rate the following in Table 2.1.4:

TABLE 2.1.4

MAINTENANCE OF BUILDING

	(1) Very Good	(2) Good	(3) Fair	(4)[a] Poor	(5)[b] Very Poor
Apartment size					
Building maintenance					
Apartment maintenance					
Safety in area					
Public transportation available					
Location (near what I would like to be near)					
Garbage disposal					
Other concerns (specify and rate)					

[a]If this category, give detailed information.
[b]If this category, give detailed information.

Now that we've rated these items, let's take a look at some special areas of maintenance.

17A. What do you have to do to get repairs done in this apartment?
17B. When was your apartment last painted?
17C. Have you had any specific problems with rats?
17D. Have you had any specific problems with roaches?
17E. Have you had any specific problems with garbage disposal?
17F. Have there been any violations filed against the landlord by the city, to your knowledge?
17G. Have you had any organized rent strikes in your building? If yes, how successful were they?
18. If you rent your apartment, how do you pay your rent?
1. Daily
2. Weekly
3. Monthly
4. Other (explain)
19. What is your total rent? What are additional payments made up of? (Check each one that is included — approximate cost if exact figure is not known)
1. Rent for apartment/house
2. Electricity*
3. Gas*
4. Telephone company (in manual)
5. Heating fuel
6. Other (explain)
7. Don't know
Total Cost
20. Did your landlord require a security deposit?
1. Yes If yes, how much?
2. No
3. Other (explain)
21. Did Welfare pay this amount?
1. Yes If yes, how much?
2. No
22. Were any other real estate broker fees required?
1. Yes If yes, how much?
2. No
3. Other (explain)
23. Did Welfare pay?
1. Yes If yes, how much?
2. No
24. For which utilities did you have to pay deposits?
1. Gas Amount__________
2. Electricity Amount__________
3. Telephone company Amount__________
4. None
5. Other (specify)
25. Has full or partial deposit been returned?
26. Did Welfare pay for the deposits?
1. Yes If yes, how much?
2. No

* Clarify if supplemental heat for apartment was included, i.e., number of rooms heated, what respondent does if there is no heat.

26A. Has the head of the household been employed at any time within the last year.
1. Yes
2. No
If yes, check one of the following:
1. Employed full-time
2. Employed part-time
3. In training
4. Other (explain)
If no, check one of the following:
1. Business discontinued
2. Laid off
3. Moved away from place of employment
4. Plant relocation
5. In school
6. Acute illness/accident
7. Chronic illness/long-term disability
8. Needed at home (child care)
9. Retired
10. Other (explain)

27. How much money does the family have to live on per month?

TABLE 2.1.5

	1970		1969	
	$ Amount	% Total	$ Amount	% Total
Employment income				
Welfare grants				
Savings				
Support contribution				
Other (explain)				
Total				

28. How would you feel if a part of your rental payments built up partial ownership of an apartment?
Additional question to be asked:
Is there anyone else in the household (besides assigned respondent) receiving welfare assistance? (If more than one other, list separately.
1. Yes
2. No
If yes, give the type and monthly amount of the assistance.
Relationship to head of household
Total amount of welfare grants (Including respondents and other members of household)

29. What do you want most in a place to live that you don't have now?
Additional comments:

30. What type of assistance are you receiving from welfare?
    1. Aid to Dependent Children (ADC)
    2. Old Age Assistance (OAA)
    3. Aid to the Disabled (AD)
    4. Aid to the Blind (AB)
    5. Aid to Dependent Children of unemployed parents (ADC)
    6. General Assistance (GA)
    7. Veterans benefits
    8. Other (explain)
    9. Don't know

31. Are you active with any welfare rights groups?
    1. Yes
    2. No

31A. If yes, how often do you attend meetings of this organization?

32. How satisfied are you with the place you are living in now? (Give reasons below)
    1. Very satisfied
    2. Satisfied
    3. Undecided
    4. Dissatisfied
    5. Very dissatisfied

33A. Looking at your present situation, where do you expect to be living one year from now?

33B. What are your chances of reaching this goal?
    1. Excellent
    2. Good
    3. Fair
    4. Poor
    5. Very poor

34A. Do you have any other plans for the future?
    1. Yes
    2. No

34B. If yes, briefly tell in your own words what they are (Code: specific short-term versus specific long-term):

34C. If you have plans for the future, in about how long do you hope they will be achieved? (Preferences?)
    1. One month or less
    2. Two to six months
    3. Six months to one year
    4. One to three years
    5. Four years or more

34D. Do you feel the achievement of these plans will be worth the effort on your part? (Expectations?)
    1. Well worth it
    2. Worth it
    3. Undecided
    4. Not worth it
    5. A waste of time

35. There is an old saying "A bird in the hand is worth two in the bush." To what extent do you agree with this statement?
    1. Strongly agree
    2. Mildly agree
    3. Undecided
    4. Mildly disagree
    5. Strongly disagree

36. How long have you lived in (name of city)?
 1. Less than one year
 2. One to two years
 3. Three to four years
 4. Five to nine years
 5. Ten to 14 years
 6. 15 years or over
 7. Always lived here (skip to question no. 42)

36A. What were your reasons for moving to New York City?

37. What type of place did you live in just before coming here?
 1. Large city
 2. Small city
 3. Small town
 4. Rural

38. What state did you live in just before coming here?
 1. New Jersey
 2. Pennsylvania
 3. Other northern or western state
 4. Southern state
 5. Out of country

39. What state were you born in?
 1. New Jersey
 2. New York
 3. Pennsylvania
 4. Other northern or western state
 5. Southern state
 6. Out of country

40. Altogether, during your lifetime, how many different cities or towns have you lived in?
 1. One
 2. Two
 3. Three
 4. Four
 5. Five
 6. Six
 7. Seven
 8. Eight or more
 9. Don't know

41. What are your plans for staying in this city?
 1. Definitely will stay
 2. Probably will stay
 3. Probably will not stay
 4. Definitely will not stay
 5. Don't know

42. All of us want certain things out of life. When you think about what really matters in your own life, what are your wishes and hopes for the future?

43. Now, taking the other side of this picture, what are your fears and worries about the future? In other words, if you imagine your future in the worst possible light, what would your life look like then? Take your time in answering.

Note: Here is a picture of a ladder (flash card #1—see Appendix 6.1). Suppose we say that the top of the ladder (pointing) represents the best possible life for you and the bottom (pointing) represents the worst possible life for you.

44. Where on the ladder (moving finger rapidly up and down ladder) do you feel you personally stand at the present time (step number)?
45. Where on the ladder would you say you stood five years ago (step number)?
46. And where do you think you will be on the ladder five years from now (step number)?
47. Now, what are your wishes and hopes for the future of our country? If you picture the United States in the best possible light, how would things look, let us say ten years from now?
48. And what about your fears and worries for the future of our country? If you picture the future of the United States in the worst possible light, how would things look in about ten years?
49. Now, looking at the ladder again (flash card #1) suppose your greatest hopes for the United States are at the top (pointing); your worst fears at the bottom (pointing), where would you put the United States on the ladder (moving finger rapidly up and down ladder) at the present time (step number)?
50. Where did the United States stand five years ago (step number)?
51. Just as your best guess, where do you think the United States will be on the ladder five years from now (step number)?

Introduction to the semantic differential

The purpose of this measure is to see how you feel about certain things. There is no right answer and no wrong answer. Your answer will be used in no way to judge you. We just want your frank opinion. On each page of this section you will find a series of word pairs arranged in the following way:

Good _______:_______:_______:_______:_______:_______:_______ Bad

Here is how you are to use the scales. You will put an X in the middle of the line section that best describes how you feel about the word to be rated. Each line section has a meaning.

My Family

Good _______:_______:_______:_______:_______:_______:_______ Bad

feel strongly good	feel pretty good	feel only slightly good	neither good or bad or don't know	feel slightly bad	feel pretty bad	feel strongly bad

If, for example, in giving your opinion you felt the word was very bad, you would mark as follows:

Good _______:_______:_______:_______:_______:_______:___X___ Bad

If you thought it was pretty good, you would mark:

Good _______:___X___:_______:_______:_______:_______:_______ Bad

If you can't make up your mind or if you felt it was neither good or bad, you would mark:

Good _______:_______:_______:___X___:_______:_______:_______ Bad

On the following pages — one page for each word presented — you are to rate the word according to all 16 of the scales on the page.

Remember

1. Make your mark in the middle of the space

_______:___X___:_______ this

_______:_______X_______ not this

2. Please do not skip any scales. Mark the middle line if you cannot make up your mind.

3. Never put more than one X on a scale.

Important: If you don't understand the instructions, ask the person who is administering the session. If you want to, you may remove the instruction sheet to refer to as you go through the questions.

Welfare

Good _____:_____:_____:_____:_____:_____:_____ Bad

Soft _____:_____:_____:_____:_____:_____:_____ Hard

Active _____:_____:_____:_____:_____:_____:_____ Passive

Cruel _____:_____:_____:_____:_____:_____:_____ Kind

Strong _____:_____:_____:_____:_____:_____:_____ Weak

Calm _____:_____:_____:_____:_____:_____:_____ Excitable

Clean _____:_____:_____:_____:_____:_____:_____ Dirty

Light _____:_____:_____:_____:_____:_____:_____ Heavy

Hot _____:_____:_____:_____:_____:_____:_____ Cold

Unsuccessful _____:_____:_____:_____:_____:_____:_____ Successful

Masculine _____:_____:_____:_____:_____:_____:_____ Feminine

Slow _____:_____:_____:_____:_____:_____:_____ Fast

Important _____:_____:_____:_____:_____:_____:_____ Unimportant

Small _____:_____:_____:_____:_____:_____:_____ Large

Foolish _____:_____:_____:_____:_____:_____:_____ Wise

Healthy _____:_____:_____:_____:_____:_____:_____ Sick

Repeat the scales using the code words "My Apartment", "Myself" and "Public Housing".

Public Housing

If you or a friend of yours got an apartment in the project (public housing) do you think you or they would feel:
1. Very happy
2. Moderately happy
3. Not so happy
4. Very unhappy
Why? Give reasons

To be completed by interviewer

a. Date completed

Month	Day (2 digits)	Time Completed
		1. Before noon 2. Noon to 5 p.m. 3. 5 to 7 p.m. 4. After 7 p.m.

b. Day of interview

c. Type of Interview
   1. Personal — first visit
   2. Personal — second visit
   3. Personal — third visit
   4. Personal — fourth visit
   5. Personal — fifth visit
   6. Telephone interview
   7. No interview
   8. Final follow-up interview
   9. Other

d. No interview
   1. No one home
   2. Temporarily absent
   3. Refused
   4. Moved
   5. Condemned, vacant, demolished
   6. Other (specify)

e. Name of person interviewed
   Telephone number of person interviewed

Inspector Interviewer # Parcel #
Date

Inside Condition Analysis

1. Vestibule appearance: A. Good B. Fair C. Poor
   Paint, light or litter
2. Mailbox condition: A. Good B. Fair C. Poor
   Are there mailboxes present? If so, do they have adequate doors and are they locked?
3. Bell system: A. Good B. Fair C. Poor
   Do the bells seem to be in proper condition for usage or are there some which are either missing or ripped out?
4. Are there elevators in the building? A. Yes B. No
5. If yes, what is the condition of the elevator cabs themselves?
   A. Good B. Fair C. Poor
   We refer here to paint, litter, smell, automatic or manual
6. Is the elevator self-operating? A. Yes B. No
   Note that in some cases there may be elevator men on duty, but only part of the day. If it is any significant part of the day answer yes.
7. Banisters and stairwells: A. Good B. Fair C. Poor
   Paint, sturdiness, littering conditions, missing rungs, etc.
8. Fire extinguishers: A. Present B. Not present

8a. If present, is the inspection date which should be pinned onto one of them within one year? A. Yes B. No

9. Appearance of hallways: A. Good B. Fair C. Poor
   We refer here to paint, cracks in plaster, litter and so on.
10. Hallway lighting quality: A. Good B. Fair C. Poor
    Are the lights adequate? Are there any lights? Are they properly shielded?
11. Condition of doors: A. Good B. Fair C. Poor
    Are hallway doors in reasonable condition in terms of paint and general capacity to operate properly? Are there evident signs of crude carpenter-type repairs?
12. Basement maintenance condition: A. Good B. Fair C. Poor
    General appearance of basement in terms of its present utilization. Is there an accumulation of garbage and litter in the basement? Does there seem to be adequate lighting? Does it smell?
13. Central heat: A. Yes B. No
    If yes, what type fuel? A. Oil B. Gas C. Coal D. Other
    Note above, if there is no central heat, list what type of heating is used.

14. General opinion of the interior of the building's maintenance numerical rating:
A. Excellent = 100 B. Good = 80 C. Fair = 60
D. Poor = 40 E. Very poor = 20
Note once again that we are interested in this building in terms of its interior maintenance as compared with the interior maintenance of building of similar age, size category, i.e., new law tenements over 50 units, and so on. Therefore use a comparative rather than an absolute standard.

Appendix 3.1

CHARACTERISTICS OF HOUSEHOLDS WITH CHILDREN

The proportion of sample households with children under ten is 52.4 percent. In this appendix we will highlight some of the salient variations in welfare households with children under ten compared to those who do not have them.

Age of Head of Household

Two-thirds of the heads of households with children under ten are under the age of 26. In other households barely 12 percent of the heads of household are this young.

Ethnicity

Households with minors under the age of ten are nearly exclusively black or Spanish speaking. Each of these groups makes up slightly more than 45 percent of the total with white non-Spanish speaking consisting of only 8.3 percent. By contrast, the households without children under ten have a broad spread with 23.5 percent white non-Spanish speaking, 41.8 percent, black and 33.2 percent Spanish speaking.

Marital Status

Less than 30 percent of these households are headed by married individuals (22.2 percent) or divorced (7.4 percent). The equivalent combination for households with no children under ten is 48 percent. Of those with children under ten, 11.1 percent are divorced, 43.5 percent are separated, 15.3 percent are single, and less than 1 percent indicate a common law arrangement. The lack of both a mother and father in the household is the predominate pattern.

Levels of Education

In general, heads of households with children under ten are better educated than are those without such minors. Thirty-four percent of the former, have less than a ninth grade education compared to nearly two-thirds of the latter. However, an additional 22.7 percent of the households with children under ten are headed by people with less than an eleventh grade education.

More than three out of five of the households with children under ten are headed by a person with less than an eleventh grade education. If the capacity of a parent to be of support to a youngster's education is determined by his own level of education, it is clear that children under ten raised in welfare families suffer a substantial disability.

Number of Rooms in the Apartment

Only 5.1 percent of these families have two or fewer rooms. Another 18.1 percent, however, have three rooms and the largest single proportion is in four room apartments. In 17 percent of the cases there is only one room for sleeping; 41.7 percent have two sleeping rooms. With few exceptions, they are all renters. In about one out of six cases, the household shares the rent with another family.

There is a comparably high level of transiency. Fully 30 percent of the families with small children have been in their present apartments less than a year. (The equivalent figure for the other group is only 20 percent.) Another 22 percent have been in their apartments for more than one, but less than two years. Only a minority had leases on their present apartments.

Number of People in Household

Less than 30 percent (27.8) of the households with small children have three or fewer members of the household. Four member households are 22.2 percent, five member households are 16.2 percent, 13.4 percent are six member households, and households with seven or more are about 20 percent. In slightly more than half the cases, at least one child is between ten and 18. Typically, there are no old people in the household. Fewer than one out of five (18.5 percent) have somebody in the household over the age of 50. Nearly one-third of the households without small children have someone over age 50.

Method of Finding Housing

Families with small children are slightly less likely to use relatives or friends to find accommodations and slightly more likely to live in public housing. For all categories, however, use of the Welfare Department is relatively infrequent.

Feelings of Prejudice

More than a quarter (27.8 percent) of the heads of households with children under ten feel they were treated unfairly in finding housing. This is more than double the proportion (11.2 percent) of those who do not have children under the age of ten. About one-fourth of the respondents indicate race as the cause (16 out of 60), substantially less then those without children (ten out of 22). Twenty-seven (45 percent) of those with small children indicate that the discrimination was because of welfare status while 21 (35 percent) feel it was the size of household that created the difficulty.

Assistance from the Welfare Department

Some assistance from the Welfare Department is indicated by 28.7 percent of the respondents with small children. In nearly three out of four cases it is financial assistance with rent deposits. Less than a dozen indicate specific help in finding housing. Most of the respondees indicate the assistance is useful, but strictly from a financial point of view.

Levels of Amenities

Barely 10 percent of the housing units occupied by families with young children are furnished (10.6 percent) compared to nearly one-third of those without such children (32.1 percent). In 95 percent of the cases, these families have hot and cold running water and toilets, baths or showers for their exclusive use; 2.8 percent indicate that these facilities are shared and a surprising 2 percent indicate that they are not in the building.

In 88 percent of the cases, the landlord furnishes the stove. In 8.3 percent of the cases the tenant claims that he must supply it, while 3.2 percent indicate that they share their cooking facilities.

Nearly one-fourth (23.6 percent) indicate that they provide their own refrigerator. One-third are housed in buildings with no resident superintendent. Less than 1 percent have private washing machines furnished by the landlord. Nearly 30 percent provide their own with an additional 10 percent sharing with a specific household. In nearly 60 percent of the cases, however, there is no washing machine in the building, and in 90 percent of the households there are no dryers. Five percent indicate that they have to provide their own exterminator service.

Rating of Apartment Amenities

Approximately 30 percent find their *apartment size* poor or very poor, compared to 15 percent of those without children under the age of 10.

Approximately one-third find *building maintenance* poor or very poor. (This is exceeded by the good or very good.) Apartment maintenance figures are substantially the same but tended toward a slightly higher good or very good level.

Safety in the area is the lowest rated amenity. Only 27.8 percent indicate it is good or very good while fully 48.6 percent say bad or very bad. This is substantially in excess of the negatives given by those without children under ten where the equivalent figures are 20.4 percent and 18.4 percent, while fully 35 percent of those who do not have children under the age of ten indicate very good or good.

Both groups of respondents view *public transportation* with considerable approval. But people with children under the age of ten are slightly more negative about *location:* 16.2 percent indicated poor or very poor compared to less than 10 percent of those without small children.

Both groups rate *garbage disposal* positively. However, 18.3 percent of those with small children rate it poor or very poor, and only 10.2 percent of those without such children. Of the 39 who gave negative responses, 22 indicate that the problem is caused by the landlord, typically due to lack of storage space for garbage.

Fully 47.7 percent of all families with children under the age of ten had problems with *rats.* In two-thirds of the cases this is not merely a trivial or occasional problem but a significant one.

Roach problems are voiced by more than 70 percent of the respondents with small children, and in 60 percent of the cases they are significant. Yet, at the same time, most of the respondents indicate no difficulty with garbage disposal.

Families with small children, perhaps because of their relatively new tenure, typically have apartments which have been relatively recently painted. More than half indicating painting within the past two years and 10 percent within three years. Sixteen percent simply didn't know, with 5 percent indicating some period of greater length.

Age, Planning Area and Violations in the Structure

Twenty-two percent of the families with young children live in Old Law Structures, with 54.4 percent in New Laws, and 23.3 percent in buildings built after 1929. Notice that 62.7 percent live in Major Action Planning Areas, 29.2 percent in Planning Area 2 (requiring a more modest level of intervention) with only eight percent in Sound Areas. Only 43 percent of the structures have no violations, 11.2 percent have two to five violations, 9.8 percent have six violations, and the balance of the sample have more than that.

The typical welfare family with young children lives in a six story or more structure (approximately 50 percent of those for whom we have data); another 30 percent live in a three or four story structure with less than 6 percent in a one or two story configuration.

Interior Maintenance Rating

In general the interior maintenance ratings are quite similar to those of the balance of the sample; three out of eight respondents rate it poor or very poor.

Plans to Stay in New York

Of the households with children under ten, 43.5 percent say that they will stay in the city; 24.1 percent indicate that they probably will; 11.1 percent indicate that they probably will not while only 2.8 percent indicate that they definitely will not. Fully 18.5 percent say that they simply do not know. A slightly heavier level of transiency is evident in this group than for other people on welfare with the difference essentially in the Old Age group.

Previous Location

Typically, the vast majority (78.5 percent) of the respondents with small children have only lived in two cities. Heads of households with children under ten have lived in New York a somewhat shorter time than the balance of the sample. Approximately one-fourth (24.1 percent) were born in New York. An additional 33.8 percent have lived in New York for 15 years or more (15.7 percent in from five to nine years and 15.7 percent from ten to 14 years). Only 10.7 percent are recent arrivals, i.e., less than five years in New York.

Reasons for Moving to New York

Heads of households with children under 10 give reasons for moving to New York similar to those of other respondents—jobs and family.

Slightly less than 30 percent lived in a large city prior to coming here, with slightly under one-fourth from a small city and the balance from small towns or rural surroundings.

Like most of the respondents, about a third were born in some Southern state, while 60 percent were born outside the country, typically in Puerto Rico. For most of the respondents, the move to New York was their first.

Appendix 4.1

THE FURNISHED APARTMENT DWELLER

EXHIBIT 4.1
WELFARE TYPE BY FURNISHED/UNFURNISHED APARTMENT

WELFARE TYPE	Furnished[a]	Unfurnished[b]
Home Relief	20.9%	17.5%
Old Age Assistance	26.8	9.8
Aid to Disabled[c]	24.4	11.0
Aid to Dependent Children	27.9	61.7
	100.0	100.0

a. N = 86.
b. N = 326.
c. Includes Aid to the Blind and Veterans Assistance.

Sex. The furnished apartment dweller is more likely to be male than the unfurnished apartment dweller; forty-three percent of the furnished apartments had male heads of household versus only 16.9 percent of the unfurnished units.

Age. In general, furnished apartments house older people. Over 40 percent are occupied by people over age 58 compared to less than 20 percent of the unfurnished. Fifty-two of the 86 furnished apartments had someone over age 50 living in them. However, more than one-fourth of the heads of household in the furnished units are under age 37. In unfurnished units, 44 percent are in that same age group.

Ethnicity. A slightly higher proportion of furnished apartments is occupied by whites—23.3 percent versus 13.5 percent for the unfurnished.

Marital Status. Nearly one-fourth of the furnished units are occupied by widowed individuals versus 16 percent of the unfurnished. Fully one-fourth of the residents are people who describe themselves as single, versus 15.3 percent of those living in unfurnished units.

Number of Rooms. More than one-third (35 percent) of the furnished apartments are single rooms versus 2.1 percent of the unfurnished. Less than 20 percent of the furnished units have more than four rooms. SROs or institutions account for 26.7 percent of the furnished apartments versus less than 1 percent of the unfurnished units.

Length of Residence in Apartment. There is relatively little variation between furnished and unfurnished apartment occupants in length of residence. Only 24.4 percent of the furnished apartment residents and 26.4 percent of the unfurnished unit residents have lived there for a year or less. Rent for most furnished units is paid on a monthly basis. If the city is paying a premium for such accommodations, investment in furniture might be worthwhile.

Rent Increases. There is no great variation between furnished and unfurnished units in rent increases over time.

Number of Persons in Furnished Apartments. Forty-three percent of furnished apartments are one person occupancies as compared with 11.3 percent of the unfurnished. An additional 20 percent versus 17.2 percent are two person occupancies. About 20 percent of the furnished apartments are occupied by five or more people.

Children in Furnished Apartments. Nearly 30 percent of the furnished apartments are occupied by families with children, and over 60 percent of the unfurnished. The number of children under ten years among furnished apartments is quite comparable with the unfurnished facilities. About one-fifth of the furnished apartments group have children from ten to 18 years, and slightly less than half of the unfurnished. Furnished facilities are not used only by the elderly.

Search Pattern for Apartments. Search patterns vary little between the two categories. Fifty-three percent of the 86 respondents who had furnished apartments had secured them through a relative or friend, compared to 46 percent of the unfurnished. The rest of the answers for both categories are scattered.

Did You Receive Fair Treatment? Eighty-five percent of furnished apartment dwellers felt that they had received fair treatment while they were searching for an apartment. The 15 percent who felt that they had been discriminated against gave a variety of reasons. Only three answered that race played a role, while twice that number felt they were discriminated against as welfare recipients.

Assistance of the Welfare Department in Securing an Apartment. Less than one out of five (18.6 percent) of the furnished apartment dwellers indicated that the Welfare Department had helped them get an apartment compared to 25 percent of the non-furnished recipients. Note that 8 percent of furnished apartment dwellers were already receiving welfare assistance when they secured their present accommodations compared to 18.1 percent of the non-furnished residents. Those that received assistance typically received financial help rather then help in finding the apartment. When assistance was given it was found to be quite useful.

Rating of Problems. Half of the furnished dwellers rated their apartment size as either very good or good, and less than 20 percent indicated it was poor or very poor. This was in line with ratings of non-furnished apartment dwellers. The same is true of building and apartment maintenance, with just a shade more negative feeling from residents of furnished apartments. Safety in the area was a cause of concern and was rated negatively by both furnished and unfurnished apartment dwellers. Public transportation, frequency of painting, location and garbage collection were generally rated the same. A small minority of both groups (12.8 percent of the furnished and 16.6 percent of the unfurnished) indicated a significant garbage problem. Rats were a problem for 30.2 percent of furnished apartment dwellers versus 44.8 percent of those living in unfurnished units. Roughly 60 percent of each group who had this problem indicated that it was significant. Roach problems were similar in incidence for both categories. In about 30 percent of the furnished facilities hot and cold water was shared. Nearly half (46.5 percent) of the furnished apartments shared toilet, baths and showers. Stoves were shared in half the cases and simply were not available in one out of six cases.

Frequency of Rent Payment. More than 80 percent of furnished apartment dwellers pay their rent weekly or bi-weekly. Daily payments were indicated by 13 of the 83 respondents (15.7 percent). This may account for some deviation in the actual rents paid.

Security Deposits. Perhaps because of the frequency of rent payments, only 44 percent of the landlords of the furnished apartment dwellers required security deposits in contrast to 83 percent of the non-furnished. Between 50 and 60 percent of welfare recipients were required to pay such deposits. *The employment patterns* are similar for both groups.

Employment Income in 1970. Roughly one out of every six (15.3 percent) of the furnished apartment dwellers were at least partially employed in 1970 compared to 21.8 percent of those living in unfurnished apartments. The same pattern held in 1969. Less than 4 percent of each group reported no income from welfare in 1969.

Attitudes Toward Rental/Ownership. Approximately half of each group indicated they would like their rental payments to build up to partial ownership of their apartment. Because furnished room/furnished apartment dwellers are generally older, more negative answers were given, with 20 percent indicating a negative position versus less than half that (6 percent) for the non-furnished.

When respondents were asked, "What do you want most in a place to live that you don't have now?", there were more "nothing" responses (26.7 percent) from the furnished apartment dwellers than the unfurnished (12.9 percent). One out of seven of the furnished apartment dwellers said that they would like furniture or appliances versus less than 10 percent of the unfurnished. Otherwise there was relatively little variation in this sub-area.

Few of either group were active in welfare rights groups (less than 2 percent).

Satisfaction with Present Dwelling Place. Dwellers in furnished accommodations tended to be more satisfied than dwellers in unfurnished accommodations with 64 percent of the former indicating they were very satisfied or satisfied as opposed to 46 percent of the latter. The very dissatisfied numbered one out of six in each group. The somewhat dissatisfied were 12.8 and 26.4, respectively, for the furnished and unfurnished. The basic problems that both groups pointed to were area, drugs, crime and the like.

Violations histories and interior maintenance rating of the buildings were quite comparable.

Looking Forward to a Year in the Future. Somewhat more than half of each group anticipated living in the same place. The same held true for general plans for the future and the practicability of those plans.

When the 48 furnished accommodation respondents who admitted that they had no plans for the future were asked why, 11 of them (22.9 percent) versus 14.7 percent for the 163 non-furnished said that they were too old and had no future. Other than that there was no great degree of variation.

Length of Residence in New York. Welfare recipients in furnished apartments had lived in the city as long as those in unfurnished facilities. Actually, 27.9 percent of the former were born in New York compared with 21.5 percent of the latter, and slightly over 40 percent of each group had lived in New York for 15 years or more. Similar reasons for moving to New York City were given by each group.

Their origins were substantially similar, with a slightly higher number of the furnished apartment residents coming from the South as contrasted with Puerto Rico. However, only two out of five of the furnished residents were not born in New York compared to three out of five of the unfurnished. The proportions planning to stay in the city for the two categories were the same. The quality of structure was slightly poorer for the furnished.

Planning Area. Sixty percent of the furnished apartments were in Major Action Areas, 29.4 percent in Protection Areas, and only 10.6 in Sound Areas. This is practically the same for their unfurnished equivalents.

Appendix 5.1

THE SEMANTIC DIFFERENTIAL

Attitudinal measures in four areas were developed for the study using the *Semantic Differential Approach* (Appendix 2.1) initially suggested by C.E. Osgood, G.J. Suci and P.H. Tannenbaum in 1957 and modified by H. Levin in 1964 and B. Indik in 1968.[1] The approach suggests that respondents' attitudes toward words (concepts) are organized along three basic and orthogonal (uncorrelated) dimensions known as Evaluation (E), Potency (P) and Activity (A).[2]

Evaluation specifies the positive or negative feeling or tone of an individual's attitude. *Potency* indicates the relative strength of those feelings. *Activity* implies the degree of activity or passivity of the respondents toward the idea or concept. These three dimensions have been rather consistently found in a number of studies. Some variance in the results of our study of New York City welfare recipients, using each of the four concepts "welfare," "my apartment," "myself" and "public housing," will be considered separately.

The finding usually noted when dealing with words as stimuli is what has been called the E, P, A, factor structure. This refers to the finding that when a factor analysis of people's responses to the word-pairs is undertaken, as in this particular circumstance, the tendency is for three factors (or subdimensions) to occur. As can be seen from a number of studies by Osgood and his associates,[3] the evaluative factor tends to include the following word-pairs: good/bad, kind/cruel, clean/dirty, successful/unsuccessful, wise/foolish, healty/sick and important/unimportant, with the latter being generally the least loaded on (correlated with) the evaluative factor.

EXHIBIT APPENDIX 5.1.1

STIMULUS WORD – WELFARE
(CORRELATION MATRIX)

	1	2	3	4	5	6	7	8	9	10	11	12	13	14	15	16
1. Good-Bad		–.249	.352	.462	.410	–.126	.423	.051	.216	.404	.067	.329	.298	.236	.286	.407
2. Hard-Soft			–.154	–.256	–.033	.220	–.202	.207	–.210	–.177	.036	–.202	–.038	–.020	–.028	–.160
3. Active-Passive				.399	.313	.064	.321	.076	.211	.405	.020	.302	.170	.251	.118	.329
4. Kind-Cruel					.363	.154	.531	.047	.307	.534	.055	.402	.184	.207	.333	.375
5. Strong-Weak						–.028	.458	.093	.238	.414	.150	.312	.202	.250	.262	.371
6. Excitable-Calm							–.220	.177	.062	–.185	–.041	–.039	–.110	–.030	–.160	–.135
7. Clean-Dirty								.005	.370	.474	.105	.349	.311	.249	.347	.429
8. Heavy-Light									.005	.071	.044	.085	.073	.294	.030	.055
9. Hot-Cold										.336	.118	.221	.086	.200	.283	.217
10. Successful-Unsuccessful											.062	.385	.334	.283	.367	.501
11. Masculine-Feminine												.042	.074	.042	.107	.004
12. Fast-Slow													.145	.220	.200	.334
13. Important-Unimportant														.339	.375	.297
14. Large-Small															.242	.270
15. Wise-Foolish																.396
16. Healthy-Sick																

Source: Housing of Welfare Recipients Survey, 1970.

Note: N=399; $r_{.05}$ =.16; $r_{.01}$ =.20.

The second factor, which has been usually referred to as potency, reflects intensity of feeling with reference to the stimulus word. Whereas evaluation was the relative favorable or unfavorable aspect of people's responses to the word stimulus, potency is generally shown by the response pattern to the following word pairs: hard/soft, strong/weak, heavy/light and masculine/feminine.

The third factor is activity, a kind of active versus passive dimension, indicating whether a person is likely to do anything with reference to this particular dimension or whether he is going to be passive in the area. Four word-pairs are generally found to load on (correlate with) the activity factor. These include active/passive, excitable/calm, hot/cold and fast/slow.

While the three factors described above are the general findings, they are not the only factors that have been noted from analyses of people's responses to stimulus words. Additional factors evolve in some cases, but they are frequently more difficult to describe and are much more dependent upon either the stimulus word involved or the population studied. Most of the common factors at variance in most studies using the Semantic Differential Approach seem to show that the majority of the common factor variance is explicable by the E, P, A factor structure.

Welfare

In the first attitudinal area, the stimulus word "welfare" was used to develop measures of attitudes toward welfare. Based on prior studies[4] we utilized 16 word-pairs and factor analyzed the responses for the 16 variables for the entire sample of welfare recipients. We used a total of 399 cases for whom all data were available.

The intercorrelation matrix for the variables involved with reference to the stimulus word welfare is shown in Exhibit Appendix 5.1.1. This exhibit shows the intercorrelations among the 16 word-pairs for the stimulus word welfare. The matrix was factor analyzed using the Biomed Programs and the Rutgers University 360 computer system.

Using only the number of factors that had eigenvalues larger than one, four factors were extracted. The eigenvalues shown for these are 4.732, 1.531, 1.180, 1.062. The associated cumulative proportions of total variance explained by the four factors extracted account for 53.1 percent of the variance. The eigenvalues after the first four factors go under 1.00 and therefore were not considered significant. The four factors are shown in Exhibit Appendix 5.1.2 and show, generally, that the evaluative factor is factor one, the potency factor is factor two, and a factor which is a combination of evaluation and potency seems to be present in factor three, while factor four is most effectively identified by the adjectival pair masculine/feminine. The communalities that appear between the original and final rotated factor matrices which were done by the verimax rotation method show no differences (to the fifth decimal place) between the original and final communalities.

The largest loadings on factor one occur for the adjectival pairs; kind/cruel, active/passive, fast/slow, good/bad, clean/dirty and successful/unsuccessful. It should also be noted that factor one not only has an evaluative component (based on prior studies) but seems also to indicate a considerable activity component. This is clearly a rather general factor that picks up considerable variability that normally loads on evaluation with an additional portion that usually loads on the activity dimension.

In Exhibit Appendix 5.1.2, which reflects responses to welfare as the stimulus word, factor scores were calculated for each of the four factors analyzed from the rotated factor matrix. This was done in the following manner using the computer program available from the Biomedical Program Series: For each individual, and for each word-pair, the score on a word-pair was weighted by the factor loading of that variable on that factor score in order to generate a factor score for each of the 16 variables for factors one, two, three and four in this analysis. In order to calculate these factor scores for the purposes of cross-tabulation they were multiplied by 1,000, then added to a constant of 50 and divided by 100.

EXHIBIT APPENDIX 5.1.2

STIMULUS WORD – WELFARE
(ROTATED FACTOR MATRIX)

VARIABLE WORD-PAIRS	Factor I	Factor II	Factor III	Factor IV	Communalities
1. Good-Bad	.618	–.065	.277	.014	.464
2. Hard-Soft	–.417	.563	.113	.145	.524
3. Active-Passive	.665	.099	.035	–.109	.465
4. Kind-Cruel	.729	–.120	.159	.087	.578
5. Strong-Weak	.571	.168	.194	.294	.479
6. Excitable-Calm	–.032	.617	–.360	–.018	.512
7. Clean-Dirty	.614	–.157	.340	.228	.569
8. Heavy-Light	.106	.739	.120	–.027	.573
9. Hot-Cold	.467	–.109	.046	.400	.393
10. Successful-Unsuccessful	.648	–.049	.383	.066	.573
11. Masculine-Feminine	–.011	.053	.037	.865	.753
12. Fast-Slow	.663	.065	.018	–.004	.444
13. Important-Unimportant	.109	.040	.780	–.028	.623
14. Large-Small	.298	.386	.495	–.070	.487
15. Wise-Foolish	.205	–.088	.675	.244	.565
16. Healthy-Sick	.534	–.032	.462	–.068	.504

Source: Housing of Welfare Recipients Survey, 1970.
Note: N=399.

This was the general approach in each of the four factor analyses that are discussed in this study. The factor scores were calculated in this way to insure that each of the scores would be positive for each of the four

EXHIBIT APPENDIX 5.1.3

STIMULUS WORD – MY APARTMENT
(CORRELATION MATRIX)

	1	2	3	4	5	6	7	8	9	10	11	12	13	14	15	16
1. Good-Bad		.645	.150	.673	.536	–.321	.633	–.314	.366	.625	–.111	.231	.507	.276	.454	.576
2. Hard-Soft			–.077	–.062	–.427	.337	–.538	.336	–.225	–.554	.114	–.232	–.432	–.137	–.380	–.519
3. Active-Passive				.101	.236	.183	.059	.024	.123	.150	–.021	.221	.054	.096	.127	.159
4. Kind-Cruel					.551	–.297	.582	–.307	.298	.580	–.098	.264	.549	.228	.591	.623
5. Strong-Weak						.194	.436	.190	.276	.485	–.051	.365	.387	.207	.447	.557
6. Excitable-Calm							–.315	.329	–.132	–.263	.113	.021	–.254	.019	–.181	–.195
7. Clean-Dirty								–.278	.308	.545	–.172	.206	.503	.145	.443	.544
8. Heavy-Light									–.065	–.265	.115	–.041	–.196	–.032	–.190	–.231
9. Hot-Cold										.217	.027	.225	.260	.027	.260	.299
10. Successful-Unsuccessful											–.159	.319	.504	.219	.469	.520
11. Masculine-Feminine												–.016	–.078	.019	–.125	–.120
12. Fast-Slow													.227	.139	.328	.317
13. Important-Unimportant														.174	.472	.524
14. Large-Small															.233	.228
15. Wise-Foolish																.515
16. Healthy-Sick																

Source: Housing of Welfare Recipients Survey, 1970.

Note: N=399; $r_{.05}$ =.16; $r_{.01}$ =.20.

factors, yielding meaningful measures of the four attitudinal components that were specific to the population being studied here.

These factor scores were used in analyzing welfare recipients' attitudes as related to such variables as ethnicity, welfare type, education and age of the head of the household.

My Apartment

The next attitudinal area that was explored dealt with how people felt about their own apartments. The stimulus words "my apartment" were used along with the same 16 word-pairs. The number of respondents was again 399 of the 412 in the total sample. Thirteen respondents did not respond to the format for a variety of reasons. The same approach was followed here as in the prior section.

The correlations between the responses to the 16 word-pairs are shown in Exhibit Appendix 5.1.3. The three factors indicated below became evident using the same methods as above. The eigenvalues that were found follow: factor 1 — 5.949; factor 2 — 1.544; factor 3 — 1.024. (Factor 4 was below 1.0 and therefore we stopped extracting factors.) The cumulative proportion of total variance explained by the three factors extracted is 53.2.

EXHIBIT APPENDIX 5.1.4

STIMULUS WORD – MY APARTMENT
(ROTATED FACTOR MATRIX)

VARIABLE WORD-PAIRS	Factor I	Factor II	Factor III	Communalities
1. Good-Bad	.825	.110	.048	.696
2. Hard-Soft	–.762	.015	.035	.581
3. Active-Passive	.044	.685	–.049	.474
4. Kind-Cruel	.823	.132	.046	.697
5. Strong-Weak	.636	.357	.107	.543
6. Excitable-Calm	–.523	.543	.043	.570
7. Clean-Dirty	.771	.015	–.021	.595
8. Heavy-Light	–.478	.312	.235	.382
9. Hot-Cold	.401	.095	.526	.447
10. Successful-Unsuccessful	.742	.203	–.102	.603
11. Masculine-Feminine	–.185	–.061	.824	.717
12. Fast-Slow	.302	.546	.152	.412
13. Important-Unimportant	.687	.087	.090	.488
14. Large-Small	.224	.391	–.051	.205
15. Wise-Foolish	.637	.299	.006	.495
16. Healthy-Sick	.734	.275	.039	.615

Source: Housing of Welfare Recipients Survey, 1970.
Note: N=399.

In Exhibit Appendix 5.1.4, which is the rotated factor matrix for responses to "my apartment," factor one is most heavily loaded on such word-pairs as good/bad, kind/cruel, clean/dirty, successful/unsuccess-

EXHIBIT APPENDIX 5.1.5

STIMULUS WORD – MYSELF
(CORRELATION MATRIX)

	1	2	3	4	5	6	7	8	9	10	11	12	13	14	15	16
1. Good-Bad		–.196	.136	.268	.125	–.205	.357	.004	.233	.225	–.126	.207	.157	–.000	.194	.102
2. Hard-Soft			.125	–.180	.245	.199	–.179	.149	–.064	–.021	.245	.085	.005	.240	.015	.077
3. Active-Passive				–.006	.469	.154	.079	.040	.002	.172	–.007	.293	.134	.083	.171	.366
4. Kind-Cruel					–.021	–.194	.353	.052	.155	.154	–.183	.010	.157	–.118	.304	–.035
5. Strong-Weak						.065	–.034	.046	.126	.257	–.023	.379	.207	.167	.203	.482
6. Excitable-Calm							–.215	.062	–.171	–.191	.050	.013	–.093	.090	–.177	.042
7. Clean-Dirty								–.022	.082	.130	–.154	.105	.158	–.093	.203	.003
8. Heavy-Light									.067	.078	.054	.046	.176	.204	.120	.003
9. Hot-Cold										.276	–.067	.305	.235	–.025	.225	.093
10. Successful-Unsuccessful											–.133	.325	.414	.063	.365	.231
11. Masculine-Feminine												–.062	–.236	.107	–.121	–.072
12. Fast-Slow													.324	.097	.275	.320
13. Important-Unimportant														.222	.288	.130
14. Large-Small															.058	.167
15. Wise-Foolish																.158
16. Healthy-Sick																

Source: Housing of Welfare Recipients Survey, 1970.

Note: N=399; $r_{.05}$ =.16; $r_{.01}$ =.20.

ful, important/unimportant, wise/foolish, healthy/sick and negatively loaded on hard/soft.

The first seven word-pairs listed above are all evaluative, and it is quite clear that predominantly this factor is extracting a very general and major evaluative component. It should be pointed out that the first seven word-pairs mentioned—not the first seven variables in terms of size of factor loading—were evaluative.

Factor two seems to be an activity factor, the largest loading being on active/passive at .685. This factor also shows high loadings on excitable/calm and fast/slow, which are also activity word-pairs. However, it also shows a minor tendency to pick up some word-pairs which are usually potency items, such as strong/weak, heavy/light and large/small.

Factor three in this factor analysis is much like factor four in the prior factor analysis. It seems to be most clearly indicated by masculine/feminine and secondarily indicated by hot/cold.

The communalities from the original factor extraction and final rotated factor matrix are very similar. There is no change at all to the fifth decimal place of any of the communalities. Most of the communalities are in the range between .59 and .70 for this analysis.

Factor scores were obtained for each of the three final rotated factors using the approach described for the prior analysis.

Myself

The third area using the Semantic Differential Approach was to measure self-concept. The stimulus word was "myself" in this attitudinal area. The same 16 adjectival word-pairs were used. The intercorrelations among the 16 word-pairs are shown in Exhibit Appendix 5.1.5. Using the same computer procedures as in the prior factor analyses five factors were extracted from the correlation matrix.

The eigenvalues are as follows: for factors: factor 1 — 3.215; factor 2 — 2.277; factor 3 — 1.331; factor 4 — 1.077; factor 5 — 1.045. The cumulative proportion of variance explained by the five factors was 55.9. After the five factors were extracted, the sixth factor had eigenvalues lower than 1.00. (Exhibit Apprndix 5.1.6.)

In dealing with the stimulus word "myself" the finding of five factors is not to be completely unexpected. Based on previous experience with this variable, people seem to be more discriminating with themselves than with reference to most other stimuli. What might be interesting in this analysis is how the welfare population divides its view of itself. A variety of other studies have used this stimulus word "myself" with other populations.

Data accumulated by Indik[4] and Gold[5] show that the stimulus word "myself" used with other sample populations and the same adjectival pairs tends to be somewhat different from the present findings so that it is necessary for clarity to present our data so as to see these data as possibly reflecting the characteristics of this sample as distinct from earlier samples.

EXHIBIT APPENDIX 5.1.6

STIMULUS WORD – MYSELF
(ROTATED FACTOR MATRIX)

VARIABLE WORD-PAIRS	Factor I	Factor II	Factor III	Factor IV	Factor V	Communalities
1. Good-Bad	.189	.609	−.112	.240	−.013	.477
2. Hard-Soft	.243	−.243	.497	−.093	−.388	.524
3. Active-Passive	.765	.175	.073	−.182	.009	.655
4. Kind-Cruel	−.112	.715	.050	.084	.154	.557
5. Strong-Weak	.789	−.019	.127	.119	−.023	.653
6. Excitable-Calm	.198	−.308	.241	−.544	.159	.513
7. Clean-Dirty	.028	.773	.070	−.001	.067	.608
8. Heavy-Light	−.105	.115	.728	.021	.006	.555
9. Hot-Cold	.047	.047	−.018	.737	.005	.548
10. Successful-Unsuccessful	.272	.137	.147	.593	.236	.522
11. Masculine-Feminine	−.035	−.117	.148	.002	−.860	.776
12. Fast-Slow	.548	.016	.091	.436	.100	.509
13. Important-Unimportant	.155	.111	.424	.416	.506	.645
14. Large-Small	.149	.126	.631	.021	−.048	.439
15. Wise-Foolish	.204	.409	.254	.384	.101	.431
16. Healthy-Sick	.713	−.032	−.040	.146	.027	.533

Source: Housing of Welfare Recipients Survey, 1970.
Note: N399.

Factor Analysis With Stimulus Word "Myself." As shown in Exhibit Appendix 5.1.6, the first factor seems to indicate or be indicated in the following order of factor loadings by the word-pairs used as variables: strong/weak; active/passive; healthy/sick; fast/slow.

It can be seen from prior analyses that there is a mixture of not only potency dimensions, but evaluative and activity variables. Factor two is revealed most clearly by: clean/dirty; kind/cruel; good/bad. These are all evaluative word-pairs, but it is not heavily loaded on the other evaluative word-pairs that are generally to be found on a broadscale evaluative factor.

Factor three seems to be indicated by three potency word-pairs; first, heavy/light; second, large/small; and third, hard/soft. But again, it is not fully a potency dimension although it has major indications of one.

Factor four seems to show a combination of activity and evaluation. The word-pair that is highest in its factor loading is hot/cold, followed by successful/unsuccessful and a negative loading on excitable/calm.

The fifth factor is most clearly indicated by feminine/masculine, important/unimportant and soft/hard. This possibly would tend to show something of the character of the welfare population.

EXHIBIT APPENDIX 5.1.7

STIMULUS WORD – PUBLIC HOUSING
(CORRELATION MATRIX)

	1	2	3	4	5	6	7	8	9	10	11	12	13	14	15	16
1. Good-Bad		–.160	.167	.494	.486	–.287	.545	–.023	.225	.585	–.016	.113	.431	.405	.425	.522
2. Hard-Soft			–.140	–.166	–.075	.163	–.088	.323	–.059	–.002	.116	–.127	.095	.147	–.085	–.068
3. Active-Passive				.041	.284	.115	.119	.040	.235	.135	.108	.234	.201	.178	.117	.135
4. Kind-Cruel					.324	–.365	.506	–.125	.040	.416	–.104	.125	.290	.274	.327	.404
5. Strong-Weak						–.111	.485	.031	.378	.544	.124	.179	.339	.371	.298	.512
6. Excitable-Calm							–.277	.217	.034	–.241	.070	.005	–.110	–.123	–.212	–.235
7. Clean-Dirty								–.076	.257	.541	.024	.140	.421	.344	.365	.577
8. Heavy-Light									–.092	–.015	.089	–.113	.043	.095	–.007	–.029
9. Hot-Cold										.268	.043	.124	.220	.222	.074	.252
10. Successful-Unsuccessful											.010	.169	.495	.441	.394	.552
11. Masculine-Feminine												.075	.058	.104	–.015	.038
12. Fast-Slow													.064	.158	.185	.082
13. Important-Unimportant														.456	.436	.430
14. Large-Small															.281	.388
15. Wise-Foolish																.489
16. Healthy-Sick																

Source: Housing of Welfare Recipients Survey, 1970.

Note: N=399; $r_{.05}$ =.16; n=390; $r_{.01}$ =.20.

Again, the communalities of the original factors extracted and final rotated factor matrix are very similar; very minor differences are in the fifth decimal place. As with the prior two stimulus words, factor scores were obtained for each of the factors of this analysis for each of the respondents in the study so that the comparative reflections of differential self-concepts for this population could be investigated.

Public Housing

There were 390 respondents to the stimulus words "public housing" and the same 16 adjectival word-pairs were used.

Exhibit Appendix 5.1.7 shows the correlation coefficients among the responses to these 16 variable word-pairs. The factor analysis was extracted: three factors prior to the eigenvalues going lower than 1.00. The eigenvalues were as follows: factor 1 — 4.857; factor 2 — 1.731; factor 3 — 1.439.

The cumulative proportion of total variance explained by the three factors extracted was 50.2.

Exhibit Appendix 5.1.8 deals with the final rotated factor matrix for the three factors extracted with reference to public housing and includes also the final rotated factor matrix communalities.

EXHIBIT APPENDIX 5.1.8

STIMULUS WORD – PUBLIC HOUSING
(ROTATED FACTOR MATRIX)

VARIABLE WORD-PAIRS	Factor I	Factor II	Factor III	Communalities
1. Good-Bad	.766	−.125	.112	.615
2. Hard-Soft	.001	.758	−.224	.624
3. Active-Passive	.091	.007	.718	.524
4. Kind-Cruel	.658	−.319	−.129	.551
5. Strong-Weak	.611	.033	.440	.569
6. Excitable-Calm	.435	.424	.358	.498
7. Clean-Dirty	.751	−.126	.109	.592
8. Heavy-Light	.012	.706	−.069	.503
9. Hot-Cold	.236	−.011	.578	.390
10. Successful-Unsuccessful	.777	.027	.155	.628
11. Masculine-Feminine	−.015	.329	.318	.210
12. Fast-Slow	.095	−.221	.532	.341
13. Important-Unimportant	.660	.238	.140	.512
14. Large-Small	.596	.301	.198	.485
15. Wise-Foolish	.620	−.057	.039	.389
16. Healthy-Sick	.762	−.022	.120	.595

Source: Housing of Welfare Recipients Survey, 1970.

Note: N=399.

Factor 1 is very clearly an evaluative factor—all seven of the word-pairs that usually appear on an evaluative factor show factor loadings above .6—the highest is successful/unsuccessful, followed by good/bad, healthy/sick, clean/dirty, important/unimportant, kind/cruel, wise/

foolish and finally a potency variable, strong/weak, which appears to be loaded strongly on this factor.

Factor 2 seems to be a clear potency factor, though not as well defined as sometimes appears in other studies. It is most clearly indicated by hard/soft, heavy/light, and positive indication of potency is indicated by minor loadings of masculine/feminine and large/small. However, it should be noted that the usual potency item strong/weak does not appear loaded on this factor. Also, there is a minor loading on this factor of an activity variable excitable/calm of + .42.

The third factor is relatively clear in relating to an activity factor. It is most heavily loaded or explained by the active/passive variable followed by hot/cold and fast/slow, which are all activity word-pairs. The fourth loading in terms of size is a potency item, strong/weak. The fifth is excitable/calm.

The E, P, A structure seems to hold fairly well for the stimulus words "public housing"; the communalities also seem to show no difference between the final rotated factor matrix and the original factors extracted. Factor scores were again developed for each respondent on the three factors developed in this analysis following the procedures outlined earlier. This, of course, facilitated the analyses done in the various chapters where attitudes toward public housing are discussed.

NOTES

1. C.E. Osgood, G.J. Suci and P.H. Tannenbaum, *The Measurement of Meaning,* Urbana, Illinois: University of Illinois Press, 1957. Hannah Levin, *A Psycholinguistic Investigation,* (unpublished doctoral dissertation, New Brunswick, New Jersey, Rutgers University, 1964). B.P. Indik, "Police and Citizen Attitudes During the Development of a Crisis" (unpublished manuscript, New Brunswick, New Jersey, Rutgers University, 1968).

2. C.E. Osgood, "On the Whys and Wherefores of E, P, and A" *(Journal of Personality and Social Psychology,* Vol. 12, 3, pp. 194-198, 1969).

3. H. Levin, *op. cit.,* B. Indik, *op. cit.,* and B.P. Indik, R.J. Zito and J. Roth, *An Analysis of the Affective Meaning of Racial and Interracial Photographs,* New Brunswick, New Jersey, Social Work Research Center, Graduate School of Social Work, Rutgers University, 1970.

4. *B.P. Indik, Police and Citizen Attitudes During the Development of a Crisis* (unpublished manuscript, New Brunswick, New Jersey, Rutgers University, 1968).

5. Sandra Gold, *The Effect of Counselor-Client Dissimilarity on Counselor Judgment* (unpublished doctoral dissertation, New Brunswick, New Jersey, Rutgers University, 1970).

Appendix 6.1

THE CANTRIL SELF-ANCHORING STRIVING SCALE

The objective of this appendix is to explain the methodology used in exploring peoples' aspirations, hopes and fears. The Cantril[1] approach takes a transactional point of view; it assumes that for the researcher to tap into an individual's unique reality world the person must define his own assumptions, perceptions, goals and values—his own anchor points. Having been used widely, the scale provides a variety of comparative results.

The Cantril Self-Anchoring Striving Scale was utilized in this study to discover the spectrum of values a person is preoccupied or concerned with and by means of which he evaluates his own life. He describes as the top anchoring point his wishes and hopes as he personally conceives them, the realization of which would constitute for him the best possible life. At the other extreme, he describes the worries and fears, the preoccupations and frustrations, embodied in his conception of the worst possible life he could imagine.

Utilizing a nonverbal ladder scale, he is asked where he thinks he stands on the ladder today, with the top being the best life *as he has defined it,* the bottom the worst life *as he has defined it.* He is also asked where he thinks he stood in the past and where he thinks he will stand in the future. Similar questions are asked about the best and worst possible situations he can imagine for his country so his aspirations and fears on the national level can be measured.

The ladder is used to find out where he thinks his country stands today, where it stood in the past, and where it will stand in the future.

The actual questions, together with the parenthetical instructions to inverviewers, follow:

1. (A) All of us want certain things out of life. When you think about what really matters in your own life, what are your wishes and hopes for the future? In other words, if you imagine your future in the *best* possible light, what would your life look like then, if you are to be happy? Take your time in answering; such things aren't easy to put into words.
   Permissible probes: What are your hopes for the future? What would your life have to be like for you to be completely happy? What is missing for you to be happy? (Use also, if necessary, the words "dreams" and "desires.")
   Obligatory probe: Anything else?
   (B) Now, taking the other side of the picture, what are your fears and worries about the future? In other words, if you imagine your future in the *worst* possible light, what would your life look like then? Again, take your time in answering.
   Permissible probe: What would make you unhappy? (Stress the words "fears" and "worries.")
   Obligatory probe: Anything else?
   Here is a picture of a ladder. Suppose we say that the top of the ladder *(pointing)* represents the best possible life for you and the bottom *(pointing)* represents the worst possible life for you.
   (C) Where on the ladder *(moving finger rapidly up and down ladder)* do you feel you personally stand at the present time? Step number___.
   (D) Where on the ladder would you say you stood five years ago? Step number___.
   (E) And where do you think you will be on the ladder five years from now? Step number___.

2. (A) Now, what are your wishes and hopes for the future of our country? If you picture the future of (name of country) in the *best* possible light, how would things look, set us say, ten years from now?
   Obligatory probe: Anything else?
   (B) And what about your fears and worries for the future of our country? If you picture the future of (name of country) in the *worst* possible light, how would things look about ten years from now?
   Obligatory probe: Anything else?
   (C) Now, looking at the ladder again, suppose your greatest hopes for (name of country) are at the top *(pointing);* your worst fears at

the bottom *(pointing)*. Where would you put (name of country) on the ladder *(moving finger rapidly up and down ladder)* at the present time? Step number___.

(D) Where did (name of country) stand five years ago? Step number___.

(E) Just as your best guess, where do you think (name of country) will be on the ladder five years from now? Step number___.

The questions were translated when necessary to match the preferred language of the respondent.

A detailed explanation of the code categories used to explore the hopes and fears mentioned in this study appears in Appendix 6.2.

NOTES

1. Hadley Cantril, *The Pattern of Human Concerns* (New Brunswick, New Jersey, Rutgers University Press, 1965).

Appendix 6.2

THE COMPLETE CANTRIL CODE

CODE FOR QUESTIONS 42 AND 43, 47 AND 48.
PERSONAL HOPES AND ASPIRATIONS; PERSONAL WORRIES AND FEARS [1]

CONCERNED WITH SELF AND/OR FAMILY

OWN PERSONAL CHARACTER

Col. 8

1. *Emotional stability and maturity* — peace of mind, mental health and well-being; sense of humor, understanding of others, etc.; harmonious life.
2. *Be a normal, decent person* — leading a quiet life, harming no one.
3. *Self-development or improvement* — opportunity for independence of thought and action, for following through with own interests; further study; reading for non-leisure purposes; no "rut."
4. *Acceptance by others* — recognition of my status by others; to be liked, respected or loved (exception: where reference is restricted to family or marriage, code under Col. 6-1).
5. *Achieve sense of my own personal worth* — self-satisfaction; feeling of accomplishment; lead a purposeful life. (Note: recognition by *self* as contrasted to recognition by others.)
6. *Resolution of one's own religious, spiritual, or ethical problems.*

7. *To lead disciplined life.*
8. *Miscellaneous* aspirations regarding one's own personal character.
9. Nothing to code in this column.

Col. 9

1. *Emotional instability and immaturity* — lack of peace of mind, of mental health or well-being; no sense of humor or understanding of others, etc.; life of disharmony.
2. Become *antisocial;* take to *crime.*
3. *No self-development or improvement* — getting in a "rut"; no opportunity for independence of thought and action, for following through with own interests; no further study or reading, etc.
4. *Not be accepted by others* — no recognition of my status by others; not be liked, respected, or loved (exception: where mention is restricted to family or marriage, code under Col. 17-1).
5. *No sense of personal worth* — feel personally inadequate; unable to achieve aspirations as to occupation or role in life; feel worthless; have no purpose in life.
6. *To be a person without character.*
7. *Miscellaneous* worries and fears regarding one's own personal character.
9. Nothing to code in this column.

PERSONAL ECONOMIC SITUATION

Col. 10

1. *Improved or decent standard of living for self or family;* sufficient money to live better or to live decently, freedom from debt; make ends meet; relief from poverty; not suffer want, hunger, etc.
2. *Have own business;* ability to increase or expand one's business.
3. Have *own land or own farm.*
4. Have own *house,* apartment or garden; or get better ones.
5. Have *modern conveniences,* such as a car, bathroom, fine clothes, large appliances such as washing machine, radio, television, etc.
6. Have *wealth* — money to do anything I/we wish.
7. *Miscellaneous* aspirations having to do with economic situation of self or family.
9. Nothing to code in this column.

Col. 11

1. *Deterioration in or inadequate standard of living for self or family;* not sufficient money to live better or to live decently; debt; poverty; suffer want, hunger, etc.
2. *Miscellaneous* worries and fears having to do with the economic situation of self or family.
9. Nothing to code in this column.

JOB OR WORK SITUATION

Col. 12

1. *Good job, congenial work* for self, spouse or other family member; independence in choice of occupation; pleasant, interesting job or work situation; chance of advancement.
2. *Employment* — steady work for self, spouse or other family member.
3. *Success* in one's work for self, spouse or other family member; make a contribution to one's field.
4. *Miscellaneous* aspirations regarding job or work situation.
9. Nothing to code in this column.

Col. 13

1. *Poor job, uncongenial work* for self, spouse or other family member; no independence in choice of occupation; unpleasant, uninteresting job or work situation; no chance for advancement.
2. *Unemployment* — no steady work for self, spouse or other family member; inability to find or hold a job; unable to work because of sickness or old age.
3. *Failure* in one's work for self, spouse or other family member; contribute little or nothing to one's field.
4. *Miscellaneous* worries and fears regarding job or work situation.
9. Nothing to code in this column.

OTHER REFERENCES TO "SELF"

Col. 14

1. One's own *health* — continued or regained health (physical or mental) for self; strength to enjoy life.
2. *Happy old age* — long and happy life; peaceful, pleasant, secure old age.
3. *Recreation, travel, leisure time;* sports, reading for pleasure, etc.
4. *Miscellaneous* aspirations involving other references to "self."
9. Nothing to code in this column.

Col. 15

1. *Ill health, accident, death* or continued illness (physical or mental) for self; no strength to enjoy life.
2. *To be dependent on others.*
3. *Miscellaneous* worries and fears involving other references to "self."
9. Nothing to code in this column.

OTHER REFERENCES TO FAMILY

Col. 16

1. *Happy family life* — happy marriage; pleasant home; love within family; have a (good) husband or wife; have children.

2. *Relatives* — concern for spouse, children, parents or other relatives; be close to them; keep them together or get them together again; help or take care of them; live up to their expectations.
3. *Health of family* — continued good health or improved health (physical or mental) for members of family.
4. *Children* — adequate opportunities for them (including education); children themselves do well, be happy, successful.
5. *Miscellaneous* aspirations regarding family.
9. Nothing to code in this column.

Col. 17

1. *No or unhappy family life* — no husband, wife or children; no marriage or unhappy marriage; no home or unhappy home; no love within family.
2. *Relatives* — separation from (or abandonment by) spouse, children, parents or other relative; not to be able to help or take care of them; not to live up to their expectations.
3. *Ill health, accident, death,* or continued poor health (physical or mental) for members of family.
4. *Children* — inadequate opportunities for them (including education); children themselves do poorly, be unhappy, unsuccessful.
5. *Miscellaneous* worries and fears regarding family.
6. Worries about family member drug use.
9. Nothing to code in this column.

CONCERNED ABOUT OTHER PEOPLE, COMMUNITY OR NATION

POLITICAL

Col. 18

1. *Freedom,* including specifically freedom of speech, of religion, of occupation, of movement, etc.
2. *Miscellaneous* aspirations having to do with the political situation.
9. Nothing to code in this column.

Col. 19

1. *Lack of freedom,* including specifically lack of freedom of speech, or religion, of occupation, or movement, etc.
2. *No improvement in present government;* fear present government will continue.
3. *Political instability;* chaos; confusion; lack of internal peace; civil war; etc.
4. *Miscellaneous* worries and fears having to do with the political situation.
9. Nothing to code in this column.

GENERAL ECONOMIC SITUATION

Col. 20

1. *Economic stability* (in general); freedom from inflation; fair prices.
2. *Miscellaneous* economic aspirations not restricted to self or family.

9. Nothing to code in this column.

Col. 21

1. *Economic instability* (in general); inflation; unfair or high prices.
2. *Deterioration in or inadequate standard of living for nation or group* (not restricted to self or family) — people unable to live decently; poverty, want, hunger, etc.
3. *Miscellaneous* economic worries and fears not restricted to self or family.
9. Nothing to code in this column.

SOCIAL

Col. 22

1. *Social justice* — greater equality, in the treatment, benefits and opportunities afforded all elements of the population, irrespective of race, color, class, caste, religion, etc.; integration; fairer distribution of wealth; elimination of discrimination or exploitation.
2. *Future generations* — better prospects and opportunities. (Note: if restricted to "own children," code under Col. 6-4.)
3. *Social security,* including pensions, annuities, etc.
4. *Miscellaneous* aspirations having to do with the social situation.
9. Nothing to code in this column.

Col. 23

1. *Social injustice;* continued inequality in the treatment, benefits and opportunities afforded various elements of the population; discrimination or exploitation based on race, color, class, caste, religion, etc.; continuing unfair distribution of wealth.
2. *Future generations* — no better prospects or worse prospects; no opportunities. (Note: if restricted to "own children," code under Col. 17-4.)
3. *No social security;* no pensions, annuities, etc.
4. *Miscellaneous* worries and fears having to do with the social situation.
5. Concern about addicts, pushers, etc.
9. Nothing to code in this column.

RELIGION, MORALITY, PUBLIC SERVICE

Col. 24

1. *Desire to be useful to others;* ability and opportunity to serve the people, community, nation, world; or to hold public office.

2. *Miscellaneous* aspirations having to do with public service or with religion or morality where the reference is not restricted to self or family.
9. Nothing to code in this column.

Col. 25

1. *Not to be useful to others;* not to serve the people, community, nation, world.
2. *Spiritual, ethical, moral or religious disintegration, deterioration or complacency on the part of society.*
3. *Miscellaneous* worries and fears having to do with public service or with religion or morality where the reference is not restricted to self or family.
9. Nothing to code in this column.

CONCERN ABOUT INTERNATIONAL SITUATION AND WORLD

Col. 26

1. *Peace* — maintenance of; no war; no threat of war.
2. *Better world* — more international cooperation; countries working together; more international understanding and responsibility; relaxation of international tensions; stronger U. N.; world government.
3. *Miscellaneous* aspirations having to do with the international or world situation.
9. Nothing to code in this column.

Col. 27

1. *War;* nuclear war; living in fear of war.
2. *Militarism and armaments; misuse of nuclear energy;* fallouts from nuclear tests.
3. *Threat, aggesssion, domination,* or conquest by Russia, Communist China, Cuba or other Communist powèr; become a Communist satellite.
4. *Miscellaneous* worries and fears having to do with the international or world situation.
9. Nothing to code in this column.

GENERAL

Col. 28

1. *Maintain status quo* (in general); person is happy with things as they are now.
2. *Miscellaneous* aspirations that do not fit under any of the preceding categories.
8. Don't know; no answer.
9. Nothing to code in this column.

Col. 29

1. *Can't think of any fears or worries.*
2. *Miscellaneous* worries and fears that do not fit under any of the preceding categories.
8. Don't know; no answer.
9. Nothing to code in this column.

NATIONAL HOPES AND ASPIRATIONS;
NATIONAL WORRIES AND FEARS
CONCERNED WITH
NATIONAL SITUATION

POLITICAL

Col. 30-31

1. *Honest government* — fair and just; no corruption or nepotism.
2. *Efficient government* — competent leadership and administration; effective party system; no excessive bureaucracy.
3. *Balanced government* — adequate system of checks and balances; no excessive power in hands of government; less central government; more power to states or provinces.
4. *Democratic or representative government* — maintain present democracy or become a democracy; have more democracy or more representative government.
5. *Socialistic government* — aspiration to become a socialistic or welfare state.
6. *Freedom* — with specific reference to freedom of speech, of religion, or occupation, of movement, etc.
7. *Law and order* — maintenance of the public peace; decrease or no increase in crime, juvenile delinquency, etc.; fair courts, good or improved juridical practices, penal system, etc.
8. *National unity* — absence of unrest, tensions and antagonisms based on regional, class, caste, religious, etc., differences.
10. *Political stability, internal peace and order.*
11. *Miscellaneous* aspirations having to do with the national political situation.
9. Nothing to code in this column.

Col. 32-33

1. *Dishonest government* — unfair and unjust; corruption and nepotism.
2. *Inefficient government* — weak, indecisive leadership and administration; no effective party system; excessive bureaucracy.
3. *Communism* — fear of the Communist danger or of the consequences of Communist control. (Note: if specific reference to the external threat from the U.S.S.R., Communist China, or other Communist powers, code under Col. 44-5.)
4. *No democracy or representative government;* loss of democracy; totalitarianism. (Note: if specific reference to Communism, code under Col. 32-33-3.)
5. *Fear country will become socialistic.*
6. *Lack or loss of freedom* — in general, or with specific reference to freedom of speech, of religion, of occupation, of movement, etc. (Note: If loss

of freedom is specifically connected with Communism, code under Col. 32-33-3.)

7. *Lack of law and order* — failure to maintain public peace; prevalence of or increase in crime, juvenile delinquency, etc.; unfair courts; poor or unfair juridical practices, penal system, etc.
8. *Disunity among people of the nation* — unrest, tensions, antagonisms based on regional, class, caste, religious, etc., differences.
10. *Political instability, chaos, civil war.*
11. *High or increased taxes.*
12. *Miscellaneous* worries and fears having to do with the national political situation.
9. Nothing to code in this column.

ECONOMIC

Col. 34

1. *Improved or decent standard of living* (in general); greater national prosperity (in general).
2. *Improved standard of living* or greater national prosperity *through technological advances* — increase in rate of mechanization, use of modern scientific advances, nuclear energy; greater *productivity* in industry or agriculture; development of natural resources.
3. *Economic stability;* no inflation; fair prices.
4. *Employment* — jobs for everyone; no unemployment problem.
5. *Miscellaneous* aspirations having to do with the national economic situation.
9. Nothing to code in this column.

Col. 35

1. *No improvement in or inadequate standard of living* (in general); not be a prosperous nation (in general).
2. *No improvement in standard of living* or no increase in national prosperity *through technological advances; economic backwardness;* no industrialization; *low productivity* in industry or agriculture; no use of modern scientific advances or of nuclear energy; no development of natural resources.
3. *Failure to preserve present standard of living;* decrease in national prosperity.
4. *Economic instability;* inflation; unfair or high prices; depression; national bankruptcy.
5. *Unemployment.*
6. *Miscellaneous* worries and fears having to do with the national economic situation.
9. Nothing to code in this column.

SOCIAL

Col. 36-37

1. *Social justice* (in the most general, positive sense); greater

3. *Eliminate discrimination* or *exploitation* based on differences in *class* or *economic status* (e.g., with reference to the poor, the workers, the common people, etc.); fairer distribution of wealth, income and opportunities regardless of class.
4. *Education* — more and/or better schools; technical and trade schools; fight ignorance and illiteracy.
5. *Improved labor conditions* — shorter working hours, etc.
6. *Control of labor* — no strikes or labor unrest or pressures; regulation of labor practices and labor unions.
7. *Social security* — adequate annuities, pensions, etc.; security for aged, handicapped, indigent.
8. *Housing* — adequate or improved housing conditions; no slums.
10. *Agrarian reform*, especially "land for the landless"; agricultural development; help for the peasants.
11. *Public health* — improved medical care; more doctors, hospitals; combat disease, epidemics; people healthy.
12. *Limited population growth* — no excess of population; control of birth rate; immigration.
13. *Sense of social and political responsibility and awareness* on the part of the people; less complacency; people working for the common good.
14. *Morality, ethical standards, religion, honesty, self-discipline* on the part of the public generally.
15. *Miscellaneous* aspirations having to do with social matters.
16. Drug addiction down.
9. Nothing to code in this column.

Col. 38-39

1. *Social injustice* (in the most general sense); continued inequality in the treatment, benefits and opportunities afforded various elements of the population.
2. *Continued discrimination* and prejudice based on *race, color, caste, religion*, etc.; segregation.
3. *Continued discrimination* or *exploitation* based on differences in *class* or *economic status* (e.g., with reference to the poor, the workers, the common people, etc.); continuing unfair distribution of wealth, income and opportunities based on class differences.
4. *Inadequate educational facilities and schooling;* lack of technical and trade schools; ignorance and illiteracy.
5. *Poor or unfair working conditions* — long working hours; forced labor.
6. *Abuses by labor* — strikes, labor pressures and unrest; abuse of power by labor unions; inadequate or no regulation of labor practices or labor unions.

7. *Unlimited population growth* — excessive population; excessive birth rate; too much immigration.
8. *No sense of social and political responsibility or awareness* on the part of the people; complacency; people not working for the common good.
10. *Lack of morality, ethical standards, religion, honesty, self-discipline* on the part of the public generally.
11. Too much *mechanization* and *standardization; materialism; conformity.*
12. *Miscellaneous* worries and fears having to do with social matters.
13. Concern about drug problems.
9. Nothing to code in this column.

CONCERNED WITH INTERNATIONAL SITUATION
INTERNATIONAL RELATIONS, COLD WAR, PEACE, ETC.

Co. 40-41

1. *Peace* — no war or nuclear war; freedom from fear of war or devastation.
2. *Disarmament, limitation of armaments, control or banning of nuclear weapons;* cessation of nuclear tests.
3. *Lessening of cold war;* reduction of tensions between East and West; coexistence.
4. *Better relations with Communist bloc* or individual members of Communist bloc.
5. *Friendly relations with all countries.*
6. *Better world* — more international cooperation in general (without specific reference to cold war); countries working together; more international understanding and responsibility; stronger United Nations; world government.
7. *Maintain neutrality* — keep aloof from conflicting ideologies, blocs, etc.; have no enemies; not take sides.
8. *Help other nations* (especially the underdeveloped); promote world-wide prosperity.
10. *Increased foreign trade or exports.*
11. *Miscellaneous* aspirations having to do with international relations, the cold war, peace, etc.
9. Nothing to code in this column.

Col. 42

1. *War;* nuclear war; living in fear of war; devastation from war's consequences (e.g., destruction, famine, imprisonment, etc.
2. *Continued armament; no control or banning of nuclear weapons;* misuse of nuclear energy; continuation of nuclear tests; fear of fallout.
3. *No lessening of cold war;* no reduction of tensions between East and West; no coexistence.

4. *Be isolated* from other nations; no friends; foreign relations deteriorate.
5. *Inability to maintain neutrality* or to keep aloof from conflicting ideologies, blocs, etc.; make enemies; have to take sides.
6. *Miscellaneous* worries and fears having to do with international relations, the cold war, peace, etc.
9. Nothing to code in this column.

INDEPENDENCE, STATUS AND IMPORTANCE OF NATION

Co. 43

1. *Be militarily strong.*
2. Maintain or attain the position of a *world power.*
3. *Enhancement of status and importance* of the nation in general in international affairs; play a more important role in international affairs and negotiations.
4. Play a more important role specifically in *regional affairs or of a regional leadership.*
5. *Exert ideological or moral leadership;* exercise potential influence abroad for peace and freedom; convey own ideas and culture to rest of world; be a mediating power; bring about understanding or reconcile opposing views of nations.
6. *National independence* — attain or preserve independence or gain greater independence; freedom from interference or excessive influence from other powers; pursuing independent foreign policy; achieve economic self-sufficiency or independence.
7. *Miscellaneous* aspirations having to do with the independence, status or importance of the nation.
9. Nothing to code in this column.

Col. 44

1. Not to maintain or attain the position of a *world power.*
2. *Lose or have no status or importance* in international affairs in general; no important role in international affairs or negotiations.
3. *Failure to exert ideological or moral leadership* — failure to exercise potential influence abroad for peace and freedom, to convey own ideas and culture to rest of world, to be a mediating power, or to bring about understanding and reconcile differing points of view among other nations.
4. *Lack or loss of national independence* — to live on sufferance of others; be subject to interference or excessive influence from other powers; to have no independent foreign policy; economic dependence; have to accept foreign aid.
5. *Threat, aggression, domination,* or conquest by Russia, Communist China, Cuba or any other

Communist power; become a Communist satellite.
6. *Threat, aggression, domination,* or conquest by any *foreign power* (not specifically Communist).
7. *Miscellaneous* worries and fears having to do with the independence, status or importance of the nation.
9. Nothing to code in this column.

GENERAL

Col. 45

1. *Maintain status quo;* content as things are; present trends satisfactory.
2. *No hopes* or aspirations for the country.
3. *Miscellaneous* aspirations for the country not covered by any of the preceding categories.
8. Don't know; no answer.
9. Nothing to code in this column.

Col. 46

1. *No fears* or worries for the country.
2. *Miscellaneous* worries and fears for the country not covered by any of the preceding categories.
8. Don't know; no answer.
9. Nothing to code in this column.

__ Col. 47	Frequency	Personal Hopes	
__ Col. 48	Frequency	Personal Fears	
__ Col. 49	Frequency	National Hopes	
__ Col. 50	Frequency	National Fears	
__ Col. 50-56		Personal Ladder	
__ Col. 51-52		Present Position	0-10
__ Col. 53-54		Past Position	0-10
__ Col. 55-56		Future Position	0-10
__ Col. 57-62		National Ladder	
__ Col. 57-58		Present Position	0-10
__ Col. 59-60		Past Position	0-10
__ Col. 61-62		Future Position	0-10
__ Col. 80		Card 7	

NOTES

1. This in the main follows Cantril, with some slight modifications.